Contemporary
American
Architects

Volume III

Philip Jodidio

Contemporary **American** Architects

Volume III

TASCHEN

KÖLN LISBOA LONDON NEW YORK PARIS TOKYO

Page 2 | Seite 2
Richard Rauh, Cinema, Duluth, Georgia, 1994–96.
An inventive use of inexpensive construction materials.

Richard Rauh, Multiplex-Kino, Duluth, Georgia, 1994–96.
Eine einfallsreiche Verwendung preiswerter Baumaterialien.

Richard Rauh, Cinéma, Duluth, Géorgie, 1994–96.
Une utilisation inventive de matériaux de construction économiques.
© Photo: Peter Mauss/Esto

© 1997 Benedikt Taschen Verlag GmbH
Hohenzollernring 53, D-50672 Köln

Edited by Christine Fellhauer, Silvia Kinkel, Cologne
Design: Sylvie Chesnay, Paris; Samantha Finn, Mark Thomson, London
Cover Design: Angelika Taschen, Cologne; Mark Thomson, London
French translation: Jacques Bosser, Paris
German translation: Franca Fritz, Heinrich Koop, Cologne

Printed in Italy
ISBN 3-8228-8187-2

Contents | Inhalt | Sommaire

Pluralism reigns
American Architects in the mid 1990s

Die Herrschaft des Pluralismus
Amerikanische Architekten Mitte der 90er Jahre

Le règne du pluralisme
Architectes américains du milieu des années 90

Few figures have had as extensive an influence on modern American architecture as Philip Cortelyou Johnson. Born in Cleveland, Ohio in 1906, founding director of the Department of Architecture and Design at the Museum of Modern Art in New York (1932–34 ; 1945–54), he was the author, with Henry-Russell Hitchcock, of the seminal 1932 book *The International Style: Architecture Since 1922*. Focusing on the work of Le Corbusier, Oud, Gropius and Mies van der Rohe, Johnson's book, published on the occasion of an exhibition at MoMA, marked its time, and the decades that followed. More recently, Philip Johnson returned to the Museum of Modern Art to curate an exhibition on "Deconstructivist Architecture," with Mark Wigley in 1988, this time turning his attention to mostly unbuilt work by Frank O. Gehry, Daniel Libeskind, Rem Koolhaas, Peter Eisenman, Zaha Hadid, Bernard Tschumi and Coop Himmelblau. His comments, in the catalog preface, define the present mood : "In art as well as architecture, however, there are many – and contradictory – trends in our quick-change generation. In architecture, strict-classicism, strict-modernism, and all sorts of shades in between, are equally valid. No generally persuasive 'ism' has appeared. It may be none will arise unless there is a worldwide, new religion or set of beliefs out of which an aesthetic could be formed. Meanwhile pluralism reigns, perhaps a soil in which poetic, original artists can develop."[1] Johnson has been taxed with being something of a quick-change artist himself, moving easily, and with appropriate media attention, from the pure Modernism of his 1949 Glass House (New Canaan, Connecticut) to the Chippendale flourish on top of his 1984 AT&T Corporate Headquarters Building on Madison Avenue in New York. More recently, he has designed a guest house in the shape of a purple octopus for the as yet unbuilt Lewis Residence (Lyndhurst, Ohio, with Frank O. Gehry, 1993). His source of inspiration for this bit of bravura, a 1930 watercolor fantasy sketch by the German expressionist Hermann Finsterlin, shows that even at the age of 90 he retains a sure taste for fashion. In 1993, Philip Johnson wrote, "I am interested only in the art of architecture. Even the art of painting leaves me less than ecstatic, perhaps with few exceptions –

Kaum jemand hat die Entwicklung der modernen amerikanischen Architektur derart beeinflußt wie Philip Cortelyou Johnson. Der 1906 in Cleveland, Ohio, geborene Johnson gründete und leitete das Department of Architecture and Design am New Yorker Museum of Modern Art (1932–34; 1945–54) und veröffentlichte 1932, zusammen mit Henry-Russell Hitchcock, das zukunftsweisende Buch »The International Style: Architecture Since 1922«. Dieses Werk, das sich vor allem mit den Arbeiten von Le Corbusier, Oud, Gropius und Mies van der Rohe befaßte und anläßlich einer Ausstellung im MoMA präsentiert wurde, erwies sich als richtungsweisend für seine Zeit und die kommenden Jahrzehnte. Vor knapp einem Jahrzehnt kehrte Johnson als Kurator an das Museum of Modern Art zurück: Zusammen mit Mark Wigley veranstaltete er 1988 die Ausstellung »Deconstructivist Architecture« (Dekonstruktivistische Architektur), in der er die größtenteils unrealisierten Arbeiten von Frank O. Gehry, Daniel Libeskind, Rem Koolhaas, Peter Eisenman, Zaha Hadid, Bernard Tschumi und Coop Himmelblau präsentierte. Seine Anmerkungen im Vorwort des Katalogs umreißen die augenblickliche Situation: »Sowohl in der Kunst als auch in der Architektur unserer schnellebigen Generation gibt es viele – teilweise auch gegensätzliche – Trends. Im Bereich der Architektur besitzen der Klassizismus, die Moderne und alle Spielarten dazwischen die gleiche Wertigkeit. Kein allgemein überzeugender ›ismus‹ ist uns erschienen. Es kann durchaus sein, daß dies so bleibt, solange sich keine weltumspannende neue Religion oder Glaubensanschauung entwickelt, aus der sich eine Ästhetik formen läßt. Inzwischen regiert der Pluralismus – und vielleicht ist dies der Nährboden, in dem poetische, originelle Künstler heranwachsen.«[1] Dabei galt Johnson selbst als schnellebiger Künstler, der sich mühelos – und unter großer Anteilnahme der Medien – von der reinen Moderne seines Glass House (New Canaan, Connecticut, 1949) zu den Chippendale-Schnörkeln am Giebel seines 1984 entstandenen AT&T Corporate Headquarters Building an der New Yorker Madison Avenue weiterentwickelte. Vor kurzem entwarf er zusammen mit Frank O. Gehry ein Gästehaus in Form einer purpurfarbenen Krake für die noch nicht realisierte

Philip Johnson, Gate House, New Canaan, Connecticut, 1995. An homage by the dean of American architecture to the "kids" who invented the deconstructivist style.

Philip Johnson, Gate House, New Canaan, Connecticut, 1995. Hommage einer der führenden Persönlichkeiten der amerikanischen Architektur an die »Kids«, die den Dekonstruktivismus erfanden.

Philip Johnson, Gate House, New Canaan, Connecticut, 1995. Hommage du doyen de l'architecture américaine aux «gamins» qui ont inventé le déconstructivisme.

Peu de personnalités ont exercé une influence aussi étendue sur l'architecture moderne américaine que Philip Cortelyou Johnson. Né à Cleveland, Ohio, en 1906, fondateur et directeur du Département d'architecture et de design du Museum of Modern Art de New York (1932–34, 1945–54); il est l'auteur avec Henry-Russell Hitchcock de l'ouvrage fondamental (1932): «The International Style: Architecture Since 1922». Centré sur les œuvres de Le Corbusier, Oud, Gropius et Mies van der Rohe, le livre de Johnson, publié à l'occasion d'une exposition du Museum of Modern Art de New York, a marqué son temps et les décennies qui suivirent. Plus récemment, en 1988, Philip Johnson est revenu au Museum of Modern Art pour organiser, avec Mark Wigley, une exposition sur «l'Architecture déconstructiviste», tournant cette fois son attention vers les œuvres pour la plupart non construites de Frank O. Gehry, Daniel Libeskind, Rem Koolhaas, Peter Eisenman, Zaha Hadid, Bernard Tschumi et Coop Himmelblau. Quelques commentaires, extraits de sa préface au catalogue, définissent l'atmosphère actuelle: «En art comme en architecture (...) notre génération qui connaît des changements rapides est confrontée à des tendances multiples et contradictoires. En architecture, le classicisme strict, le modernisme strict, et toutes leurs nuances intermédiaires, sont tout aussi valables. Aucun ‹isme› nouveau et décisif n'a fait son apparition. Peut-être la situation restera-t-elle ainsi tant que n'apparaîtra une nouvelle religion ou philosophie universelle à partir de laquelle une esthétique puisse s'élaborer. Pendant ce temps, le pluralisme règne, et c'est peut-être un terrain sur lequel peuvent se développer des talents artistiques poétiques et originaux.»[1] Johnson a été lui-même accusé d'être un artiste insaisissable, qui a évolué avec aise sous le regard attentif des médias, du pur modernisme de sa Maison de Verre de 1949 (New Canaan, Connecticut) au couronnement style Chippendale du siège social d'AT&T sur Madison Avenue à New York. Plus récemment, il a dessiné une maison d'invités en forme de pieuvre pourpre pour la Lewis Residence, jusque-là non construite (Lyndhurst, Ohio, avec Frank O. Gehry, 1993). Sa source d'inspiration pour ce morceau de bravoure – une fantaisie à l'aquarelle de l'expressionniste

Caspar David Friedrich, Paul Klee, Piero della Francesca. Politics interest me only in so far as it fosters or impedes the production of architectural beauty." In these clear terms, Johnson bids for recognition as an artist, tied to few if any social concerns, an arbiter of taste. From the moment when Louis Kahn died in 1974, and through the 1980s, Philip Johnson was undoubtedly the most important American architect, not only because of his own work, but because of the careers he helped launch, including those of Michael Graves or Eric Owen Moss.

Though he is arguably more creative and consistent than Johnson, it is Frank O. Gehry who has now taken on his mantle as the reigning sage of the profession. Born in Toronto in 1929, Gehry has long been established in Santa Monica, California, where his example has given rise to a generation of architects freed from many of the formal constraints that plagued their predecessors. Named one of "America's 25 Most Influential People," by *Time Magazine* (June 17, 1996), Gehry attempted to define his own importance: "It's not my formal vocabulary as much as the way I explore, deal with the world and respond. I don't think my ideas, my designs, my architecture should be emulated by kids as much as for them to know that somebody like them was able, by some kind of relentless pursuit, to make space in the world for this kind of work. And because of that, they can do it too."

The examples of Johnson and Gehry might be interpreted as encouraging an "anything goes" attitude: the architect as demiurge with little or no interest in social, economic or environmental issues. In fact, in the mid 1990s, these forces shape much of contemporary American architecture, obliging some to seek out new, less expensive materials while others make clever use of existing buildings, for example. To the charge that American architecture has lost its inventiveness, a new generation of designers, such as the New Yorkers Tod Williams and Billie Tsien, respond with a sophistication and a breadth of inquiry that is the equal of anything being done in Europe. As Philip Johnson said in 1988, "Meanwhile pluralism reigns, perhaps a soil in which poetic, original artists can develop."

Lewis Residence (Lyndhurst, Ohio, 1993). Johnsons Inspirationsquelle für dieses Bravourstück – eine Phantasieskizze, die der deutsche Expressionist Hermann Finsterlin 1930 als Aquarell schuf – zeigt, daß er sich selbst mit 90 Jahren einen sicheren Geschmack für aktuelle Trends bewahrt hat. 1993 schrieb Johnson: »Ich interessiere mich nur für die Kunst der Architektur. Selbst die Kunst der Malerei läßt mich kalt, von einigen wenigen Ausnahmen abgesehen – Caspar David Friedrich, Paul Klee, Piero della Francesca. An der Politik interessiert mich nur, inwieweit sie architektonische Schönheit fördert oder behindert.« Mit diesen klaren Worten bemüht Johnson sich um die Anerkennung als Künstler, der sich nur wenig um soziale Fragen kümmert – ein Hüter des guten Geschmacks.

Von Louis Kahns Tod 1974 bis zum Ende der 80er Jahre war Philip Johnson zweifellos der bedeutendste amerikanische Architekt – nicht nur dank seiner eigenen Arbeiten, sondern auch aufgrund der Karrieren anderer, von ihm geförderter Architekten, wie zum Beispiel Michael Graves oder Eric Owen Moss.

Obwohl man ihn als kreativer und konsequenter bezeichnen könnte als Johnson, hat Frank O. Gehry erst jetzt dessen Nachfolge als geistiger Führer seines Berufsstandes angetreten. Der 1929 in Toronto geborene Gehry lebt seit langem in Santa Monica, Kalifornien, wo sein Beispiel eine ganze Generation von Architekten dazu veranlaßte, sich von den Fesseln formaler Beschränkungen zu befreien, unter denen noch ihre Vorgänger litten. Gehry, der von »Time Magazine« zu den »25 einflußreichsten Menschen Amerikas« gezählt wird, umreißt seine eigene Bedeutung so: »Es ist weniger meine Formensprache als die Art, in der ich etwas erforsche, mich mit der Welt auseinandersetze und darauf reagiere. Ich glaube nicht, daß die Jugendlichen von heute meine Ideen, meine Entwürfen, meine Architektur nachahmen müssen; sie sollten daraus nur lernen, daß jemand wie sie in der Lage war, durch nie nachlassende Zielstrebigkeit für seine eigenen Arbeiten einen Raum in der Welt zu schaffen. Und genau dies können sie auch erreichen.«

Die Beispiele von Johnson und Gehry könnten als Unterstützung einer »anything goes«-Haltung interpretiert werden – der

allemand Hermann Finsterlin – montre que même à l'âge de 90 ans, Johnson conserve un goût affirmé pour la mode. En 1993, il écrivait: «Je ne m'intéresse qu'à l'art de l'architecture. Même la peinture me laisse moins qu'extatique, avec peut-être quelques exceptions, comme Caspar David Friedrich, Paul Klee, Piero della Francesca. La politique ne m'intéresse que dans la mesure où elle favorise ou empêche la production de la beauté architecturale.» Johnson cherche clairement à être reconnu comme artiste et arbitre du goût, et ne se sent pas ou guère lié par des préoccupations sociales.

De la mort de Louis Kahn en 1974, et tout au long des années 80, Philip Johnson a été sans conteste le plus important architecte américain, non seulement pour son œuvre, mais aussi pour les carrières qu'il aidé à lancer, comme celles de Michael Graves ou d'Eric Owen Moss.

Éventuellement plus créatif et plus cohérent que Johnson, Frank O. Gehry a repris le bâton de sage de la profession. Né à Toronto en 1929, il est installé de longue date à Santa Monica, Californie, où son exemple a favorisé la naissance de toute une génération d'architectes libérés d'un grand nombre de contraintes formelles dans lesquelles s'étaient empêtrés leurs prédécesseurs. Nommé l'un des «25 Américains les plus influents» par «Time Magazine» (17 juin 1996), Gehry tente ainsi de définir son rôle: «Ce n'est pas tant mon vocabulaire formel qui compte, que la façon dont j'explore, dont je me confronte avec le monde et lui réponds. Je ne pense pas que l'important soit que mes idées, mes plans, mon architecture inspirent des jeunes, mais qu'il sachent que quelqu'un comme eux a été capable, à travers une sorte de quête inlassable, de faire un peu de place dans le monde tel qu'il est pour ce type de travail. Et parce que j'ai pu le faire, ils le peuvent également.»

Les exemples de Johnson et Gehry peuvent être interprétés comme encourageant une attitude du «tout est possible», d'architecte démiurge, peu préoccupé par les enjeux sociaux, économiques, ou environnementaux. En fait, au milieu des années 90, ces enjeux influent sur une grande partie de l'architecture américaine, obligeant certains à rechercher des maté-

Frank O. Gehry, Minden-Ravensberg Electric Company Offices, Bad Oeynhausen, Germany, 1991–95. A symphony of different materials and unusual shapes in a largely traditional area.

Frank O. Gehry, Bürogebäude des Elektrizitätswerkes Minden-Ravensberg, Bad Oeynhausen, Deutschland, 1991–95. Eine Symphonie aus unterschiedlichen Materialien und ungewöhnlichen Formen in einer weitestgehend traditionellen Umgebung.

Frank O. Gehry, Bureaux de la compagnie d'électricité Minden-Ravensberg, Bad Oeynhausen, Allemagne, 1991–95. Symphonie de formes et de matériaux inhabituels dans une région essentiellement traditionnelle.

Centerbrook, Nauticus, National Maritime Center, Norfolk, Virginia, 1988–94. Education and entertainment in one facility, or the triumph of "edutainment."

Centerbrook, Nauticus, National Maritime Center, Norfolk, Virginia, 1988–94. Bildungsstätte und Freizeitcenter in einem – oder: der Triumph des »Edutainment«.

Centerbrook, Nauticus, National Maritime Center, Norfolk, Virginie, 1988–94. Éducation et divertissement réunis, ou le triomphe de la pédagogie ludique.

That's Entertainment!

American cities, like those in Europe or Japan, invested heavily in the 1970s and 1980s in art museums, new symbols of civic pride and achievement. Unfortunately, forming art collections is a costly business, and the more economically minded 1990s have seen fewer art museums created. A relatively modest project such as Venturi, Scott Brown's recent expansion and renovation of the San Diego Museum of Contemporary Art in La Jolla still fits in with the spirit of the times, however. With such visible museum edifices as I.M. Pei's 1978 East Building for the National Gallery of Art (Washington, D.C.) it was shown that calling on a "name" architect in the United States could make sense not only in terms of the quality of the final product, but also in attracting large numbers of visitors. This lesson has been retained in new and unusual ways in different types of public structures in the 1990s. As the English news weekly *The Economist* points out ("America smiles at itself," June 22, 1996), "Certain types of museum are thriving. There has been a boomlet, for example, in science-and-technology centers (some fifty have opened in the 1990s), in children's museums (thirty-six new ones over the past five years) and in aquariums... New museums bring innovation. 'Interaction' and 'edutainment' are buzzwords. Visitors to the Nauticus National Maritime Center in Norfolk, Virginia, can play at shooting down enemy aircraft from a destroyer or embark on a virtual-reality search for the Loch Ness monster."

Founded in 1682 in a tobacco-growing area, the deep natural port of Norfolk was home to the Hampton Roads Operating Base, which grew during World War II to be the largest naval facility in the world, home to the Atlantic Fleet and the Supreme Allied Command. After 1945, however, the 14,000 housing units built rapidly during the war turned into slums, causing Norfolk to be the first city in the United States to start a federal urban renewal program, in 1950. Still home to the largest naval base in the United States, the city of Norfolk appropriately enough decided that maritime technology, shipping, and marine science provided the ideal subject for a combined educational and entertainment facility. After the idea of an oceanic center under the

Architekt als Weltenschöpfer mit geringem oder keinem Interesse an sozialen, wirtschaftlichen oder ökologischen Themen. Dabei prägen gerade diese Kräfte die zeitgenössische amerikanische Architektur in der Mitte der 90er Jahre: Sie bringen die Architekten dazu, nach neuen, preiswerten Materialien zu suchen oder existierende Gebäude interessant und effektiv umzugestalten. Auf den Vorwurf, die amerikanische Architektur habe ihre Kreativität verloren, reagiert eine neue Generation von Designern, wie die New Yorker Tod William und Billie Tsien, mit einer Kultiviertheit und intellektuellen Bandbreite, die sich durchaus mit den aktuellen Entwicklungen in Europa messen kann. Wie sagte Philip Johnson 1988: »Inzwischen regiert der Pluralismus – und vielleicht ist dies der Nährboden, in dem poetische, originale Künstler heranwachsen.«

That's Entertainment!

In den 70er und 80er Jahren investierten amerikanische, europäische und japanische Städte in großem Umfang in Kunstmuseen – die neuen Symbole für die Errungenschaften einer Stadt und der Stolz ihrer Bürger. Leider ist der Aufbau einer Kunstsammlung ein teures Vergnügen, so daß in den wirtschaftlicher orientierten 90er Jahren nur noch wenige Kunstmuseen entstanden. Daher entspricht ein vergleichsweise bescheidenes Projekt wie die von Venturi, Scott Brown durchgeführte Erweiterung und Neugestaltung des San Diego Museum of Contemporary Art in La Jolla dem Geist der heutigen Zeit. Aufsehenerregende Museumsgebäude wie I.M. Peis Ostflügel der National Gallery of Art (Washington, D.C., 1978) traten den Beweis an, daß die Berufung eines »namhaften« Architekten nicht nur eine bessere Qualität des Endproduktes garantierte, sondern auch eine große Zahl von Besuchern anzieht. Diese Lektion behielt man in den 90er Jahren auch beim Bau neuer und ungewöhnlicher öffentlicher Gebäude im Gedächtnis. Das englische Wochenmagazin »The Economist« schreibt dazu (in dem Artikel »America smiles at itself«, 22. Juni 1996): »Gegenwärtig erfreuen sich bestimmte Museumstypen großer Beliebtheit. Bei den Wissenschafts- und Technologiezentren (in den 90er Jahren

riaux nouveaux et moins coûteux, tandis que d'autres, par exemple, vont s'accommoder avec intelligence de bâtiments existants. À la critique selon laquelle l'architecture américaine aurait perdu de sa créativité, une nouvelle génération de concepteurs, comme les New-Yorkais Tod Williams et Billie Tsien, répondent par une sophistication et une largeur de vue tout à fait équivalentes à ce que l'on trouve en Europe. Ceci confirme l'idée de Philip Johnson selon laquelle le pluralisme pourrait favoriser l'éclosion de pratiques poétiques originales et artistiques.

Du grand spectacle!

Au cours des années 70 et 80, les cités américaines, comme celles d'Europe ou du Japon, ont beaucoup investi dans les musées, nouveaux symboles de fierté et de réussite des collectivités locales. Malheureusement, constituer une collection d'œuvres d'art s'est révélé coûteux, et les années 90, plus économes, ont freiné ce mouvement. Un projet relativement modeste, comme la récente extension et rénovation du San Diego Museum of Contemporary Art de La Jolla par Venturi, Scott Brown, correspond cependant à l'esprit du temps. Depuis la construction d'édifices aussi spectaculaires que l'aile Est de la National Gallery of Art (Washington D.C.) par I.M. Pei en 1978, il était admis que le choix d'un architecte célèbre se justifiait non seulement par la qualité du résultat, mais également parce que l'on mettait de son côté toutes les chances d'attirer un public plus vaste. Cette leçon a été retenue et adaptée de manière nouvelle dans plusieurs équipements publics des années 90. Comme le fait remarquer l'hebdomadaire «The Economist», «L'Amérique se sourit» (22 juin 1996): «Certains types de musées sont florissants. On a assisté à un petit *boom* des musées de sciences et de technologie (50 ont ouvert dans les années 90), des musées pour enfants (36 ces cinq dernières années), et des aquariums. Les nouveaux musées sont innovants. ‹Interactivité› et ‹éducation par le jeu› sont les nouveaux mots de passe. Les visiteurs du Nauticus National Maritime Center de Norfolk, Virginia, peuvent jouer à détruire des avions

auspices of Jacques Cousteau was rejected by the city, the National Maritime Center Authority, a semi-public organization, and the exhibition design consultants Herb Rosenthal & Associates began work with Centerbrook Architects on a complex containing an aquarium, university research labs, a wide-screen theater and the Hampton Roads Naval Museum.

Centerbrook began its existence in 1965 when Charles Moore left Berkeley to become Chairman of the Yale University Department of Architecture. Originally located in New Haven, under the name Charles Moore Associates, and later Moore Grover Harper, his firm purchased an abandoned 19th century factory in the village of Centerbrook, located about 50 kilometers to the east of New Haven. Although he was ailing at the time, Charles Moore was brought into the Nauticus project as a design consultant. Completed by Centerbrook principal Mark Simon, the building seems right at home on the Elizabeth River downtown waterfront, at the foot of Main Street. According to Simon, "Visually, it refers to all things maritime, yet they come together to make a very special place that is its own invention. It's science fiction." The structure actually brings to mind some of the very modern warships that often pass by. The pier in front of the facility was specifically designed to accommodate 183 meter long Aegis class cruisers, which occasionally dock there for public visits.

Akron, Ohio is another American city with grand memories and a somewhat less brilliant present. Once the "tire capital of the world" its factories have been largely abandoned since the mid 1980s, and the municipality has sought to reinvigorate the economy by declaring the city "polymer capital of the world." Together with new university facilities devoted to the study of polymers, Akron, a city of 225,000 people, has recently invested in a new museum for the National Inventors Hall of Fame. Coupled with an area called the Inventors Workshop, which invites visitor participation, Inventure Place is the work of the New York architect James Stewart Polshek. A native of Akron, Polshek also designed the city's new convention center. Remarkable because of the close cooperation between the architect and the exhibition

wurden bisher etwa 50 eröffnet), den Museen für Kinder (36 Neueröffnungen in den letzten fünf Jahren) und den Aquarien könnte man fast von einem Boom sprechen... Neue Museen bringen Innovation. ›Interaktion‹ und ›Edutainment‹ sind die Schlagworte der Zeit. So können die Besucher des Nauticus National Maritime Center in Norfolk, Virginia von einem Zerstörer aus feindliche Flugzeuge abschießen oder auf eine virtuelle Suche nach dem Ungeheuer von Loch Ness gehen.«

Der natürliche Tiefwasserhafen Norfolk, der 1682 in einem Tabakanbaugebiet entstand, entwickelte sich während des Zweiten Weltkriegs zur größten Marinebasis der Welt, zur Heimat der US-Atlantikflotte und zum Sitz des Alliierten Oberbefehlshabers. Nach 1945 verkamen die während des Krieges erbauten 14 000 Wohneinheiten zu einem Slum, weshalb Norfolk 1950 als erste Stadt der USA mit einem staatlichen Stadtsanierungsprogramm begann. Da Norfolk auch heute noch die größte Marinebasis der USA beherbergt, war es nur passend, hier eine lehrreiche und gleichzeitig unterhaltsame öffentliche Einrichtung zu den Themen Marinetechnologie, Schiffbau und Marinewissenschaften zu errichten. Nachdem die Idee eines ozeanographischen Zentrums unter Schirmherrschaft von Jacques Cousteau von den Stadtvätern abgelehnt worden war, begann die National Maritime Center Authority in Zusammenarbeit mit den Ausstellungsdesignern Herb Rosenthal & Associates und Centerbrook Architects mit der Planung eines Komplexes, der ein Aquarium, Forschungslabors, ein Breitwandkino und das Hampton Roads Naval Museum umfassen sollte.

Centerbrook wurde 1965 gegründet, als Charles Moore Berkeley verließ und eine Stelle als Leiter des Fachbereichs Architektur an der Yale University antrat. Die ursprünglich in New Haven unter dem Namen Charles Moore Associates (später Moore Grover Harper) ansässige Firma erwarb in der Kleinstadt Centerbrook, etwa 50 km östlich von New Haven, eine verlassene Fabrik aus dem 19. Jahrhundert. Obwohl er zu dieser Zeit erkrankt war, gewann man Charles Moore als Designberater für das Nauticus-Projekt. Das von Mark Simon, dem Leiter von Centerbrook, fertiggestellte Gebäude fügt sich perfekt in das Hafen-

ennemis à partir d'un destroyer, ou s'embarquer dans une recherche du monstre du Loch Ness, en réalité virtuelle.»

Fondé en 1682 dans une région de plantations de tabac, le port naturel en eaux profondes de Norfolk est le site de la Hampton Roads Operating Base, qui se développa pendant la seconde guerre mondiale jusqu'à devenir la plus grande base navale du monde, abritant la Flotte de l'Atlantique et le Commandement suprême allié. Après 1945, cependant, les 14 000 unités d'habitation rapidement construites pendant la guerre se transformèrent vite en taudis. Dès 1950, Norfolk à été la première ville américaine à bénéficier d'un projet fédéral de rénovation urbaine. Toujours siège de la plus importante base de la marine américaine, la ville a décidé que la technologie maritime, la construction navale et les sciences de la mer pourraient faire le thème d'un parc de loisirs et d'éducation. Après qu'un projet de Centre océanique sous les auspices de Jacques Cousteau eut été rejeté, la National Maritime Center Association, organisme semi-public, et les concepteurs d'expositions Herb Rosenthal & Associates collaborèrent avec l'agence Centerbrook Architects sur un ensemble comprenant un aquarium, des laboratoires universitaires de recherche, une salle à écran géant, et le Hampton Roads Naval Museum.

Centerbrook naît en 1965 lorsque Charles Moore quitte Berkeley pour devenir président du département d'architecture de l'Université de Yale. Installée à l'origine à New Haven, sous le nom de Charles Moore Associates, puis de Moore Grover Harper, l'agence fait l'acquisition d'une fabrique du XIXe siècle abandonnée dans le village de Centerbrook, à 50 km à l'est de New Haven. Bien qu'il ait été souffrant à l'époque, Charles Moore fut appelé en consultation sur le Projet Nauticus. Achevé par le principal responsable de Centerbrook, Mark Simon, le bâtiment semble tout à fait chez lui au bord de l'Elizabeth River, en plein centre ville. Pour Simon, «cette construction fait réellement penser à certains des bateaux de guerre ultra-modernes qui passent devant elle. La jetée a été dessinée pour recevoir les croiseurs de 183 m de long de la classe Aegis qui y accostent parfois et sont visités par le public.»

Centerbrook, Nauticus, National Maritime Center, Norfolk, Virginia, 1988–94. An exterior view showing the "aircraft carrier" bulk of the structure.

Centerbrook, Nauticus, National Maritime Center, Norfolk, Virginia, 1988–94. Die Außenansicht zeigt den an einen Flugzeugträger erinnernden Teil der Konstruktion.

Centerbrook, Nauticus, National Maritime Center, Norfolk, Virginie, 1988–94. Vue extérieure montrant la masse du bâtiment en forme de porte-avions.

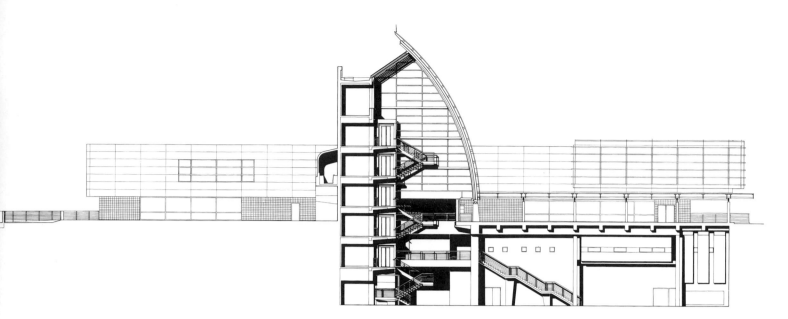

Polshek and Partners, Inventure Place, Akron, Ohio, 1993–95. A cross-section showing the sail-like form at the entry and the large underground activity space.

Polshek and Partners, Inventure Place, Akron, Ohio, 1993–95. Ein Querschnitt, der den segelartig geformten Eingangsbereich und den großen, unterirdischen Mehrzweckraum zeigt.

Polshek and Partners, Inventure Place, Akron, Ohio, 1993–95. Coupe montrant la forme en voile de bateau de l'entrée et les vastes espaces souterrains.

designers, Inventure Place is readily visible on its hilltop site because of the large stainless steel curve that defines the main facade. Although it should not be suggested that any of these projects directly inspired James Stewart Polshek, it is interesting to note that the 1995 Akron building's curving sail-like form resembles that of at least three other recent buildings: Sir Norman Foster's University of Cambridge Faculty of Law (Cambridge, Great Britain, 1993–95); Arata Isozaki's Domus: La Casa Del Hombre (La Coruña, Spain, 1993–95); and most directly, the National Theater School (Churubosco, Mexico), completed in 1993 by Ten Arquitectos. These similarities should undoubtedly be attributed to the new capacity of computer-driven design and manufacturing to resolve the technical problems posed by complex curves in architecture. Dramatic curves are also quite fashionable in current architectural design.

One of the more interesting projects to grow out of the combined influence of economic pressures and the American taste for places of entertainment is a new multiplex cinema built in Duluth, Georgia by the architect Richard Rauh. Designed for O'Neil Theaters, a Louisiana firm specializing in roadside "second-run" movie theaters, Rauh's complex features a total seating capacity of 1,808 divided between twelve auditoriums. Incorporated into an existing, but nearly vacant mall on the sprawling urban periphery of Atlanta, the theater was built for the extremely low price of $55 per square foot. This was achieved through the extensive use of materials most often found in agricultural and industrial applications, such as corrugated galvanized steel on the outside, or corrugated tin within. Although the architect encountered resistance from workers who balked at carefully fashioning "chicken coop material" he succeeded in convincing them that the quality of their workmanship was essential to the success of the design. Although other talented architects have confronted the problem of putting "ordinary" materials to use in "quality" designs, the Duluth cinema complex also deals convincingly with the integration of popular roadside imagery into an inexpensive structure. The architect compares the 140 meter long composition, illuminated with

viertel am Elizabeth River ein, das am Anfang der Main Street liegt. Simon sagt dazu: »Visuell bezieht es sich auf alles Maritime; aber diese Dinge vereinigen sich zu einem ganz besonderen Ort, der sich selbst erfunden hat. Es ist Science-fiction.« Tatsächlich erinnert das Bauwerk an die Formen der modernen Kriegsschiffe, die häufig vor dem Museum vorübergleiten. Der Pier vor dem Komplex wurde speziell den Bedürfnissen der 183 m langen Kreuzer der Aegis-Klasse angepaßt, die hier von Zeit zu Zeit für öffentliche Besichtigungen anlegen.

Akron in Ohio ist ebenfalls eine Stadt mit einer großartigen Vergangenheit und einer etwas weniger beeindruckenden Gegenwart. Seit Mitte der 80er Jahre sind die Fabriken der ehemaligen »Reifenhauptstadt der Welt« größtenteils stillgelegt, und die Stadtverwaltung versuchte, die Wirtschaft wiederzubeleben, indem sie Akron zur »Polymerhauptstadt der Welt« ernannte. Neben den neuen Universitätseinrichtungen, die der Polymerforschung gewidmet sind, entstand in dieser Stadt mit 225 000 Einwohnern die neue National Inventors Hall of Fame, ein Museum für die größten amerikanischen Erfinder. Der mit dem »Inventors Workshop« – hier können Besucher selbst an Erfindungen teilnehmen – gekoppelte Komplex trägt den Namen »Inventure Place« und ist das Werk des in Akron geborenen und in New York lebenden Architekten James Stewart Polshek. Der in bemerkenswert enger Zusammenarbeit zwischen dem Architekt und den Ausstellungsdesignern entstandene Inventure Place erhebt sich auf einem Hügel, so daß die große, gebogene Edelstahlfassade weithin sichtbar ist. Dabei erinnert die gekurvte, segelartige Form des 1995 in Akron fertiggestellten Gebäudes an zumindest drei erst kürzlich entstandene Bauten – Sir Norman Fosters Juristische Fakultät der University of Cambridge (Cambridge, Großbritannien 1993–95), Arata Isozakis Domus: La Casa Del Hombre (La Coruña, Spanien 1993–95) und vor allem an die National Theater School im mexikanischen Churubosco, die 1993 von Ten Arquitectos entworfen wurde. Zweifellos müssen diese Ähnlichkeiten den neuen computerunterstützten Design- und Herstellungsverfahren zugeschrieben werden – und vor allem ihrer Fähigkeit, die technischen Probleme beim Bau komplexer

Akron, Ohio, est une autre de ces villes américaines riches de souvenirs et confrontées à un présent moins brillant. Jadis capitale mondiale du pneu, ses usines sont en grande partie abandonnées depuis le milieu des années 80, et la municipalité a cherché à revigorer l'économie locale en déclarant la ville «capitale mondiale des polymères». Avec les nouvelles installations universitaires consacrées à l'étude des polymères, cette cité de 250 000 habitants a récemment investi dans un nouveau musée pour le National Inventors Hall of Fame. Couplé à une installation baptisée l'Inventors Workshop (l'atelier des inventeurs) qui invite les visiteurs à participer, Inventure Place est l'œuvre de l'architecte new-yorkais James Stewart Polshek. Né à Akron, Polshek a également conçu le nouveau centre de congrès de la ville. Remarquable par l'étroite coopération entre l'architecte et les concepteurs des espaces d'expositions, Inventure Place se détache au sommet de sa colline grâce à sa grande courbe d'acier inoxydable qui le fait repérer de loin. Même si l'on ne peut parler d'inspiration directe, les formes en voiles de bateau de ce bâtiment édifié en 1995 font penser à au moins trois constructions récentes: la faculté de droit de l'Université de Cambridge de Sir Norman Foster (Cambridge, Grande-Bretagne, 1993–95), La Casa del Hombre d'Arata Isozaki (La Corogne, Espagne, 1993–95), et plus directement encore l'École nationale du théâtre de Churubosco (Mexique) achevée en 1993 par Ten Arquitectos. Ces similitudes s'expliquent peut-être par les nouveaux moyens informatiques de conception et de construction qui permettent de résoudre les problèmes architecturaux complexes posés par ces courbes spectaculaires, assez à la mode dans l'architecture contemporaine.

L'un des projets les plus intéressants nés de l'influence combinée des pressions économiques et du goût américain pour les lieux de divertissement est un nouveau cinéma multisalles édifié à Duluth, Géorgie, par l'architecte Richard Rauh. Construit pour O'Neil Theaters, société de Louisiane spécialisée dans les cinémas de banlieue de non-exclusivité, le complexe de Rauh offre 1 808 places réparties en douze salles. Intégré dans un centre commercial existant mais presque vide, l'ensemble a été réalisé

continuous fluorescent billboard lights, which are visible from the neighboring interstate highway, to a "Star Wars light saber." Despite the theoretical approach to popular culture set forth in books like *Learning from Las Vegas* (Venturi, Scott Brown, Izenour; MIT Press, 1977), few architects have actually succeeded in assimilating the imagery of the American roadside into their designs as effectively as Richard Rauh seems to have done in this case.

Learning from Culver City

Though Venturi's Las Vegas certainly is rich in a particular type of American architectural imagery, a less spectacular urban area may, thanks to the efforts of at least two talented architects, provide more insight into the future possibilities of blighted cities. Incorporated in 1917, Culver City is for all intents and purposes part of Los Angeles, located midway between the downtown area and Santa Monica. It is here that the motion picture industry began its spectacular development in about 1915 before moving to nearby Hollywood. A population of less than 40,000 people indicates that Culver City's atmosphere of abandoned industrial or warehouse-type buildings is hardly conducive to a thriving community. This is where a developer named Frederick Norton Smith and the architect Eric Owen Moss come into the picture. Born in Los Angeles in 1943, and educated at UCLA, Moss opened his own office in Culver City in 1976. Through his affiliation with Smith, Moss has had the opportunity to build complexes that incrementally connect together, such as the Paramount Laundry-Lindblade Tower-Gary Group Complex, completed between 1987 and 1989. More recent rehabilitation of these large warehouse-type structures originally built for the movie industry includes The Box and IRS buildings, located nearby. Making very inventive use of common materials such as sewer pipes serving as columns, or bolts bent in a U shape to form fluorescent light fixtures, Moss has managed to create an impetus for forward-looking advertising or recording companies to install themselves in an area that was all but abandoned a few years ago. No less a figure than Philip Johnson has dubbed him

Rundungen zu lösen. Darüber hinaus sind aufsehenerregende Kurven in der zeitgenössischen Architektur sehr beliebt.

Zu den interessantesten Projekten, die der wirtschaftliche Druck und die amerikanische Vorliebe für Unterhaltungszentren hervorbrachten, gehört ein neues Multiplex-Kino, das der Architekt Richard Rauh in Duluth, Georgia erbaut. Der für O'Neil Theaters – eine in Lousiana ansässige Firma, die sich auf Programmkinos an Highways spezialisiert hat – entworfene Komplex bietet in zwölf Sälen insgesamt 1808 Plätze. Das in ein nahezu leerstehendes Einkaufszentrum am Rande von Atlanta integrierte Kino wurde für den extrem günstigen Preis von 592 $ pro m² erbaut. Dies gelang vor allem dank der weitreichenden Verwendung von Materialien aus agrarischer oder industrieller Architektur, wie gewelltem, verzinktem Stahl an der Außenfassade und Wellblech im Inneren. Obwohl Rauh auf starken Widerstand der Arbeiter stieß, die den Umgang mit diesem »Hühnerfarm-Material« ablehnten, gelang es ihm, sie davon zu überzeugen, daß der Erfolg seines Entwurfs von der Qualität ihrer Arbeit abhing. Zwar haben sich auch andere talentierte Architekten mit dem Problem der Verwendung »gewöhnlicher« Materialien im Rahmen einer »Qualitätsarchitektur« befaßt, aber Rauhs Kino-Komplex gelingt darüber hinaus die überzeugende Integration populärer Highway-Bildsprache in ein preiswertes Bauwerk. Der Architekt vergleicht die 140 m lange Komposition – die von leuchtenden Werbetafeln illuminiert wird und daher sogar vom benachbarten Interstate Highway aus zu sehen ist – mit einem Lichtschwert aus »Krieg der Sterne«. Trotz der theoretischen Annäherung an die Populärkultur, die von Büchern wie »Learning from Las Vegas« (Venturi, Scott Brown, Izenour, MIT Press 1977; dt. »Lernen von Las Vegas«, Vieweg 1979) eingeleitet wurde, ist es nur wenigen Architekten gelungen, die Bildsprache der amerikanischen Highways so überzeugend in ihre Entwürfe zu integrieren wie Richard Rauh.

Lernen von Culver City

Obwohl Venturis Las Vegas sicherlich in hohem Maße über eine ganz bestimmte Art amerikanischer architektonischer Bildspra-

pour le prix extrêmement bas de 3 000 FF le m² environ, grâce au recours à des matériaux généralement utilisés en agriculture ou dans l'industrie, comme l'acier galvanisé ondulé en façade, ou la tôle ondulée à l'intérieur. Bien que l'architecte ait rencontré quelques difficultés avec les ouvriers qui rechignaient à ajuster avec soin «ces matériaux pour cages à poules», il réussit à les convaincre que la qualité de leur travail était essentielle au succès du projet. D'autres architectes de talent ont déjà utilisé des matériaux ordinaires dans des réalisations «de qualité», mais le cinéma de Duluth joue également de manière convaincante avec l'intégration de l'esthétique populaire de banlieue dans une construction bon marché. L'architecte compare sa composition de 140 m de long, illuminée en continu de projecteurs fluorescents, au «sabre de lumière» de «La Guerre des étoiles». Si l'approche théorique de la culture populaire est bien développée (à travers en particulier «L'Enseignement de Las Vegas», de Venturi, Scott Brown, Izenour, MIT Press, 1977), peu d'architectes ont en fait aussi efficacement réussi à assimiler l'imagerie des bords de route américains que Richard Rauh dans ce cas.

L'enseignement de Culver City

Si le Las Vegas de Venturi est certainement très riche en exemples de cette imagerie architecturale typiquement américaine, une zone urbaine moins spectaculaire peut prétendre, grâce aux efforts d'au moins deux grands architectes, offrir des perspectives renouvelées à des cités écrasées de difficultés. Fondée en tant que commune en 1917, Culver City fait partie de Los Angeles, et se trouve entre le centre de la mégalopole et Santa Monica. C'est ici, vers 1915, que l'industrie cinématographique a commencé à connaître un développement spectaculaire avant de se déplacer vers le tout proche Hollywood. Avec 40 000 habitants, Culver City et ses entrepôts et usines abandonnés ne semblait guère dynamique il y a quelques années encore. C'est pourtant là que le promoteur Frederick Norton Smith et l'architecte Eric Owen Moss ont décidé d'intervenir. Né à Los Angeles en 1943, formé à UCLA, Moss ouvre sa propre agence à Culver City en 1976. Grâce à son association avec Smith, il se voit offrir

Richard Rauh, Cinema, Duluth, Georgia, 1994–96. A powerful architectural vocabulary situated somewhere between "high-tech" and deconstruction.

Richard Rauh, Multiplex-Kino, Duluth, Georgia, 1994–96. Eine ausdrucksstarke architektonische Formensprache zwischen »Hightech« und Dekonstruktion.

Richard Rauh, Cinéma, Duluth, Géorgie, 1994–96. Un puissant langage architectural, quelque part entre «high-tech» et déconstruction.

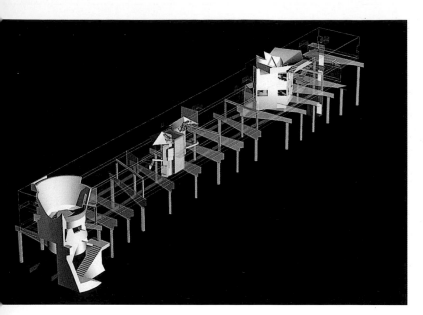

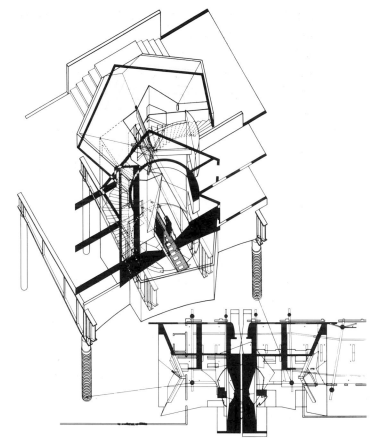

"the jeweler of junk." The latest building by Eric Owen Moss,
called Samitaur, is one of his most poetic and significant works.
It takes advantage of the principal of air rights, to build over an
existing road, and thus addresses the problem of vast areas of
unused or underused urban space. Typically, Moss describes his
project in very unexpected terms. He says, "When you see the
steel frame that supports the flying block (I hesitate because this
is easily misunderstood), it looks like a freeway designed by a
drunk. He's not sloshed and mumbling incoherently. The drunk
is talking very seriously and very articulately – explaining what
the project is about. But he's talking in a dream. The drunk sees
the world precisely, but very differently – This is an argument for
Coleridge and Xanadu. Conventional analytical references are
gone, and a privatized version appears."[2] The names of Xanadu
and Coleridge are of course a reference to the poem "Kubla
Khan": "In Xanadu did Kubla Khan a stately pleasure-dome
decree..."; which ends with the words, "That with music loud
and long, I would build that dome in air, That sunny dome! Those
caves of ice!" Lifted up on girders supported by pipes in the
heart of what used to be the home of the movie industry,
Samitaur is a kind of "pleasure dome" for the 21st century, a
floating form bringing life back to an abandoned urban area.

One of the clients for whom Frederick Norton Smith and Moss
have designed structures in Culver City is the Japanese media
giant Sony. Sony has already invested more than $100 million in
the area in a renovation program of a site taken over from MGM
involving several architects, including Steven Ehrlich, who built
the large Sony Music Entertainment complex in Santa Monica
(1991–93). Born in New York in 1946, Steven Ehrlich received his
degree from the Rensselaer Polytechnic Institute in Troy, New
York in 1969. An unusual aspect of his experience is that he
studied indigenous vernacular architecture in North and West
Africa from 1969 to 1977. Ehrlich recently completed the Game
Show Network building for Sony (1995), a complete rehabilitation
of a 1930s garage for a station that broadcasts game shows
24 hours a day. As he says, it is "a very low-tech building that has
been turbocharged into a very high-tech use." Although the

che verfügt, bietet ein anderes, weniger spektakuläres städtisches Areal dank der Anstrengungen zumindest zweier talentierter Architekten einen tieferen Einblick in die Zukunftsmöglichkeiten ehemals verwahrloster Städte. Culver City, das 1917 von Los Angeles eingemeindet wurde und heute auf halbem Weg zwischen der Innenstadt und Santa Monica liegt, ist in jeder Hinsicht Teil der Stadt. Hier begann die Filmindustrie 1915 ihre aufsehenerregende Entwicklung, bevor sie in das nahegelegene Hollywood umzog. Eine Bevölkerung von unter 40 000 Menschen deutet darauf hin, daß die Atmosphäre der Stadt Culver City mit ihren stillgelegten Fabriken und leeren Lagerhäusern nicht unbedingt dem Idealbild einer blühenden Kommune entspricht. An diesem Punkt kommen ein Bauunternehmer namens Frederick Norton Smith und der Architekt Eric Owen Moss ins Bild. Moss wurde 1943 in Los Angeles geboren, studierte an der UCLA und eröffnete 1976 in Culver City sein eigenes Büro. Aufgrund seiner Verbindung zu Smith erhielt Moss Gelegenheit zum Bau großer Komplexe, die zunehmend aneinander anschließen, wie etwa der Paramount Laundry-Lindblade Tower-Gary Group Complex (1987–89). Zu den jüngsten Sanierungsarbeiten dieses ursprünglich für die Filmindustrie errichteten Lagerhauskomplexes zählen das nahegelegene The Box und das IRS Building. Durch die einfallsreiche Verwendung herkömmlicher Materialien – Abwasserrohre, die als Säulen dienen oder U-förmig gebogene Bolzen als Leuchtstoffröhrenhalter – gab Moss fortschrittlich orientierten Werbeagenturen oder Plattenfirmen den Anstoß, sich in einer noch vor wenigen Jahren nahezu ausgestorbenen Gegend niederzulassen. Niemand Geringeres als Philip Johnson taufte ihn den »Juwelier des Schrotts«. Eric Owen Moss' bisher letztes Projekt namens Samitaur gehört zu seinen poetischsten und charakteristischsten Arbeiten. Es macht sich das Prinzip des Luftraumrechts zunutze, das es erlaubt, über einer bereits existierenden Straße zu bauen, und bietet auf diese Weise eine Lösung für das Problem der Nutzung riesiger Flächen bisher kaum genutzten städtischen Raums. Moss beschreibt dieses Projekt in völlig unerwarteten Worten: »Wenn man den Stahlrahmen betrachtet, der den fliegenden Block trägt (ich

l'opportunité d'édifier des ensembles qui se relient peu à peu les uns aux autres, comme le Paramount Laundry-Lindblade Tower-Gary Group Complex, achevé entre 1987 et 1989. La réhabilitation de ces grandes structures de type entrepôt a été récemment complétée par The Box et l'IRS Building, situés non loin. Grâce à une utilisation très inventive de matériaux communs comme des tuyaux d'égout formant colonnes ou des tiges filetées recourbées pour créer des luminaires, Moss a réussi à attirer des agences de publicité ou des maisons de production de disques qui se sont installées dans ce quartier encore abandonné peu de temps auparavant. Le grand Philip Johnson a qualifié Moss de «joaillier de la ferraille». La dernière de ses constructions, Samitaur, est l'une de ses œuvres les plus poétiques et les plus significatives. Il a mis à profit des *air rights* existants (droits de construire en hauteur), pour construire au-dessus d'une voie existante, abordant du même coup le problème des vastes espaces inutilisés de l'espace urbain. À sa manière caractéristique, l'architecte décrit son projet en termes inattendus: «Lorsque vous voyez l'ossature métallique qui soutient le ‹bloc volant› (j'hésite parce que l'on peut facilement mal me comprendre), vous pouvez penser à une autoroute dessinée par un ivrogne. Il n'est pas complètement ivre et n'est pas incohérent. Il parle très sérieusement et de façon très articulée – expliquant les tenants et aboutissants du projet. Mais il parle comme dans un rêve. Il voit le monde avec précision mais très différemment – et fait penser à Coleridge et à son Xanadu. Les références analytiques conventionnelles ont disparu, et une version personnelle, privatisée, apparaît.»[2] Les noms de Xanadu et de Coleridge sont une référence au poème «Kubla Khan»: «Kubla Khan décide d'élever à Xanadu un temple du plaisir...» qui se termine par: «Au son d'une musique splendide, j'élèverai ce temple dans les airs, ce temple ensoleillé! Ces cavernes de glace!» Surélevé sur des poutres soutenues par des colonnes au cœur de ce qui fut la patrie de l'industrie du cinéma à ses origines, Samitaur est une sorte de «temple du plaisir» pour le XXIe siècle, forme flottante qui ramène la vie dans une zone urbaine délaissée.

L'un des clients pour lesquels Frederick Norton Smith et Moss

architect admits that tearing down the existing building might have been a less expensive solution, he says of the original garage, "It had heart and soul, and that made it worth doing all this." A second building in Culver City by Ehrlich, the Sony Child Care Center (1992–94), is a new structure, located directly behind the Game Show Network building. The sensitivity shown by the architect to the needs of children in a day care center in this instance, is indicative of an approach that succeeds in convincing a large corporate client like Sony that it is indeed worth calling on a talented designer rather than using unimaginative industrial buildings to house its activities.

By mixing the use of existing structures and the rehabilitation of old ones in Culver City, and aiming their work at high-technology or entertainment companies, Eric Owen Moss and Steven Ehrlich, with the enlightened backing of a developer or a client, have shown that contemporary architecture can have a positive impact on abandoned urban areas.

La Jolla on my mind
In 1959, when the microbiologist Dr. Jonas Salk went to ask the architect Louis Kahn to build a new laboratory, he said that he wanted it to be the kind of place where "Picasso could come to visit." Salk believed that medical research could not be confined to science alone. The result was the famous Salk Institute for Biological Studies (1959–65), located on a spectacular site overlooking the Pacific Ocean on North Torrey Pines Road in La Jolla, California. La Jolla, a district within the confines of the city of San Diego, is also home to the Scripps Institution of Oceanography, which was endowed by the newspaper publisher Edward Wyllis Scripps (1854–1926). It is a small and apparently wealthy resort town, which is not subject to the kind of urban sprawl that characterizes the environment of Los Angeles.

Another client, undoubtedly as remarkable in his own way as Jonas Salk, has just enriched La Jolla with a building that may one day be considered as significant as Louis Kahn's masterpiece. Gerald Maurice Edelman was born in New York in 1929. He became a professor of biochemistry at Rockefeller University

zögere, weil dies leicht mißzuverstehen ist), wirkt er wie ein Freeway, der von einem Betrunkenen entworfen wurde. Der Trinker ist nicht völlig besoffen oder murmelt unzusammenhängend; er spricht sehr ernsthaft und sehr artikuliert – und erklärt, um was es bei diesem Projekt geht. Aber er redet in einem Traum. Der Betrunkene sieht die Welt genau vor sich, aber völlig anders als alle anderen – und dies ist ein Argument für Coleridge und Xanadu. Die Zeit der konventionellen analytischen Bezüge ist vorüber; eine privatisierte Version ist im Kommen.«[2] Die Namen Xanadu und Coleridge sind natürlich eine Anspielung auf das Gedicht »Kubla Khan«: »In Xanadu ließ Kubla Khan ein stolzes Freudenschloß entstehn...«, das mit den Worten endet, »Daß ich aus den Melodien / Erbaute in der Luft die Pracht / Das Sonnenschloß, das Eisverlies!« Das auf Trägern errichtete und von stählernen Röhren gestützte Samitaur liegt mitten im Herzen der ehemaligen Heimat der Filmindustrie – eine Art »Freudenschloß« des 21. Jahrhunderts, eine schwebende Form, die einem verlassenen Stadviertel wieder neues Leben einhaucht.

Einer der Auftraggeber von Frederick Norton Smith und Moss ist der japanischen Medienriese Sony. Die Firma investierte bereits mehr als 100 Millionen $ in die Region, unter anderem im Rahmen eines Sanierungsprogramms für ein von MGM übernommenes Baugelände, an dem mehrere Architekten beteiligt waren. Unter ihnen befand sich auch Steven Ehrlich, der 1991–93 den großen Sony Music Entertainment Komplex in Santa Monica erbaute. Der 1946 in New York geborene Ehrlich machte 1969 seinen Abschluß am Rensselaer Polytechnic Institute in Troy, New York. Zu den ungewöhnlichsten Aspekten seiner Karriere zählt seine intensive Auseinandersetzung mit der Architektur Nord- und Westafrikas, wo er zwischen 1969 und 1977 arbeitete. Kürzlich beendete Ehrlich die Arbeiten am Game Show Network Building für Sony (1995) – die völlige Neugestaltung einer Autowerkstatt aus den 30er Jahren für einen Fernsehsender, der rund um die Uhr Gameshows ausstrahlt. Laut Aussage des Architekten handelt es sich um »ein Low Tech-Gebäude, das für einen High Tech-Verwendungszweck aufgerüstet wurde«. Obwohl Ehrlich einräumt, daß ein Abriß die preiswertere Lösung

ont réalisé ces bâtiments de Culver City est la grande firme japonaise Sony. Sony a déjà investi plus de 100 millions de $ dans le programme de rénovation d'un site repris à la MGM et confié à plusieurs architectes dont Steven Ehrlich, qui a édifié le Sony Music Entertainment Complex à Santa Monica (1991–93). Né à New York en 1946, Ehrlich est diplômé en architecture du Rensselaer Polytechnic Institute de Troy, New York, en 1969. Aspect inhabituel de son cursus: il a étudié l'architecture vernaculaire de l'Afrique du Nord et de l'Ouest de 1969 à 1977. Il a récemment achevé l'immeuble du Game Show Network pour Sony (1995), réhabilitation globale d'un garage des années 30 pour une chaîne de télévision qui diffuse des jeux 24 heures sur 24. Comme il l'indique: «Il s'agit d'un bâtiment très *low-tech*, qui a été turbo-chargé pour une utilisation très *high-tech*.» Admettant que la destruction du bâtiment et sa reconstruction à neuf auraient peut-être été moins coûteuses, il dit de ce garage: «Il avait un cœur et une âme, cela valait donc la peine de dépenser tant d'efforts.» Le second bâtiment construit à Culver City par Ehrlich directement derrière le précédent, le Sony Child Care Center (1992–94) est une construction entièrement nouvelle. La sensibilité dont témoigne l'architecte envers les besoins des enfants dans cette crèche est indicative d'une approche qui réussit à convaincre un client aussi important que Sony qu'il est plus intéressant de faire appel à des créateurs de talent que de se contenter d'immeubles industriels sans imagination.

En associant réutilisation de constructions existantes et constructions nouvelles à Culver City, pour le compte de sociétés du spectacle ou de haute technologie, Eric Owen Moss et Steven Ehrlich, avec le soutien éclairé d'un promoteur et d'une grande entreprise, ont montré que l'architecture contemporaine pouvait revitaliser des quartiers urbains abandonnés.

L'exemple de La Jolla

En 1959, lorsque le biologiste Jonas Salk demande à l'architecte Louis Kahn de lui construire un nouveau laboratoire, il lui précise qu'il veut élever un endroit où «Picasso pourrait venir en visite». Salk pensait que la recherche médicale ne pouvait se

Tod Williams, Billie Tsien, Neurosciences Institute, San Diego, La Jolla, California, 1993–95. Unlike Louis Kahn's nearby Salk Institute, the Neurosciences Institute is turned in on itself in a more protected or "monastic" design.

Tod Williams, Billie Tsien, Neurosciences Institute, San Diego, La Jolla, Kalifornien, 1993–95. Im Gegensatz zu Louis Kahns nahegelegenem Salk Institute zeichnet sich das Neurosciences Institute durch ein abschirmendes bzw. »klösterliches« Design aus.

Tod Williams, Billie Tsien, Neurosciences Institute, San Diego, La Jolla, Californie, 1993–95. À la différence du Salk Institute de Louis Kahn voisin, ce Neurosciences Institute est refermé sur lui-même, selon un plan plus «monastique.»

in New York in 1966, and founded the Neurosciences Institute there. He received the Nobel Prize for medicine in 1972. Known for the theory he calls "Neural Darwinism", which postulates that the brain develops in relation to the circumstances that it is confronted with, Edelman is a figure to be reckoned with not only in scientific terms, but also in relation to his opinions about art. In an essay written for the catalog of the 1995 Whitney Biennial Exhibition, he said,

"The experience of a work of art defies direct translation into language. At best, it can be handled in terms of metaphor – saying one thing and meaning another...
New ideas about the brain have suggested, for example, how the metaphorical functions of art may be grounded in our bodies. These ideas provide a strong case against mechanical views of the world and the mind. Indeed, modern scientific discoveries contradict the old notion that the world is a machine and the more recent one that the mind is another kind of machine, a computer for understanding the world machine...
As a result of competition and selection constrained by values, particular circuits in the brain are in time favored over others among the myriad possible choices. This view of the brain makes it more akin to an evolutionary jungle (or as Darwin put it, a 'tangled bank') than a computer. It is for this reason that I have called the theory Neural Darwinism.
The intriguing question is: does artistic activity reflect a similar bodily-based set of metaphors?... I am representing here a stronger and more general claim: that almost all our earliest thoughts and images that are grounds for artistic expression arise during development from the form and motion of the human body."[3]

Edelman's comments on the brain and art are of interest because his ideas undoubtedly had an influence on the shape of the new Neurosciences Institute (NSI), a complex designed by the New York architects Tod Williams and Billie Tsien. Located on the grounds of the Scripps Institution, one mile away and across North Torrey Pines Road from the Salk, the NSI is a three-building complex including laboratories, offices, a library and

gewesen wäre, sagt er über die ehemalige Werkstatt: »Sie besaß Herz und Seele, und deshalb war sie die ganze Mühe wert.« Ein weiteres, von Ehrlich errichtetes Gebäude ist das Child Care Center (1992–94), das als Neubau direkt hinter dem Game Show Network Building entstand. Die Sensibilität, mit der der Architekt auf die Bedürfnisse von Kindern in einer Tagesstätte einging, ist typisch für einen Ansatz in der Architektur, der große Firmenkunden wie Sony davon überzeugt, daß sich die Auftragsvergabe an einen talentierten Architekten eher lohnt, als weiterhin phantasielose Industriebauten errichten zu lassen.

Indem sie existierende Bauten weiterverwandten, sie mit völlig neugestalteten alten Gebäuden kombinierten und diese Projekte Firmen aus dem Bereich der Elektronik- und Unterhaltungsindustrie anboten, haben Eric Owen Moss und Steven Ehrlich – mit der verständnisvollen Unterstützung eines Bauunternehmers oder Auftraggebers – bewiesen, daß die zeitgenössische Architektur einen positiven Einfluß auf heruntergekommene Stadtviertel ausüben kann.

La Jolla on my mind

Als der Mikrobiologe Dr. Jonas Salk 1959 den Architekten Louis Kahn bat, ein neues Laborgebäude zu bauen, sagte er ihm, daß es ein Ort werden solle, den »auch Picasso besuchen würde«. Salk glaubte, daß die medizinische Forschung sich nicht nur auf die Wissenschaft beschränken dürfe. Das Ergebnis war das berühmte Salk Institute for Biological Studies (1959–65), das in La Jolla – einem Stadtteil von San Diego – an der North Torrey Pines Road liegt, auf einem aufsehenerregenden Gelände mit Blick über den Pazifik. Hier befindet sich auch die Scripps Institution of Oceanography, die von dem Zeitungsverleger Edward Wyllis Scripps (1854–1926) gestiftet wurde.

Ein weiterer Auftraggeber hat La Jolla vor kurzem um ein Gebäude bereichert, das eines Tages als ebenso bedeutend angesehen werden könnte wie Louis Kahns Meisterwerk. Gerald Maurice Edelman, 1929 in New York geboren, wurde 1966 Professor für Biochemie an der New Yorker Rockefeller University. Er gründete das dortige Neurosciences Institute und erhielt 1972

confiner à la seule science. C'est ainsi que naquit le célèbre Salk Institute for Biological Studies (1959–65) construit sur un site spectaculaire au-dessus de l'océan Pacifique sur North Torrey Pines Road, à La Jolla, Californie. La Jolla est un secteur de la ville de San Diego qui abrite également la Scripps Institution of Oceanography, financée par le propriétaire de journaux Edward Wyllis Scripps (1854–1926). Il s'agit d'une petite ville apparemment riche qui n'est pas sujette à cette forme de «banlieurisation» qui caractérise les environs de Los Angeles.

Personnage aussi remarquable à sa façon que Jonas Salk, un autre savant vient d'enrichir La Jolla d'un immeuble qui sera peut-être un jour jugé aussi important que le chef-d'œuvre de Louis Kahn. Gerald Maurice Edelman est né à New York en 1929. Il devient professeur de biochimie à New York en 1966 et y fonde le Neurosciences Institute. Il reçoit le prix Nobel de médecine en 1972. Connu pour sa théorie du «darwinisme neuronal» qui postule que le cerveau se développe en fonction des circonstances auxquelles il est confronté, Edelman est une grande figure avec laquelle il faut compter non seulement pour ses découvertes scientifiques, mais également pour ses opinions sur l'art. Dans un essai rédigé pour l'exposition biennale du Whitney en 1995, il écrit: «L'expérience d'une œuvre d'art défie sa translation directe dans le langage. Au mieux, elle peut être traitée en termes de métaphore – dire une chose en en signifiant une autre...

De nouvelles idées sur le cerveau ont suggéré, par exemple, que les fonctions métaphoriques de l'art sont peut-être enracinées dans nos corps. Ces idées s'opposent avec force aux vues mécanistes du monde et de l'esprit. En fait les découvertes scientifiques récentes contredisent la notion ancienne selon laquelle le monde est une machine et, plus récente, pour laquelle l'esprit est une sorte de machine, un ordinateur qui permettrait de comprendre la machine-monde...

Il résulte de l'esprit de compétition et de sélection contenu dans les valeurs que, avec le temps, des circuits particuliers du cerveau sont favorisés par rapport à d'autres parmi la myriade de choix possibles. Cette conception du cerveau en fait plus une

reading room, a refectory and an auditorium. Edelman, who was a fellow at the Salk Institute from 1973 to 1985, admits that the Kahn building was very much in his mind, if only by way of contradiction: "The Salk is a triumph of monumental architecture," he maintains, " but I didn't want to capture that quality. I wanted a sense of commitment to excellence and artistic vision." Architect Billie Tsien is more direct in her appraisal of the contrast between the buildings: "The purity of view and space is not something we're looking for," she says. "That's my problem with the Salk-people seem like litter in it. Our whole thought about making places is that people can enter them without destroying the clarity of space." Rather than monumentality, the architects and their client have opted for a complexity and a discretion that honor them and undoubtedly mark a new maturity in contemporary American architecture. As Herbert Muschamp, the architecture critic of *The New York Times*, wrote: "To see the world, in Dr. Edelman's view, is to construct the world. And the Institute's architecture... introduces us to a world in which perception, intuition and mood are as real as concrete, stone and glass... The building conveys a philosophical outlook in architectural terms. It makes no appeal to the external authority of theory. In the unfolding of its imagery and spaces, in its ethereal use of materials, the building invites us to appreciate the simultaneous separateness and connectedness of things – minds and bodies, objects and ideas, people and their environments. This is a magnificent piece of work."[4] As Gerald Edelman points out, the machine, which was long the metaphor sought out by modern architecture, has less to do with art than does the body or the brain itself, which is by no means a machine. A building such as the Neurosciences Institute in La Jolla, which cannot really be perceived as a whole from any particular angle, promises a more profound, more humanistic approach to the art of design and building, without the superficial "return to the past" suggested by post-modernism.

Tod Williams and Billie Tsien have undoubtedly shown a part of their considerable talents with the NSI complex. Another of their projects, the renovation and expansion of the Phoenix

den Nobelpreis für Medizin. Edelman, der für seine Theorie zum »Neuraldarwinismus« (das menschliche Gehirn entwickelt sich in Relation zu den Umständen, mit denen es konfrontiert wird) bekannt wurde, gilt nicht nur in wissenschaftlicher, sondern auch in kunstkritischer Hinsicht als anerkannte Größe. In einem Essay für den Katalog der Biennial Exhibition (1995) des Whitney Museum of American Art schrieb er:

»Das Erleben eines Kunstwerks widersetzt sich einer direkten Übersetzung in Sprache. Es könnte bestenfalls mit den Mitteln der Metaphorik erfaßt werden – man sagt das eine und meint das andere...
Neue Theorien über das menschliche Gehirn besagen, daß die metaphorischen Funktionen der Kunst in unserem Körper verankert sind. Diese These wendet sich gegen eine mechanische Betrachtungsweise der Welt und des Geistes. Und tatsächlich widersprechen moderne wissenschaftliche Entdeckungen der alten Auffassung von der Welt als Maschine sowie der Theorie, derzufolge der Geist ebenfalls eine Art Maschine ist – ein Computer, mit dem sich die Weltmaschine verstehen läßt...
Als Ergebnis eines Wettbewerbs und einer von Werten eingeengten Selektion werden unter den Myriaden von Möglichkeiten bestimmte Schaltkreise des Gehirns im Laufe der Zeit vor anderen bevorzugt. Nach dieser Auffassung ähnelt das Gehirn eher einem evolutionären Dschungel (oder, in Darwins Worten, einem ›wirren Knäuel‹) als einem Computer. Aus diesem Grund habe ich meine Theorie als ›Neuraldarwinismus‹ bezeichnet. Die faszinierende Frage lautet: Greift die künstlerische Aktivität ebenfalls auf im Körper verankerte Gruppen von Metaphern zurück?... Ich stelle hier eine noch stärkere Behauptung auf – nämlich, daß unsere frühesten Gedanken und Bilder, die den Ursprung künstlerischer Ausdruckskraft bilden, während der Entwicklung durch Form und Bewegung des menschlichen Körpers entstehen.«[3]

Edelmans Thesen über das Gehirn und die Kunst sind deshalb so interessant, weil sie mit Sicherheit Einfluß auf die Form des neuen Neurosciences Institute (NSI) ausübten – ein Komplex, den die New Yorker Architekten Tod Williams und Billie Tsien

sorte de jungle évolutionniste qu'un ordinateur. C'est pour cette raison que je l'ai appelée la théorie du darwinisme neuronal.

La question qui se pose est celle-ci: l'activité artistique reflète-t-elle un ensemble similaire de métaphores à base physique? Je prétends ici à une revendication plus forte et plus générale: que presque toutes nos premières pensées et images qui sont le terrain d'une expression artistique naissent lors du développement de la forme et du mouvement du corps humain.»[3]

Les idées d'Edelman sur le cerveau et l'art sont d'autant plus intéressantes qu'elles ont sans aucun doute exercé une influence sur l'apparence du nouveau Neurosciences Institute (NSI), ensemble conçu par les architectes new-yorkais Tod Williams et Billie Tsien. Implanté sur le terrain de la Scripps Institution, à un kilomètre et demi du Salk Institute, le NSI est constitué de trois bâtiments abritant des laboratoires, des bureaux, une bibliothèque avec salle de lecture, une salle de conférence, et un réfectoire. Edelman, qui a travaillé au Salk Institute de 1973 à 1985, admet qu'il a beaucoup réfléchi au chef-d'œuvre de Kahn, ne serait-ce que par esprit de contradiction: «Le Salk est un triomphe d'architecture monumentale», affirme-t-il, «mais mon objectif n'était pas d'atteindre à cette qualité. Je voulais que l'on sente une recherche de l'excellence et une vision artistique.» L'architecte Billie Tsien est plus directe quand elle juge le contraste entre les deux constructions: «La pureté de la vue et de l'espace n'est pas ce que nous recherchons», précise-t-elle, «c'est mon problème avec le Salk. On a l'impression que ceux qui s'y trouvent le perturbent. Notre volonté, quand nous dessinons un lieu, est que l'on puisse le parcourir sans détruire la clarté de lecture de l'espace.» Plutôt que la monumentalité, ces architectes et leur client ont opté pour une complexité et une discrétion qui les honore, et marque sans aucun doute une nouvelle étape de la maturité de l'architecture américaine. Comme le critique d'architecture du «New York Times», Herbert Muschamp, l'a écrit: «Voir le monde, selon la vision du Dr. Edelman, est le construire. Et l'architecture de l'Institut... vous introduit à un monde dans lequel la perception, l'intuition et l'atmosphère sont aussi réelles que le béton, la pierre et le verre. Le bâtiment

Tod Williams, Billie Tsien, Phoenix Art Museum, Phoenix, Arizona, 1992–96. A $25 million expansion and renovation of this thirty-five-year-old museum, including a new 4,200 square meter gallery.

Tod Williams, Billie Tsien, Phoenix Art Museum, Phoenix, Arizona, 1992–96. Die Erweiterung und Neugestaltung dieses 35 Jahre alten Museums, das nun auch eine neue, 4 200 m² große Galerie beherbergt, kostete 25 Millionen Dollar.

Tod Williams, Billie Tsien, Phoenix Art Museum, Phoenix, Arizona, 1992–96. L'extension et la rénovation de ce musée vieux de 35 ans, dont une nouvelle galerie de 4 200 m², a coûté 25 millions de $.

Venturi, Scott Brown, Museum of Contemporary Art, San Diego, La Jolla, California, 1986–96. An expansion and renovation of the 1915 Scripps House originally designed by Irving Gill.

Venturi, Scott Brown, Museum of Contemporary Art, San Diego, La Jolla, Kalifornien, 1986–96. Erweiterung und Neugestaltung des von Irving Gill 1915 entworfenen Scripps House.

Venturi, Scott Brown, Museum of Contemporary Art, San Diego, La Jolla, Californie, 1986–96. Extension et rénovation de Scripp House (1915), conçue à l'origine par Irving Gill.

Museum, opened on September 20, 1996. Doubling the size of the former 35 year-old facility, their design features a 28 meter high conic sculpture pavilion with walls of cast translucent fiberglass resin. This element, together with an exterior cladding of "celadon green" panels made of an aggregate of green glacier quartz from Utah mixed with white sand and mica from Georgia, confers a sculptural quality to the whole composition. With the new public library designed by Will Bruder, and an upcoming U.S. Federal Courthouse by Richard Meier (1995–2000), Phoenix has become a city to be reckoned with in the area of contemporary architecture, as befits its recent prosperity.

Though less ambitious than the Neurosciences Institute, the renovation and expansion of the San Diego Museum of Contemporary Art, also in La Jolla, by Venturi, Scott Brown, gives palpable evidence too of a new-found maturity in American architecture. And at that, from the very inventor of the post-modern attitude, the author of *Complexity and Contradiction in Architecture* himself, Mr. Robert Venturi. Since 1941, the museum has occupied the former house of Ellen Browning Scripps, a villa built in 1915 by Irving Gill, one of the outstanding pioneers of modern architecture in the United States. Voted the ninth most important building in America since 1850 in a 1957 poll by the magazine *Architectural Record,* the Scripps house is close to other Irving Gill buildings near downtown La Jolla, such as his Women's Club (1912–14) across the street. For a total cost of $9,250,000, the Philadelphia architects harmonized the various

entwarfen. Das auf dem Gelände der Scripps Institution entstandene NSI liegt nur 1,5 km auf der North Torrey Pines Road vom Salk Institute entfernt. Es handelt sich um einen Komplex aus drei Gebäuden, mit Laboratorien, Büros, einer Bücherei mit Lesesaal, einer Mensa und einem Auditorium. Edelman, der von 1973 bis 1985 am Salk Institute lehrte, gibt zu, daß er Kahns Bauwerk immer vor Augen hatte – wenn auch nur als Negativbeispiel: »Das Salk ist ein Triumph der monumentalen Architektur«, sagt Edelman, »aber ich wollte diese Eigenschaft nicht einfangen. Mir schwebte ein Gefühl der Hingabe an die Einzigartigkeit und die künstlerische Vision vor.« Die Architektin Billie Tsien ist in ihrem Vergleich der beiden Gebäude etwas direkter: »Wir haben keine Reinheit der Ansicht und des Raums angestrebt«, sagt sie. »Das ist auch mein Problem mit dem Salk – Menschen wirken darin wie Müll. Unsere Auffassung von Gebäuden beruht darauf, daß Menschen sie betreten können, ohne die Klarheit des Raumes zu zerstören.« Statt für die Monumentalität haben sich Architekten und Auftraggeber für eine Komplexität und Zurückhaltung entschieden, die sie ehrt und zugleich eine neue Reife in der zeitgenössischen amerikanischen Architektur kennzeichnet. Herbert Muschamp, der Architekturkritiker der »New York Times«, schrieb: »Die Welt mit Dr. Edelmans Augen zu sehen, heißt, die Welt neu zu konstruieren. Und die Architektur des Instituts... entführt uns in eine Welt, in der Wahrnehmung, Intuition und Stimmung so real sind wie Beton, Stein und Glas.... Das Gebäude vermittelt eine philosophische Weltanschauung in architektonischen Begriffen; es wendet sich nicht an die externe Autorität der Theorie. Durch die Entfaltung seiner Bildsprache und seiner Räume, durch die vergeistigte Verwendung seiner Materialien lädt es uns ein, die simultane Trennung und Verbindung von Dingen zu erleben – Geist und Körper, Objekte und Ideen, Menschen und ihre Umgebung. Dies ist ein großartiges Bauwerk.«[4] Wie Gerald Edelman erläutert, hat die Maschine, die von der modernen Architektur lange als Metapher erforscht wurde, weniger mit der Kunst zu tun als der Körper oder das menschliche Gehirn, das keineswegs eine Maschine ist. Ein Gebäude wie das NSI in La Jolla, das aus kei-

est chargé d'une présence philosophique qui se traduit en termes architecturaux. Il ne fait pas appel à l'autorité extérieure de la théorie. En déployant son imagerie et ses espaces, dans son usage éthéré des matériaux, il nous invite à apprécier la séparation et la connexion simultanée des choses – esprits et corps, objets et idées, gens et environnement – c'est un superbe travail.«[4] Comme Gerald Edelman le fait remarquer, la machine, qui a longtemps été la métaphore recherchée par l'architecture moderne, a moins de rapports avec l'art que le corps ou le cerveau, qui n'est certainement pas une machine. Un bâtiment comme le Neurosciences Institute de La Jolla, qui ne peut être perçu dans sa totalité sous quelque angle que ce soit, annonce une approche plus profonde et plus humaniste de l'architecture et de la construction, sans ce «retour au passé» superficiel qu'avait suggéré le postmodernisme.

Tod Williams et Billie Tsien ont fait preuve d'un incontestable talent dans ce NSI. Un autre de leurs projets, la rénovation et extension du Phoenix Museum, a été inauguré le 20 septembre 1996. Pour doubler la taille de l'ancien bâtiment vieux de 35 ans, ils ont conçu un pavillon de forme conique de 28 m de haut à murs en résine et fibre de verre moulée translucide. Cet élément, ainsi qu'un revêtement extérieur de panneaux vert céladon en agrégat de quartz vert glacier de l'Utah mélangé à du sable blanc et du mica de Géorgie, confère une qualité toute sculpturale à leur composition. Avec la nouvelle bibliothèque de Will Bruder et la future cour fédérale de justice de Richard Meier (1995–2000), Phoenix, profitant de sa prospérité récente, est devenue une ville avec laquelle il faudra compter dans le domaine de l'architecture contemporaine.

Moins ambitieuses que le Neuroscience Institute, la rénovation et l'extension du Museum of Contemporary Art de San Diego, également à La Jolla, par Venturi, Scott Brown, donnent une nouvelle preuve palpable de cette maturité affirmée de l'architecture américaine, offerte par l'inventeur de l'attitude postmoderne, l'auteur de «Complexité et contradiction en architecture», Robert Venturi lui-même. Depuis 1941, le musée occupe l'ancienne résidence d'Ellen Browning Scripps, villa

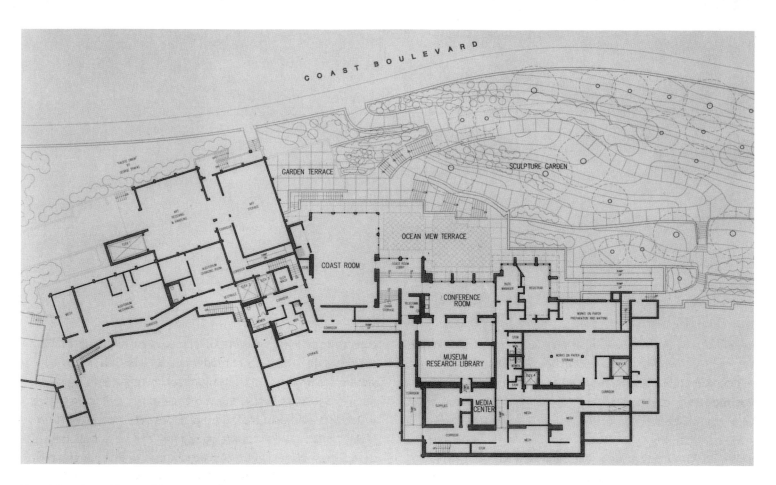

Venturi, Scott Brown, Museum of Contemporary Art, San Diego, La Jolla, California, 1986–96. A floor plan shows the relationship of newer spaces to the existing house.

Venturi, Scott Brown, Museum of Contemporary Art, San Diego, La Jolla, Kalifornien, 1986–96. Der Grundriß zeigt die Beziehung zwischen den neuen Räumen und den bereits vorhandenen Gebäudebereichen.

Venturi, Scott Brown, Museum of Contemporary Art, San Diego, La Jolla, Californie, 1986–96. Plan de niveau montrant la relation entre les nouveaux espaces et la maison originale.

additions that had been made to the original house over time, and added new facades, and in particular, a new entrance lobby providing access to the bookstore, auditoriums and extra gallery space. The most visually spectacular element of Venturi, Scott Brown's work is the "star-shaped clerestory" over the new lobby, a fact that calls attention to the relative modesty of the project, and the respect that it shows for the work of Irving Gill.

An interesting sidelight to the work of Venturi, Scott Brown is the insistence of the firm on the collaborative nature of their work. A cover story in the June 1996 issue of the professional magazine *Architecture* on husband and wife teams called attention to the fact that Venturi, but not his wife and partner Denise Scott Brown, was honored with the 1991 Pritzker Prize. As Martin Filler wrote, "Using the flimsy excuse that the award is meant for individuals, not firms, the Pritzker committee dishonored itself by snubbing the world's most distinguished woman architect, with no other female of her stature on the horizon. That scandal still rankles enough for Venturi to have informed the AIA that he will not accept its proffered Gold Medal unless his partner is included. 'There is this old-fashioned idea that the architect is a 19th century Romantic genius who works alone,' Venturi says, 'but in fact it is an intensely collaborative effort.'"[5]

Big in Asia

Although it is in large part a matter of coincidence, it happens that two of the most impressive projects being built in the world by American architects are in fact the work of émigré designers, both born in Latin America. Both too are located in Asia, and that is less of a coincidence. The first of these projects, the twin

nem Blickwinkel als vollständiges Ganzes erfaßt werden kann, zeigt eine tiefergehende, menschlichere Auseinandersetzung mit der Kunst des Designs und der Architektur als die von der Postmoderne angestrebte, oberflächliche »Rückkehr zur Vergangenheit«.

Mit dem NSI-Komplex haben Tod Williams und Billie Tsien einen Teil ihrer bemerkenswerten Fähigkeiten unter Beweis gestellt. Ein weiteres ihrer Projekte, die Neugestaltung und Erweiterung des Phoenix Museum, wurde am 20. September 1996 eröffnet. Der Entwurf, der die Größe des 35 Jahre alten Museumsbaus verdoppelt, umfaßt als Mittelpunkt einen 28 m hohen, konischen Skulpturenpavillon, dessen Wände aus gegossenem, lichtdurchlässigem Fiberglas bestehen. Zusammen mit der Fassadenverkleidung aus blaßgrünen Platten, die aus einer Mischung von grünem Gletscherquartz aus Utah, weißem Sand und Glimmer aus Georgia bestehen, verleiht dieses Element der Gesamtkomposition eine skulpturale Qualität. Mit der von Will Bruder entworfenen öffentlichen Bibliothek und Richard Meiers geplantem US-Bundesgerichtshof (1995–2000) hat sich Phoenix zu einer bedeutenden Stadt auf dem Gebiet der zeitgenössischen Architektur entwickelt – ganz wie es sich für ihren momentanen Wohlstand gehört.

Die von Venturi, Scott Brown – ebenfalls in La Jolla – durchgeführte Neugestaltung und Erweiterung des San Diego Museum of Contemporary Art kann ebenfalls als Beweis für eine neue Reife in der amerikanischen Architektur stehen. Dies gilt umso mehr, als der Entwurf von Robert Venturi höchstpersönlich stammt, dem Erfinder der Postmoderne und Autor des Buches »Complexity and Contradiction in Architecture« (Komplexität und Widerspruch in der Architektur). Seit 1941 befindet sich das Museum im ehemaligen Haus von Ellen Browning Scripps, das 1915 von Irving Gill erbaut wurde, einem herausragenden Pionier der modernen Architektur in den USA. Das Scripps House, das 1957 in einer Umfrage des Magazins »Architectural Record« unter die zehn wichtigsten Bauten Amerikas seit 1850 gewählt wurde, liegt nahe der Innenstadt von La Jolla, in unmittelbarer Nähe einiger anderer Bauten Irving Gills. Für eine Gesamt-

construite en 1915 par Irving Gill, l'un des plus remarquables pionniers de l'architecture moderne aux États-Unis. Élue neuvième plus importante réalisation architecturale américaine depuis 1850 lors d'une enquête menée en 1957 par le magazine «Architectural Record», la Scripps House est proche des autres réalisations de Gill au centre de La Jolla, comme son Women's Club (1912–14), de l'autre côté de la rue. Pour un budget total de 9 250 000 $ les architectes de Philadelphie ont harmonisé les diverses additions apportées au bâtiment d'origine au fil du temps, ajouté de nouvelles façades, et en particulier un nouveau hall d'entrée qui donne accès à la librairie, à des salles de conférence et à des galeries nouvelles. L'élément visuel le plus spectaculaire de l'intervention de Venturi et Scott Brown sont les «ouvertures en forme d'étoile» au-dessus du nouveau hall, qui montrent la modestie relative du projet et le respect de l'œuvre d'Irving Gill.

Un aspect secondaire intéressant du travail de Venturi, Scott Brown est leur insistance sur la nature de collaboration de leur travail. Un dossier paru dans le numéro de juin 1996 de la revue professionnelle «Architecture» sur les équipes d'architectes mariés rappelait que c'est Venturi et non son épouse et associée Denise Scott Brown qui avait reçu le Prix Pritzker en 1991. Comme le notait Martin Filler: «Avec l'excuse fragile selon laquelle ce prix était destiné à des individus, le comité Pritzker s'est déshonoré en snobant la plus remarquable architecte du monde, alors qu'aucune consœur de sa stature n'existe à l'horizon. Ce scandale est suffisamment resté sur le cœur de Venturi pour qu'il informe l'AIA qu'il refuserait sa médaille d'or si elle n'était pas également attribuée à sa partenaire, précisant qu'‹il existe une idée démodée qui veut que l'architecte est une sorte de génie romantique travaillant en solitaire, alors qu'en fait son travail est le résultat d'un intense effort de collaboration›. »[5]

Aux dimensions de l'Asie

Bien qu'il s'agisse en grande partie d'une coïncidence, deux des plus impressionnants chantiers actuellement en cours dans le monde sont l'œuvre d'architectes américains tous deux immi-

Petronas Towers in Kuala Lumpur, Malaysia have wrested a coveted title from the city of Chicago – that of the tallest office building in the world. At 452 meters above street level they are at least 7 meters higher than the Sears Tower in Chicago, the former record holder. This fact in itself is the reflection of the very high economic growth rates in some Asian countries, and in Malaysia in particular. With a total land area of 328,550 square kilometers, or a little more than the state of New Mexico, and a population of 19,723,000 (July 1995 estimate), Malaysia has posted a remarkable record of 9% average annual growth in the period 1988–94. The real growth rate of the national product in 1994 was estimated at 8.7%. For this Islamic country with a large Chinese minority, Cesar Pelli, born in Tucuman, Argentina in 1926, chose to view the very tall building in a new manner. As he says, "The new towers should not look as if they could have been built in America or Europe, but as somehow belonging to Malaysia. The most important artistic decision was to make the towers figurative and symmetrically composed. In the modern movement architects have endeavored to compose pairs of buildings in an asymmetrical composition, preferably by making the two buildings of differing heights, or if the same height, organized diagonally, following the examples of Mies van der Rohe's Lakeshore Drive Apartment Towers and as Minoru Yamasaki did at the World Trade Center Towers in downtown Manhattan. The symmetrical arrangement was avoided by early modernists precisely because of its symbolic quality. The towers we designed are not only symmetrical but figurative, creating an also figurative space between them. This space is the key element in the composition. The power of the void is increased and made more explicit by the pedestrian bridge that connects the two towers at the 41st and 42nd floors, the skylobby floors. The bridge with its supporting structure creates a portal to the sky, a 170m high portal, a door to the infinite... The plan of the buildings is based on the geometry of two interlocked squares, which is perhaps the most important geometric form underlying Islamic designs." Some firmly contest the utility of twin eighty-eight-story towers in the midst of a city which has not yet attained

summe von 9 250 000 $ brachten die in Philadelphia ansässigen Architekten die verschiedenen Anbauten miteinander in Einklang, um die das Haus im Laufe der Zeit erweitert worden war; darüber hinaus entwarfen sie neue Fassaden und vor allem einen neuen Eingangsbereich, mit Zugang zur Buchhandlung, verschiedenen Auditorien und zusätzlichen Museumsräumen. Das optisch auffälligste Element der Neugestaltung ist das »sternförmige Oberlichtfenster« über der neuen Lobby – eine Tatsache, die ein bezeichnendes Licht auf den relativ bescheidenen Umfang des Projekts wirft und zeigt, welchen Respekt es den Arbeiten von Irving Gill zollt.

Als im Juni 1996 die Fachzeitschrift »Architecture« ihre Titelgeschichte Teams miteinander verheirateter Architekten widmete, lenkte sie die Aufmerksamkeit auf die Tatsache, daß nur Venturi, nicht aber seiner Frau und Partnerin Denise Scott Brown 1991 der Pritzker Preis verliehen worden war. Martin Fuller schrieb: »Unter dem fadenscheinigen Vorwand, daß der Preis nur Einzelpersonen und keinen Firmen verliehen wird, diskreditierte sich das Pritzker-Komitee selbst und brüskierte die berühmteste Architektin der Welt. Dieser Skandal nagt immer noch so stark an Venturi, daß er der AIA mitteilte, er werde die angebotene Goldmedaille ablehnen, wenn seine Partnerin sie nicht auch erhielte. ›Es herrscht immer noch die altmodische Vorstellung, daß ein Architekt wie ein romantisches Genie aus dem 19. Jahrhundert allein arbeitet‹, sagt Venturi, ›dabei handelt es sich in Wirklichkeit um eine intensive gemeinschaftliche Anstrengung.‹«[5]

Groß in Asien

Obwohl es hauptsächlich einem Zufall zu verdanken ist, werden zur Zeit zwei der beeindruckendsten Bauprojekte der Welt von in Lateinamerika geborenen und in die USA ausgewanderten Architekten realisiert. Darüber hinaus liegen beide Projekte in Asien – und das ist kein Zufall. Das erste dieser beiden Bauwerke, die Petronas Twin Towers in Kuala Lumpur, haben der Stadt Chicago einen begehrten Titel entrissen – den der Stadt mit dem höchsten Bürogebäude der Welt. Mit einer Höhe von 452 m sind die

grés et venus d'Amérique latine. Ces deux projets concernent l'Asie, ce qui n'est pas un hasard. La première de ces réalisations, les tours jumelles Petronas, à Kuala Lumpur (Malaisie), a ravi à Chicago le titre convoité de posséder la tour la plus haute du monde. Avec 452 m de haut, elles mesurent sept mètres de plus que la Sears Tower de Chicago, ancienne détentrice du titre. Ce fait en soi reflète la croissance économique extrêmement rapide de certains pays asiatiques, et de la Malaisie en particulier. Avec 328 550 kilomètres carrés, un peu plus que l'État du Nouveau-Mexique, et une population de 19 723 000 habitants (juillet 95), la Malaisie connaît une remarquable croissance annuelle moyenne de 9% entre 1988 et 1994, et de 8,7% en 1994. Pour ce pays musulman, où vit une importante communauté chinoise, Cesar Pelli, né à Tucuman (Argentine) en 1926, a renouvelé l'art de l'immeuble de grande hauteur: «Ces nouvelles tours ne devaient pas sembler pouvoir être construites en Amérique ou en Europe, mais paraître appartenir d'une certaine façon à la Malaisie. La décision artistique la plus importante a été d'élever des tours ‹figuratives›, composées de façon symétrique. Le mouvement moderniste a vu les architectes articuler symétriquement des paires de bâtiments, essentiellement avec des hauteurs différentes, ou lorsqu'elles étaient de la même hauteur, disposées en diagonale, suivant en cela l'exemple de Mies van der Rohe pour les Lakeshore Drive Apartment Towers ou de Minoru Yamasaki pour le World Trade Center à Manhattan. La disposition symétrique fut évitée par les premiers modernistes justement pour sa symbolique. Les tours que nous avons conçues ne sont pas seulement symétriques mais figuratives, créant entre elles un espace également figuratif. Cet espace est l'élément clé de la composition. La puissance du vide est accrue et rendue encore plus explicite par la passerelle qui réunit les deux tours entre le 41e et le 42e niveau. Cette passerelle et ses supports forment une sorte de porte ouverte sur le ciel, une porte de 170 m de haut, donnant sur l'infini... Le plan du bâtiment repose sur la géométrie de deux carrés superposés et décalés, l'une des formes le plus souvent utilisées dans les motifs graphiques islamiques.» Certains contestent fortement

Cesar Pelli, Petronas Twin Towers, Kuala Lumpur, Malaysia, 1991–97. A night image taken during construction gives an idea of the stunning presence of these twin towers on the Kuala Lumpur skyline.

Cesar Pelli, Petronas Twin Towers, Kuala Lumpur, Malaysia, 1991–97. Die während der Bauphase entstandene Nachtaufnahme vermittelt einen Eindruck von der verblüffenden Präsenz dieser beiden Doppeltürme inmitten der Silhouette der Stadt Kuala Lumpur.

Cesar Pelli, Petronas Twin Towers, Kuala Lumpur, Malaisie, 1991–97. Cette vue de nuit, prise pendant la construction, donne une idée de l'étonnante présence de ces tours jumelles sur le panorama de Kuala Lumpur.

Rafael Viñoly, Tokyo International Forum, Tokyo,
Japan, 1989–96. This aerial image of the complex
shows its layout, with the oblong form of the
191 meter long Glass Hall.

Rafael Viñoly, Tokyo International Forum, Tokio, Japan,
1989–96. Die Luftaufnahme des Komplexes zeigt den
Grundriß und die langgestreckte Form der 191 m
langen Glass Hall.

Rafael Viñoly, Forum international de Tokyo, Tokyo,
Japon, 1989–96. Vue aérienne du complexe montrant
le plan et la forme oblongue du Hall de verre de 191 m
de long.

the kind of urban density that makes such high-rise development
inevitable. Located in the midst of the former Selangor Turf Club,
an area of 45 hectares in the heart of the commercial district or
"Golden Triangle," half of the site will be opened to the public as
park designed by Roberto Burle Marx, but another tall building,
the fifty-story Ampang Tower designed by Roche Dinkeloo, will
soon join Cesar Pelli's record breaker. It was undoubtedly the
architect himself who summed up the reasoning behind the
erection of such tall buildings: "Very tall structures have the power
to not only mark a place, but to become the symbol of a place."

Whereas Cesar Pelli has had extensive experience in the
realization of large projects, Rafael Viñoly had never before
attempted anything approaching the scale of the new Tokyo
International Forum. Located on a 3 hectare site formerly occupied by the Tokyo City Hall (Kenzo Tange, 1956), near the outer
gardens of the Imperial Palace and close to the Tokyo JR Station,
the Forum is the largest and most important cultural and convention center in Japan. Born in Montevideo, Uruguay in 1944,
and established in New York since 1979, Viñoly was selected by
a jury that included I.M. Pei, Fumihiko Maki, Kenzo Tange,
Vittorio Gregotti and Arthur Erickson in November 1989, which is
to say before the speculative real estate "bubble" broke in Japan.
This explains the extremely ambitious nature of this project,
whose form consists of two intersecting glass and steel ellipses

Petronas Twin Towers mindestens 7 m höher als der ehemalige Rekordhalter, der Sears Tower in Chicago. Diese Tatsache reflektiert das sehr hohe Wirtschaftswachstum in einigen Ländern Asiens, insbesondere in Malaysia. Mit einer Gesamtfläche von 328 550 km² (etwas mehr als New Mexico) und einer Bevölkerung von 19 723 000 (Schätzung, Juli 1995) ist es Malaysia gelungen, von 1988–94 den bemerkenswerten Rekord von 9 % Wirtschaftswachstum pro Jahr aufzustellen. Dabei wurde die reale Wachstumsrate des Bruttosozialprodukts für 1994 auf 8,7 % geschätzt. Für dieses islamische Land mit seiner großen chinesischen Minderheit entschloß sich der 1926 in Tucuman in Argentinien geborene Cesar Pelli, ein sehr hohes Gebäude auf völlig neue Art und Weise zu entwerfen. Er sagt: »Die neuen Türme sollten nicht an Gebäude in Europa oder Amerika erinnern, sondern in gewisser Weise typisch für Malaysia sein. Die wichtigste künstlerische Entscheidung betraf die Tatsache, die Türme metaphorisch und symmetrisch zu gestalten. Die Architekten der Moderne haben danach gestrebt, Gebäudepaare asymmetrisch zu entwerfen, also entweder zwei Türme von unterschiedlicher Höhe zu bauen oder zwei gleich hohe, aber diagonal organisierte Gebäude zu errichten. Dies gilt für Mies van der Rohes Lakeshore Drive Apartment Towers oder für den Aufbau von Minoru Yamasakis World Trade Center in Manhattan. Das symmetrische Arrangement wurde von den frühen Modernisten aufgrund seiner symbolischen Qualität bewußt vermieden. Dagegen sind die von uns entworfenen Türme nicht nur symmetrisch, sondern auch metaphorisch und schaffen zwischen sich einen ebenso metaphorischen Raum. Dieser Raum ist das zentrale Element der Komposition, und seine Kraft wird noch verstärkt und hervorgehoben durch die Fußgängerbrücke, die den 41. und 42. Stock der beiden Türme – die »Skylobby« – miteinander verbindet. Die Brücke mit ihrer Tragekonstruktion schafft ein Tor zum Himmel, ein 170 m hohes Portal, eine Tür zum Unendlichen... Der Gebäudegrundriß basiert auf der Geometrie zweier ineinandergreifender Quadrate – der wichtigsten geometrischen Form in islamischen Entwürfen.« Manche Kritiker bezweifeln hartnäckig den Nutzen zweier 88 Stockwerke hoher Türme mitten in

l'utilité de deux tours jumelles de 88 étages au milieu d'une ville qui n'a pas encore atteint le niveau de densité qui pourrait rendre ce genre de construction inévitable. Situées sur les 45 ha de l'ancien Selangor Turf Club, au cœur du quartier commercial du «Triangle d'or», elles seront entourées d'un parc public de 22 ha dessiné par Roberto Burle Marx, et bientôt rejointes par un autre immeuble de grande hauteur (50 étages), la tour Ampang de Roche Dinkeloo. L'architecte résume ainsi l'idée sous-jacente à l'érection de bâtiments aussi élevés: «Les immeubles de très grande hauteur ont le pouvoir non seulement de marquer un lieu, mais d'en devenir le symbole.»

Si Cesar Pelli possédait déjà une vaste expérience de la réalisation de projets d'envergure, Rafael Viñoly n'avait encore jamais été confronté avec un chantier approchant l'échelle du nouveau Forum international de Tokyo. Situé sur un terrain de 3 ha naguère occupé par l'hôtel de ville de Tokyo (Kenzo Tange, 1956), près des jardins extérieurs du Palais impérial et proche de la gare JR, le Forum est le plus vaste et le plus important centre de conférences du Japon. Né à Montevideo (Uruguay) en 1944, et installé à New York depuis 1979, Viñoly a été sélectionné par un jury comprenant I.M. Pei, Fumihiko Maki, Kenzo Tange, Vittorio Gregotti et Arthur Erickson en novembre 1989, soit avant l'éclatement de la «bulle financière» japonaise. Ceci explique la nature extrêmement ambitieuse du projet, dont la forme consiste en deux ellipses d'acier et de verre en intersection, enfermant un énorme hall central. Avec une surface totale au sol de 130 000 m² carrés et pour un coût de 1,6 milliard de $, le Forum international de Tokyo est peut-être le plus vaste et le plus coûteux bâtiment de ce type jamais contruit dans le monde. Son spectaculaire «Hall de verre» mesure 191 m de long, 30 de large et 57 de haut. Le Hall A, de 5 000 places, est la plus grande salle de Tokyo. Cet ensemble massif manifeste également dans sa dénomination et dans le processus qui a abouti au choix d'un architecte étranger, un effort du Japon de s'ouvrir davantage au monde extérieur. Viñoly a tenu à obtenir une licence d'architecte japonais, performance que peu d'étrangers ont accomplie, mais ses efforts portent néanmoins la marque de l'euphorie spécula-

enclosing an enormous central lobby. With a total floor area of over 130,000 square meters, and a project cost exceeding $1.6 billion, the Tokyo International Forum may indeed be the most expensive and vast building of its type in the world. It spectacular Glass Hall measures 191 meters in length, 30 meters in width and 57 meters in height. Its 5,000 seat Hall A is the largest theater in Tokyo. Massive by nature, the Tokyo International Forum represents an effort to open Japan more to the outside world, both in its very name, and in the process by which a foreign architect was chosen. Viñoly went to the trouble of becoming a registered architect in Japan, a feat that few if any other foreigners have achieved, but his effort does seem to bear the mark of the speculative euphoria of the 1980s. *The New York Times* greeted the design for the Tokyo International Forum with more than a little enthusiasm, at least some of which may have been well taken. As Herbert Muschamp wrote in 1993, "Some may find the design excessively retrospective, an evocation of yesterday's vision of things to come. Well, those things did come, but seldom with the grace Mr. Viñoly promises to confer upon the vision. He has not launched a new style. He seeks to enlarge the expressive potential and the urban dimension of a vernacular that originated a century and a half ago with Joseph Paxton's Crystal Palace in London, designed for the first world's fair. Appearing now, at the end of a century that has seen movements rise and fall with accelerating futility, the design's evolutionary stance is refreshing. Not all radiance has perished in this brutal century: that is the elevating message that the Tokyo Forum could pass on to the next."[6]

Graying rebels

One of the architects chosen for the MoMA Deconstructivist exhibition in 1988, Peter Eisenman has had a long career as a theorist, and admittedly has something of a reputation as a trouble-maker. One of the so-called "New York Five" with Meier, Hejduk, Stern and Gwathmey in the 1970s, Eisenman has been criticized for frequently changing his architectural ideas. In a scathing article written for the American monthly *Progressive*

einer Stadt, der die urbane Dichte fehlt, die derartige Hochbauten unumgänglich macht. Die Hälfte des mitten im ehemaligen Selangor Turf Club gelegenen Grundstücks – der ein Gebiet von etwa 45 ha im Herzen des Finanzviertels oder »Goldenen Dreiecks« umfaßte – soll für die Öffentlichkeit nach Entwürfen von Roberto Burle Marx als Park freigegeben werden; allerdings soll schon bald ein weiteres Hochhaus – der von Roche Dinkeloo entworfene, 50 Stockwerke hohe Ampang Tower – neben Cesar Pellis Rekordbau entstehen. Dem Architekt selbst blieb es vorbehalten, die Motive für die Errichtung solcher Hochbauten zusammenzufassen: »Sehr hohe Gebäude haben die Macht, eine Stadt nicht nur zu dominieren, sondern zum Symbol für diese Stadt zu werden.«

Während Cesar Pelli über ausgedehnte Erfahrungen bei der Realisierung von Großprojekten verfügte, hatte Rafael Viñoly nie zuvor etwas entworfen, daß in seinen Ausdehnungen dem neuen Tokyo International Forum gleichgekommen wäre. Das auf dem 3 ha großen Gelände der ehemaligen Tokyo City Hall (Kenzo Tange, 1956) entstandene Forum liegt in der Nähe der äußeren Gärten des Kaiserpalastes sowie in unmittelbarer Nachbarschaft zur Tokyo JR Station und ist das größte und bedeutendste Kultur- und Kongreßzentrum Japans. Rafael Viñoly, ein 1944 in Montevideo geborener und seit 1979 in New York lebender argentinischer Architekt, wurde im August 1989 von einer Jury ausgewählt, in der unter anderem I.M. Pei, Kenzo Tange, Vittorio Gregotti, Arthur Erickson und Fumihiko Maki saßen – also noch, bevor die spekulative Immobilien-»Seifenblase« in Japan zerplatzte. Dies erklärt die extrem ehrgeizige Natur dieses Projekts, dessen Form aus zwei sich überschneidenden Ellipsen aus Glas und Stahl besteht, die eine riesige zentrale Eingangshalle umfassen. Mit einer Gesamtfläche von über 130 000 m² und Baukosten von über 1,6 Milliarden $ dürfte das Tokyo International Forum weltweit zu den teuersten und größten Gebäuden seiner Art zählen. Seine aufsehenerregende Glass Hall ist 191 m lang, 30 m breit und 57 m hoch, und die Halle A ist mit 5 000 Plätzen das größte Theater in Tokio. Das von Natur aus gewaltige Tokyo International Forum stellt einen Versuch dar,

tive des années 1980. Le «New York Times» a salué la conception de cet ensemble avec enthousiasme. Comme l'a écrit Herbert Muschamp en 1993: «Certains peuvent trouver le dessin extrêmement rétrograde, sorte d'évocation d'une vision dépassée de ce qui allait arriver. Malheureusement ce qui est arrivé n'a que rarement témoigné de la grâce dont M. Viñoly veut le parer. Il n'a pas lancé de nouveau style. Il cherche à élargir le potentiel expressif et la dimension urbaine d'un style vernaculaire qui trouve son origine dans le Crystal Palace de Londres réalisé par Joseph Paxton il y a plus d'un siècle et demi pour la première exposition universelle. Réapparaissant aujourd'hui, à la fin d'un siècle qui a vu la naissance et la chute de divers mouvements d'une futilité de plus en plus accélérée, cette affirmation d'une évolution stylistique est rafraîchissante. Tout aspect radieux n'a pas disparu dans ce siècle brutal: tel est le noble message que le Forum de Tokyo pourrait bien transmettre au siècle qui suit.»[6]

Les rebelles, 20 ans après

Un des architectes sélectionnés pour l'exposition sur le déconstructivisme organisée par le Musée d'art moderne de New York en 1988, Peter Eisenman, possède une longue carrière de théoricien derrière lui et, il faut l'admettre, une petite réputation de trouble-fête. Membre des «New York Five» avec Meier, Hejduk, Stern et Gwathmey dans les années 70, il a été critiqué pour changer souvent son fusil théorique d'épaule. Dans un article acerbe rédigé pour le mensuel américain «Progressive Architecture», Diane Ghiradro écrivait: «De sa méthodologie d'origine, Eisenman passa rapidement d'un engouement à un autre: creusements, cube de Boole, ruban de Möbius, ADN, mise en abyme, ou ce qui allait apparaître comme un amoncellement hasardeux de fettucini trop cuits pour le Columbus Convention Center, chaque formule étant censée apporter structuration, ordre et diversité à ses plans. Elle habillait commodément d'une méthodologie rationnelle l'imagination créative, constante des projets d'Eisenman.»[7] La réalisation la plus récente d'Eisenman, l'Aronoff Center for Design and Art, à l'université de Cincinnati, à Cincinnati, Ohio, est l'élément central d'un ambitieux plan de

Rafael Viñoly, Tokyo International Forum, Tokyo, Japan, 1989–96. An interior view of the Glass Hall.

Rafael Viñoly, Tokyo International Forum, Tokio, Japan, 1989–96. Blick in die Glass Hall.

Rafael Viñoly, Forum international de Tokyo, Tokyo, Japon, 1989–96. Vue intérieure du Hall de verre.

Architecture, Diane Ghiradro said, "From the early methodology – Eisenman moved rapidly through one infatuation after another: excavations, Boolean cube, Möbius strip, DNA, scaling, or what would appear to be randomly piled strips of cooked fettuccini in the Columbus Convention Center, each of which promised to give structure, order, and diversity to his designs. They also conveniently substituted rational methodology for creative imagination, something that has been a constant in Eisenman's projects."[7] Eisenman's most recent work, the Aronoff Center for Design and Art, at the University of Cincinnati, in Cincinnati, Ohio is the centerpiece of an ambitious campus master plan that includes projects by such architects as Frank O. Gehry, Michael Graves, Cambridge Seven Associates, Pei Cobb Freed, Skidmore, Owings & Merrill and Venturi, Scott Brown. The architect's brief was to reorganize the existing 13,400 square meters of the building and build an additional 12,000 square meters of exhibition, library, theater, studio and office space, with the intention of unifying the schools of Design, Architecture, Art and Planning within the College for a budget of $35 million. According to the statement of Eisenman Architects, the building's "vocabulary derives from the curves of the land forms and the chevron forms of the existing building; the dynamic relationship between these two forms organizes the space between them... The project is designed to challenge and change the mode by which we educate people. We can no longer train people to design the superficial and the inconsequential; design disciplines must assume a far more important role in our media-dominated age."

Peter Eisenman is certainly at his most convincing when he speaks of his own view of contemporary architecture. As Diane Ghiradro says, he has had a tendency to change styles and sources of inspiration quite often, but he remains a barometer of current thinking in American architecture, if only by opposition to some of his colleagues. A recent interview gives some idea of his positions:

Philip Jodidio: *Isn't there less willingness on the part of potential clients in the United States to be forward looking in their choice of architecture now than in the recent past?*

Japan weiter der Außenwelt zu öffnen – sowohl durch seinen Namen als auch durch die Tatsache, daß man sich bei einem offenen Architekturwettbewerb für einen ausländischen Architekten entschied. Die »New York Times« begrüßte den Entwurf für das Tokyo International Forum mit Begeisterung, die zumindest zum Teil durchaus berechtigt erscheint. Herbert Muschamp schrieb 1993: »Einige werden den Entwurf für übermäßig retrospektiv halten, für die lebensechte Darstellung einer früheren Zukunftsvision. Diese Zukunft ist mittlerweile Gegenwart, aber nur selten mit der Anmut verwirklicht worden, die Rafael Viñoly der ehemaligen Vision verleiht. Er schuf keinen neuen Stil, sondern versuchte, das expressive Potential und die urbane Dimension einer dem Charakter des Landes angepaßten Bauweise zu erweitern – im Stile von Joseph Paxtons Crystal Palace in London, der vor eineinhalb Jahrhunderten für die erste Weltausstellung entworfen wurde. Heute, am Ende eines Jahrhunderts, das Architekturströmungen von zunehmender Oberflächlichkeit aufkommen und niedergehen sah, wirkt der Entwicklungsstand dieses Entwurfs erfrischend. Nicht aller strahlende Glanz ist in diesem brutalen Jahrhundert zugrunde gegangen – so lautet die Botschaft, die das Tokyo Forum dem nächsten Jahrhundert weitergeben kann.«[6]

Ergraute Rebellen

Der als einer von sieben Architekten für die MoMA-Ausstellung 1988 ausgewählte Peter Eisenman kann auf eine lange Karriere als Theoretiker zurückblicken und genießt zugegebenermaßen so etwas wie den Ruf eines Unruhestifters. Eisenman, der in den 70er Jahren zusammen mit Meier, Hejduk, Stern und Gwathmey zu den sogenannten »New York Five« gehörte, wird von Kritikern der häufige Wechsel seiner architektonischen Grundsätze vorgeworfen. In einem vernichtenden Artikel für das amerikanische Magazin »Progressive Architecture« schrieb Diane Ghiradro: »Von der frühen Methodologie bewegte sich Eisenman im Eiltempo von einer Vernarrtheit zur nächsten. Ob Ausgrabungen, Boole'sche Algebra, Möbiussches Band, DNA, maßstabsgetreue Vergrößerung oder Verkleinerung oder das wie zufällig über-

masse du campus qui comprend des projets d'architectes comme Frank O. Gehry, Michael Graves, Cambridge Seven Associates, Pei Cobb Freed, Skidmore Owings & Merrill et Venturi, Scott Brown. Le programme confié à l'architecte était de réorganiser les 13 400 m² du bâtiment existant, et de concevoir 12 000 m² supplémentaires pour une galerie d'exposition, une bibliothèque, une salle de spectacle, un atelier, des bureaux, afin de réunir les écoles de design, d'architecture, d'art et d'urbanisme du collège, le tout pour un budget de 35 millions de $. Selon le descriptif fourni par Eisenman Architects, «le vocabulaire (du bâtiment) dérive des courbes du terrain et des formes en chevron de la construction existante; la relation dynamique entre ces deux formes organise l'espace entre elles... Le projet est un défi à la façon dont nous éduquons les étudiants, et se propose de la changer. Nous ne pouvons plus former des gens pour concevoir du superficiel et de l'inconséquent; à notre époque dominée par les médias, les disciplines créatives doivent assumer un rôle beaucoup plus important.»

Peter Eisenman est certainement très convaincant lorsqu'il parle de sa propre vision de l'architecture contemporaine. Comme le dit Diane Ghiradro, il a tendance à changer de style et de source d'inspiration assez souvent, mais reste le baromètre de la réflexion dans l'architecture américaine d'aujourd'hui, ne serait-ce que par opposition à certains de ses confrères. Un entretien récent précise ses positions:

Philip Jodidio: *Ne constate-t-on pas aujourd'hui moins de volonté de la part des clients potentiels américains à opter pour des solutions architecturales d'avant-garde que dans un récent passsé?*

Peter Eisenman: Ce n'est pas seulement le cas des clients, mais aussi celui des architectes. J'ai récemment dîné avec Richard Meier, Michael Graves et Robert Stern, et la question qu'ils se posaient était: «Pourquoi avons-nous besoin de théorie? Construisons, et la théorie viendra d'elle-même.» Pour moi, le problème est que les gens ne s'intéressent pas à ce que j'appellerai «l'architecture critique». Il s'agit d'une architecture qui ne traite pas seulement d'un projet particulier, mais de la problématique générale de l'architecture.

Peter Eisenman, Aronoff Center for Design and Art, Cincinnati, Ohio, 1988–96. Upsetting the rules of rectilinear, colorless modernism.

Peter Eisenman, Aronoff Center for Design and Art, Cincinnati, Ohio, 1988–96. Gegen alle Regeln eines rechtwinkligen, »farblosen« Modernismus.

Peter Eisenman, Aronoff Center for Design and Art, Cincinnati, Ohio, 1988–96: bousculer les règles d'un modernisme rectiligne et sans couleur.

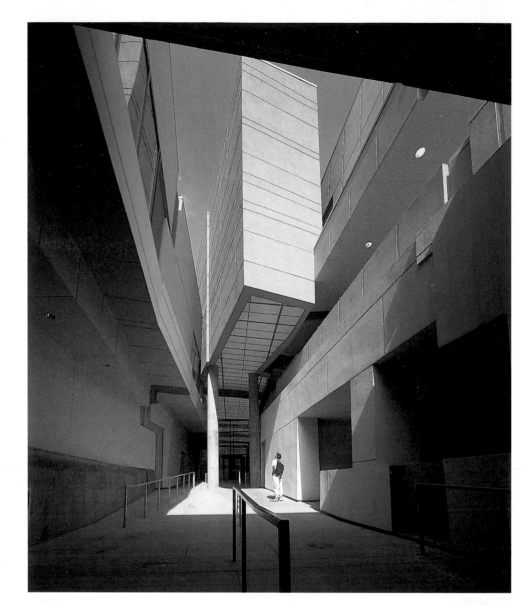

Peter Eisenman, Aronoff Center for Design and Art, Cincinnati, Ohio, 1988–96. At least in theoretical terms, the architect feels that buildings should be noticed, even at the price of making their users "uncomfortable."

Peter Eisenman, Aronoff Center for Design and Art, Cincinnati, Ohio, 1988–96. In der Theorie vertritt der Architekt die Ansicht, daß Gebäude bemerkt werden sollten – auch wenn sie den Nutzern ein Gefühl des Unbehagens bereiten.

Peter Eisenman, Aronoff Center for Design and Art, Cincinnati, Ohio, 1988–96. Sur le plan théorique du moins, l'architecte pense qu'un bâtiment doit se faire remarquer, même au prix de «l'inconfort» de ses utilisateurs.

Peter Eisenman: It's not only the clients, it's the architects as well. I had dinner with Richard Meier, Michael Graves, and Robert Stern recently, and the question they asked was "Why do we need theory? We just need to build, and theory gets in the way." In my opinion the problem is that people are not interested in what I would call "critical architecture." That is an architecture which deals not only with a particular project, but deals in general with the problematic of architecture.

Philip Jodidio: *When I last saw you, you spoke a great deal about the French philosopher Jacques Derrida. Is that still as much a focus of your intellectual process?*

Peter Eisenman: No. I believe that deconstruction runs into a big problem, which is its refusal to deal with the physical reality which is presence. Its object is to subvert the metaphysics of presence. You can subvert the metaphysics of drawing, but not of architecture. There will always be four walls in architecture. Rather than arguing against four walls, it is more relevant to argue how you can detach the four walls from the notion a casual perception of architecture. Most people want architecture to remain casual. My work is about making it uncasual.

Philip Jodidio: *You were also fascinated with scientific ideas such as plate tectonics and sound waves...*

einandergeschichtete Streifen gekochter Fettucini wirkende Columbus Convention Center – jede dieser Methoden versprach, seinen Entwürfen Struktur, Ordnung und Vielfalt zu verleihen. Gleichzeitig ersetzten sie praktischerweise kreative Phantasie durch rationale Methodologie – eine der wenigen Konstanten in Eisenmans Projekten.«[7]

Eisenmans aktuelle Arbeit, das Aronoff Center for Design and Art an der University of Cincinnatti, bildet den Mittelpunkt eines ehrgeizigen Bebauungsplans für den Campus, der auch Projekte von Frank O. Gehry, Michael Graves, Cambridge Seven Associates, Pei Cobb Freed, Skidmore, Owings & Merrill und Venturi, Scott Brown umfaßt. Eisenman erhielt den Auftrag, mit einem Budget von 35 Millionen $ das bereits bestehende, 13 400 m² große Gebäude neu zu gestalten und weitere 12 000 m² an Ausstellungs-, Bibliotheks-, Theater-, Studio- und Büroräumen zu bauen; auf diese Weise sollten die Fachbereiche für Design, Architektur, Kunst und Stadtplanung harmonisch unter einem Dach vereint werden. Nach Aussage von Eisenman Architects ist die »Formensprache des Gebäudes von den Krümmungen der Landformen und den Zickzackformen des bestehenden Gebäudes abgeleitet; die dynamische Beziehung dieser beiden Formen organisiert zugleich den Raum zwischen ihnen... Das Projekt wurde entworfen, um die Art und Weise in Frage zu stellen und zu verändern, in der wir Menschen unterrichten. Wir können den Menschen nicht länger beibringen, Oberflächliches und Inkonsequentes zu entwerfen; die Designerausbildung muß in unserer von den Medien beherrschten Zeit eine wesentlich wichtigere Rolle spielen.«

Peter Eisenman ist immer dann besonders überzeugend, wenn er seine eigene Sicht der zeitgenössischen Architektur erläutert. Wie Diane Ghiradro sagte, neigt er dazu, seinen Stil und seine Inspirationsquellen zu wechseln; dennoch bleibt Eisenman ein Barometer der aktuellen Strömungen in der amerikanischen Architektur – und sei es auch nur aus Opposition zu einigen seiner Kollegen. Ein kürzlich geführtes Interview vermittelt einen Eindruck seiner Ansichten:

Philip Jodidio: *Sind potentielle Auftraggeber in den USA heute*

Philip Jodidio: *La dernière fois que je vous ai rencontré, vous citiez beaucoup le philosophe français Jacques Derrida. Sa pensée vous préoccupe-t-elle toujours autant?*

Peter Eisenman: Non. Je pense que la déconstruction s'est trouvé confrontée à un gros problème qui est son refus de considérer la réalité physique, la présence. Son objet est la subversion de la métaphysique de la présence. Vous pouvez subvertir la métaphysique du dessin, mais non celle de l'architecture. Il y aura toujours quatre murs en architecture. Plutôt que de se battre contre quatre murs, il est plus pertinent de voir comment vous pouvez détacher les autres murs d'une perception banale de l'architecture. La plupart des gens souhaitent que l'architecture reste banale. Mon travail est de la rendre non banale.

Philip Jodidio: *Vous étiez également fasciné par des idées d'ordre scientifique comme la tectonique des plaques et les ondes sonores...*

Peter Eisenman: Je ne le suis plus. Je m'intéresse davantage aux formes liées de façon interne à l'architecture – le *morphing*, la distorsion, le détournement – ces sortes de trajectoires que vous pouvez obtenir avec les logiciels d'architecture.

Philip Jodidio: *Il semblerait que vous soyez davantage intéressé aujourd'hui par les problèmes d'esthétique que de fonction...*

Peter Eisenman: Je ne dirais pas esthétique, mais plutôt questions formelles. Les questions formelles sont proches des enjeux critiques. Nous essayons de nous servir de quelque chose qui est interne au sujet, puis de le gauchir et de le tordre jusqu'à ce que vous ne puissiez plus le reconnaître. Je recherche des façons de conceptualiser l'espace qui projette le sujet dans une relation déplacée, parce qu'il ne trouvera plus de références iconographiques aux formes traditionnelles d'organisation. C'est ce que j'ai toujours essayé de faire – déplacer le sujet – pour l'obliger à reconceptualiser l'architecture. Nous avons concrètement à changer la relation du corps à l'architecture. Le corps doit envoyer des messages au cerveau disant: «Un moment! Il y a là quelque chose auquel je dois m'ajuster, quelque chose que j'ai besoin de comprendre est en train de m'arriver.» Ce n'est plus une question de philosophie ou d'esthétique, et je n'ai pas besoin de Jacques Derrida pour me dire comment le faire. Je me

Peter Eisenman: No more. I am more interested in the kinds of forms which are related internally to architecture, – by morphing, by distorting, deflecting – the kind of trajectories that you can do with architectural software.

Philip Jodidio: *It sounds as though you are now more interested in questions of aesthetics than problems of function.*

Peter Eisenman: I would not say aesthetics, but rather formal questions. Formal questions deal with critical issues. We are trying to use something that is internal to the subject, and then warping and distorting it until you cannot recognize it. I am looking for ways of conceptualizing space that will place the subject in a displaced relationship because they will have no iconographic references to traditional forms of organization. That is what I have always been trying to do – to displace the subject – to oblige the subject to reconceptualize architecture. We have to actually change the relationship of the body to architecture. The body has to send messages to the brain saying "Wait a minute, something that I need to adjust to, something that I need to understand is happening to me." It is no longer a question of philosophy or aesthetics, and I don't need Jacques Derrida to tell me how to do that. I have also moved away from seeking new forms of organization in known, natural phenomena. I like the idea that architecture comes from some sort of molten state in forming itself, rather than starting from a container. We all design architecture from the peripheries in. I am suggesting that we should design from the inside out.

Philip Jodidio: *Even if you do succeed in getting something other than a casual reaction from a visitor to one of your buildings, what is the point of that?*

Peter Eisenman: Doesn't it go back to Tolstoy's man who is cleaning, and who finds everything so easy that he falls asleep working? He just stops being. Because of the media, we have become much more sedentary. The relationship of mind to eye and body has changed. We don't use our bodies when we watch TV. The reason we have so many health spas is that people realize that there has been a cut-off. The health spa isn't the only way. Maybe you can activate the body through one of the tradi-

weniger bereit, sich für eine progressive Architektur zu entscheiden, als noch vor wenigen Jahren?

Peter Eisenman: Es sind nicht nur die Kunden, sondern auch die Architekten. Als ich vor kurzem mit Richard Meier, Michael Graves und Robert Stern zu Abend aß, kam die Frage auf: »Warum brauchen wir die Theorie? Wir wollen nur bauen, und die Theorie ist dabei hinderlich.« Meiner Meinung nach besteht das Problem darin, daß sich niemand für eine »kritische Architektur« interessiert. So bezeichne ich einen Baustil, der sich nicht nur mit einem bestimmten Projekt, sondern ganz allgemein mit der Problematik der Architektur auseinandersetzt.

Philip Jodidio: *Bei unserem letzten Treffen sprachen Sie sehr viel über den französischen Philosophen Jacques Derrida. Steht er immer noch im Mittelpunkt ihres intellektuellen Prozesses?*

Peter Eisenman: Nein. Ich glaube, daß der Dekonstruktivismus große Schwierigkeiten bekommen wird aufgrund seiner Weigerung, sich mit der physikalischen Realität zu befassen, die die Gegenwart darstellt. Sein Ziel ist es, die Metaphysik der Gegenwart zu untergraben. Man kann die Metaphysik des Zeichnens untergraben, nicht aber die der Architektur. In der Architektur wird es immer vier Wände geben. Anstatt gegen die vier Wände vorzugehen, wäre es wichtiger, sich mit der Frage auseinanderzusetzen, wie man sie von der beiläufigen Wahrnehmung von Architektur freimachen kann. Die meisten Menschen wollen, daß Architektur beiläufig bleibt. Meine Arbeit zielt darauf, sie ungewöhnlich und auffällig zu machen.

Philip Jodidio: *Früher waren Sie auch fasziniert von wissenschaftlichen Ideen wie Plattentektonik und Klangwellen...*

Peter Eisenman: Heute nicht mehr. Ich interessiere mich mehr für die Formen, die innerlich mit der Architektur verwandt sind – durch Morphing, Verzerrung oder Umleitung –, also für die Möglichkeiten, die Architektursoftware bietet.

Philip Jodidio: *Das klingt so, als seien Sie heute mehr an Fragen der Ästhetik als an funktionalen Problemen interessiert.*

Peter Eisenman: Ich würde nicht von Ästhetik, sondern eher von formalen Fragen sprechen. Formale Fragen beschäftigen sich mit kritischen Themen. Wir versuchen, etwas zu verwenden,

suis également éloigné de la recherche de nouvelles formes d'organisation dans des phénomènes connus, naturels. J'aime l'idée que l'architecture surgisse d'une sorte d'état «mou» qui se forme lui-même plutôt que de partir d'un contenant. Nous dessinons tous l'architecture à partir de la périphérie. Je suggère que nous commencions de l'intérieur.

Philip Jodidio: *Même si vous réussissez à obtenir quelque chose d'autre qu'une réaction banale du visiteur entrant dans l'une de vos constructions, quel est l'objectif de cette recherche?*

Peter Eisenman: N'est-ce pas en revenir à l'homme de Tolstoï qui est en train de nettoyer, et trouve tout tellement facile qu'il s'endort en travaillant? Il cesse tout simplement d'être. Du fait des médias, nous sommes devenus beaucoup plus sédentaires. La relation de l'esprit à l'œil et au corps a changé. Nous n'utilisons pas nos corps quand nous regardons la télévision. Si nous avons tellement de salles de gymnastique, c'est que les gens réalisent qu'ils sont coupés de quelque chose. La gymnastique n'est pas la seule solution. Peut-être pouvez-vous activer le corps d'une des multiples façons traditionnelles, c'est-à-dire à travers l'architecture. Nous avons besoin de réintégrer à nouveau l'esprit, l'œil et le corps dans une sorte d'unité opératoire.

Philip Jodidio: *Votre idée de réveiller les gens inclut-elle la possibilité qu'ils peuvent se sentir dans une situation très inconfortable quand ils sont dans l'environnement que vous leur construisez?*

Peter Eisenman: Le premier sentiment qu'ils éprouveront sera de se sentir mal à l'aise. Ils se sentiront désorientés.

Philip Jodidio: *Fondamentalement, lorsque vous vous trouvez dans un bâtiment, est-ce que vous n'avez pas envie de vous sentir bien dans son espace?*

Peter Eisenman: C'est une question très intéressante. À partir de quel moment vous sentez-vous bien et commencez à ignorer l'espace? À partir de quel point se sentir bien implique-t-il d'ignorer l'architecture?[8]

Peter Eisenman, Aronoff Center for Design and Art, Cincinnati, Ohio, 1988–96. The complex articulation of the exterior volumes finds its logical counterpart in these interior spaces.

Peter Eisenman, Aronoff Center for Design and Art, Cincinnati, Ohio, 1988–96. Die komplexe Formensprache der äußeren Baukörper findet ihr logisches Pendant in den Innenräumen.

Peter Eisenman, Aronoff Center for Design and Art, Cincinnati, Ohio, 1988–96. L'articulation complexe des volumes extérieurs trouve sa contrepartie logique dans les espaces intérieurs.

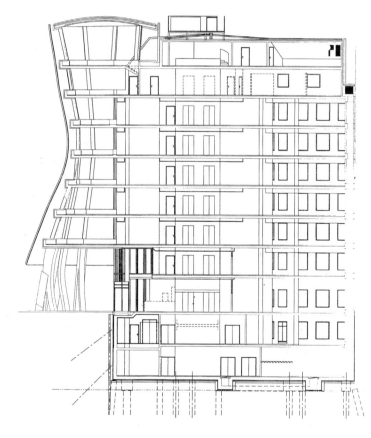

Frank O. Gehry, Nationale-Nederlanden Building,
Rasin Embankment, Prague, Czech Republic,
1994–96. A sketch by the architect and a later drawing
showing the undulating facade volume to the left.

Frank O. Gehry, Gebäude der Nationale-Nederlanden,
Rasinufer, Prag, 1994–96. Eine Skizze sowie eine später
angefertigte Zeichnung des Architekten zeigen die
geschwungene Linienführung des linken Fassaden-
bereiches.

Frank O. Gehry, Nationale-Nederlanden Building, quai
Rasin, Prague, République Tchèque, 1994–96. Esquisse
de l'architecte et dessin plus tardif montrant le volume
en courbes de la façade à gauche.

tional ways, which is through architecture. We need to reinteg-
rate mind, eye and body into some kind of operating unit again.

Philip Jodidio: *Does your idea of waking people up include the
possibility that you may make them very uncomfortable in their
surroundings?*

Peter Eisenman: The first thing they are going to be is uncomfortable. They are going to feel disoriented.

Philip Jodidio: *Fundamentally, when you are in a building, don't
you want to feel good about the space?*

Peter Eisenman: That is a very interesting question. At what
point do you feel good and begin to ignore the space? At what
point does feeling good mean ignoring architecture?[8]

Eisenman's new "formal" approach to architecture might be
opposed to the more artistic or "aesthetic" approach of another
of the major figures of contemporary American architecture,
Frank O. Gehry. Despite continuing difficulties, which have at
least temporarily halted the construction of his largest building
in the United States, the Disney Concert Hall in Los Angeles, he
is approaching the completion of the new Guggenheim Bilbao,
and most visibly the Nationale-Nederlanden Building, on the
Rasin Embankment, in Prague (1994–96). One of only three
sites in the historic district of central Prague where new construction is being permitted, located along the Vltava River
within walking distance of the National Theater and other prom-
inent cultural facilities, this building has been nicknamed "Fred
and Ginger" by some residents because of the unusual curvature
of the facade. Using CATIA software developed by Dassault for
fighter plane design and Parametric Technology's Pro/Engineer,
Gehry and local architect Vladimir Milunic have indeed obtained
forms that seem to dance, in sharp contrast to the more conser-
vative architecture of Prague. Reactions to Gehry's building have
been far from unanimously positive. Writing in the magazine
Architekt in 1993, the young Prague designer Zdenek Jiran dis-
missed Gehry's and Mulunic's project as "a case of irresponsible
exhibitionism – a bizarre, extravagant design based on a random
interplay of volumes."

das dem Subjekt eigen ist, und es dann so lange zu verwerfen und zu verzerren, bis man es nicht mehr wiedererkennen kann. Ich suche nach Möglichkeiten der Konzeptualisierung des Raumes, die das Subjekt in einen veränderten Zusammenhang stellen, da sie keine ikonographischen Bezüge zu traditionellen Organisationsformen aufweisen. Das ist es, was ich zu erreichen versucht habe – das Subjekt zu verschieben – das Thema der Architektur in neue Begriffswelten zu zwingen. Was wir verändern müssen, ist das Verhältnis des Körpers zur Architektur. Der Körper muß dem Gehirn die Botschaft senden: »Moment mal, hier ist etwas, auf das ich mich einstellen muß – hier geschieht etwas, was ich erst noch begreifen muß«. Es handelt sich nicht länger um eine Frage der Philosophie oder der Ästhetik, und ich brauche Jacques Derrida nicht, der mir sagt, was ich zu tun habe. Ich habe aufgehört, in bekannten, natürlichen Umgebungen nach neuen Organisationsformen zu suchen. Mir gefällt die Vorstellung, daß Architektur sich aus einer Art geschmolzenem Zustand heraus selbst formt, anstatt von einem Behälter auszugehen. Wir alle entwerfen Architektur vom äußeren Rand her; ich schlage vor, wir sollten beginnen, von innen nach außen vorzugehen.

Philip Jodidio: *Selbst wenn es Ihnen gelingt, mehr als nur eine beiläufige Reaktion von den Besuchern eines Ihrer Gebäude zu erhalten – was ist damit gewonnen?*

Peter Eisenman: Ist das nicht das gleiche wie bei Tolstois Mann, der aufräumt, und dem alles so leichtfällt, daß er bei der Arbeit einschläft? Er hört einfach auf, zu existieren. Aufgrund der Medien haben wir eine sitzende Lebensweise angenommen, und das Verhältnis von Geist zu Auge und Körper hat sich verändert. Wir benutzen unsere Körper nicht, wenn wir fernsehen. Wir haben so viele Fitness-Studios, daß den Menschen klar wird, daß ein Einschnitt stattgefunden hat. Aber das Fitness-Studio ist nicht der einzige Weg. Vielleicht kann man den Körper wieder auf eine traditionelle Weise aktivieren, nämlich mit Hilfe der Architektur. Wir müssen versuchen, Geist, Auge und Körper wieder zu einer funktionierenden Einheit zu verschmelzen.

Philip Jodidio: *Schließt Ihre Vorstellung vom Aufrütteln der Men-*

La nouvelle approche «formelle» de l'architecture d'Eisenman peut être opposée à celle plus artistique, ou «esthétique», d'une autre des grandes figures de l'architecture américaine contemporaine, Frank O. Gehry. Malgré de multiples difficultés qui bloquent temporairement la construction de son plus important projet aux États-Unis, le Disney Concert Hall à Los Angeles, il approche de l'achèvement du nouveau musée Guggenheim de Bilbao, et plus spectaculaire encore, du Nationale-Nederlanden Building, quai Rasin, à Prague (1994–96). Sur l'un des trois seuls emplacements du centre historique de Prague où il était encore possible de construire au bord de la Moldau, à quelques pas du Théâtre National et d'autres importants équipements culturels, cet immeuble a vite été surnommé «Fred et Ginger» par certains habitants pour le jeu de courbes hautement inhabituel de ses façades. À l'aide du logiciel CATIA mis au point par Dassault pour dessiner des avions de chasse et du Pro/Engineer de Parametric Technology, Gehry et l'architecte praguois Vladimir Milunic ont en effet obtenu des formes qui semblent littéralement danser, en contraste total avec l'architecture classique de la ville. Les réactions à ce projet de Gehry sont loin d'être toutes positives. En 1993, dans la revue «Architekt» le jeune designer praguois Zdenek Jiran a rejeté le projet de Gehry et Mulunic comme «un cas d'exhibitionnisme irresponsable – un dessin bizarre, extravagant, reposant sur un jeu hasardeux de volumes». À une époque où de plus en plus d'architectes se sentent concernés par les enjeux sociaux et environnementaux, on peut en effet à bon droit se poser des questions sur l'approche sculpturale et esthétique défendue par Frank O. Gehry. Ceci ne veut pas dire qu'il faille l'exclure de la scène actuelle. Un immeuble de bureaux comme celui qu'il a édifié pour la compagnie d'électricité Minden-Ravensberg, à Bad Oeynhausen (Allemagne, 1991–95) arrive à conserver une conception sculpturale dans le cadre d'un certain souci des conditions urbanistiques existantes, et d'un intérêt renouvelé pour les économies d'énergie.

«Je travaillerais pour le diable lui-même», avait déclaré Philip Johnson dans un entretien publié en 1973. En fait lorsque John-

At a time when more and more architects are concerned with social or environmental issues in Europe, there may indeed be some grounds to question the sculptural, aesthetic approach pioneered by Frank O. Gehry. This is not to say that Gehry should be counted out in the current architectural scene. Indeed, a building like his Minden-Ravensberg Electric Company Offices, located in Bad Oeynhausen, Germany (1991–95), manages to conserve a fully sculptural design with a certain responsiveness to existing urban conditions, as well as a new-found interest in energy conservation.

"I'd work for the devil himself," said Philip Johnson in an interview published in 1973. Indeed, when Johnson spoke knowingly in 1988 of today's "quick-change generation" he might have added that his own highly mutable architecture may well have contributed to the general lack of esthetic direction in contemporary buildings. The most recent addition to his New Canaan estate, which is a kind of museum of architectural "follies", is of course the visitors' pavilion, which he designed as an homage to the "kids" who practice deconstructivism. This 84 square meter sculptural design, completed in 1995, was built with "prefabricated panels of structural wire mesh around an insulating urethane foam core, cut and bent to the required shape and then sprayed with concrete to complete its structural integrity."

It is curious and significant that one of the most admired (and criticized) figures of modern American architecture should be a man of such considerable versatility. A critic's view of Johnson's New Canaan Glass House published in 1993 came quite close to addressing the same questions that have been raised about Gehry's Rasin building, making reference to Johnson's "hysterical exhibitionism," and concluding that "the fallacy of formalism is not in regarding architecture as an art. It is in thinking that art is served by divorcing it from social context."[9] Might it be that the freedom earned for contemporary architecture by such figures as Johnson, Gehry or Eisenman, the freedom to imagine a building as an esthetic, sculptural or formal composition, is now an issue of the past?

schen auch die Möglichkeit mit ein, daß sie sich in ihrer Umgebung sehr unwohl fühlen könnten?

Peter Eisenman: Sie werden mit Sicherheit zuerst verwirrt sein. Sie werden sich desorientiert fühlen.

Philip Jodidio: *Sollte man sich nicht eigentlich wohl fühlen, wenn man sich in einem Gebäude aufhält?*

Peter Eisenman: Das ist eine sehr interessante Frage. An welchem Punkt fühlt man sich wohl und beginnt, den Raum zu ignorieren? An welchem Punkt fühlt man sich wohl und ignoriert die Architektur?[8]

Eisenmans neue, »formale« Auffassung von Architektur steht im Gegensatz zu dem eher künstlerischen oder »ästhetischen« Ansatz einer anderen großen Persönlichkeit der zeitgenössischen amerikanischen Architektur, Frank O. Gehry. Trotz der anhaltenden Schwierigkeiten, die zum zumindest zeitweiligen Baustopp seines größten Projekts in den USA – der Disney Concert Hall in Los Angeles – führten, nähern sich Gehrys Guggenheim Museum in Bilbao und vor allem das Gebäude der Nationale-Nederlanden am Rasinufer in Prag (1994–96) ihrer Fertigstellung. Dieses Gebäude, das aufgrund der ungewöhnlich gekurvten Fassade von den Pragern den Spitznamen »Fred and Ginger« erhielt, entsteht auf einem Grundstück mitten im historischen Zentrum Prags; es liegt direkt am Ufer der Moldau, nahe dem Nationaltheater und anderen berühmten Kulturdenkmälern. Mit Hilfe von CATIA – einer Software, die die französische Firma Dassault zur Entwicklung neuer Kampfflugzeuge verwendet – und dem Programm »Pro/Engineer« der Firma Parametric Technology schufen Gehry und der ortsansässige Architekt Vladimir Milunic Formen, die tatsächlich zu tanzen scheinen und in krassem Gegensatz zu der ansonsten eher konservativen Architektur Prags stehen. Die Reaktionen auf Gehrys Bauwerk fallen daher auch nicht einhellig positiv aus. In einem 1993 erschienenen Artikel der Zeitschrift »Architekt« tat der junge Prager Designer Zdenek Jiran Gehrys und Milunics Projekt als »Beispiel eines unverantwortlichen Exhibitionismus« ab – »ein bizarrer, extravaganter Entwurf, der auf der zufälligen Wech-

son parlait à juste titre en 1988 de «la génération rapidement changeante» d'aujourd'hui, il aurait pu y inclure sa propre architecture dont les multiples évolutions ont sans doute contribué au manque général d'orientation esthétique de beaucoup de constructions actuelles. La plus récente addition à son domaine de New Canaan, qui est une sorte de musée de «folies» architecturales, est le pavillon des visiteurs qu'il a dessiné en hommage aux «gamins» qui pratiquent le déconstructivisme. Ce petit bâtiment sculptural de 84 m², achevé en 1995, a été construit avec «des panneaux préfabriqués de fers à béton entourant un cœur de mousse d'uréthane, coupés et courbés aux formes souhaitées, puis recouverts de béton projeté pour assurer leur intégrité structurelle».

Il est curieux et significatif que l'une des figures les plus admirées (et critiquées) de l'architecture moderne américaine soit un homme aussi versatile. Une critique de la nouvelle Maison de verre de New Canaan publiée en 1993 est ainsi bien proche des remarques adressées sur les mêmes sujets à l'immeuble Rasin de Gehry, et fait référence à «L'exhibitionnisme hystérique» de Johnson, et conclut que «l'erreur du formalisme n'est pas dans le fait de considérer l'architecture comme un art. Elle est de penser que l'art est servi par le divorce du contexte social».[9] Il se pourrait que la liberté gagnée au plus grand bénéfice de l'architecture contemporaine par des créateurs comme Johnson, Gehry, ou Eisenman, la liberté d'imaginer une construction en termes de compositions esthétique, sculpturale ou formelle, soit déjà un défi du passé.

Habiller la boîte

La boîte parallélépipédique est, dans toute sa splendeur, l'icône de l'architecture moderniste, que ce soit le pavillon de Barcelone de Ludwig Mies van der Rohe de 1929 ou la Maison de verre de Philip Johnson (1949). Comme Johnson aime à le dire aujourd'hui, «en architecture, le strict classicisme, le strict modernisme et toutes les nuances entre ces deux extrêmes sont également valables». Ce qui est surprenant, c'est que des variantes de la géométrie essentiellement rectiligne du moder-

Philip Johnson, Gate House, New Canaan, Connecticut, 1995. This pavilion, most probably the last of several built by the architect on his estate, will be used to greet visitors coming in for tours of the property.

Philip Johnson, Gate House, New Canaan, Connecticut, 1995. Dieser Pavillon ist wahrscheinlich das letzte Bauwerk einer Reihe von Gebäuden, die der Architekt auf seinem Grundstück errichtete. Er dient als Empfangsraum für Besucher des Anwesens.

Philip Johnson, Gate House, New Canaan, Connecticut, 1995. Ce pavillon, probablement le dernier de la série construite par l'architecte sur son domaine, servira à l'accueil des visiteurs de la propriété.

Arquitectonica, United States Embassy, Lima, Peru, 1993–95. An interesting effort to reconcile security concerns, space needs and a decor that makes a connection between the United States and Peru.

Arquitectonica, Gebäude der amerikanischen Botschaft, Lima, Peru, 1993–95. Ein interessanter Versuch, die verschiedenen Aspekte von Sicherheitsbelangen, Raumbedarf und einem Design, das eine Verbindung zwischen den Vereinigten Staaten und Peru schafft, miteinander in Einklang zu bringen.

Arquitectonica, ambassade des États-Unis, Lima, Pérou, 1993–95. Effort intéressant de conciliation des préoccupations de sécurité, des besoins d'espace et d'un décor qui fait le lien avec la tradition péruvienne.

Dressing Up The Box

The geometric box in all its splendor is the iconic image of modernist architecture, whether it be in Ludwig Mies van der Rohe's 1929 Barcelona Pavilion, or in Philip Johnson's 1949 Glass House. As Johnson says, today, "in architecture, strict-classicism, strict-modernism, and all sorts of shades in between, are equally valid." What is surprising is that variants on the largely rectilinear geometry of modernism continue to be created in a number of different modes, and by architects who range from the youngest stars of the international scene to the older masters of architecture. Three examples concerning large, rectangular buildings show just how different the approach to such a basic form can be.

The neo-modernism practiced by such younger architects as Herzog and de Meuron in Europe or Kazuyo Sejima in Japan has not yet caught on in the United States, but the Miami group Arquitectonica, headed by Bernardo Fort-Brescia, who is of Peruvian origin, and Laurinda Spear, has recently had great success with modernist designs that eschew the bland discretion of some of their European counterparts. These are buildings that you can't help but notice, such as the new U.S. Embassy in Lima, Peru. It should be noted that the rigid rectangular shape of this building was not so much an idea of the architects as it was a security requirement. Indentations or complex forms apparently can magnify the effects of a bomb blast, and a square or rectangular shape with small windows is required to better resist such an unfortunate possibility. Be that as it may, colorful cladding and geometric patterns give this fortress a decidedly contemporary look.

Located in the Casa de la Caritat, a former monastic enclave in the old part of Barcelona, Richard Meier's new Museum of Contemporary Art stands out like a beacon of white perfection. Although this too is a rectangular block, measuring 36 by 122 meters, it is marked by complex articulations which are as many elements of Meier's signature style. According to the firm's statement, "the labyrinthine nature of the site's existing paths and routes is reflected in the building's organization," but some

selwirkung von Baukörpern basiert«. In einer Zeit, in der mehr und mehr Architekten in Europa sich mit sozialen oder Umweltthemen befassen, besteht vielleicht tatsächlich die Notwendigkeit, den skulpturalen, ästhetischen Ansatz eines Frank O. Gehry zu hinterfragen. Dies soll nicht bedeuten, daß Gehry in der gegenwärtigen Architekturszene keine Rolle mehr spielt: Ein Gebäude wie das Bürohaus des Elektrizitätswerks Minden-Ravensberg in Bad Oeynhausen (1991–95) verbindet ein für Gehry typisches skulpturales Äußeres mit einem Verständnis für bereits vorhandene urbane Bedingungen und zeigt ein neuentdecktes Interesse an der Einsparung von Energie.

»Ich würde für den Teufel persönlich arbeiten«, sagte Philip Johnson 1973 in einem Interview. Und als Johnson 1988 wissend von der heutigen »schnellebigen Generation« sprach, hätte er noch hinzufügen können, daß seine eigene, höchst wandelbare Architektur ihren Beitrag zur allgemeinen ästhetischen Richtungslosigkeit vieler zeitgenössischer Gebäude geleistet hat. Die neueste Errungenschaft auf seinem Anwesen in New Canaan, das sich zu einer Art Museum für architektonische »Spielereien« entwickelt hat, ist natürlich der Besucherpavillon, den Johnson als Hommage an die »Kids« entwarf, die den Dekonstruktivismus propagieren. Der 1995 fertiggestellte, 84 m² große skulpturale Entwurf entstand aus »vorgefertigten Paneelen einer tragenden Maschendrahtkonstruktion, die zunächst rund um einen isolierenden Kern aus Urethanschaum gebogen, danach zugeschnitten und schließlich mit Beton besprüht wurden, um die Einheit der Konstruktion zu vollenden.«

Es ist seltsam und zugleich bezeichnend, daß eine der meistbewunderten (und kritisierten) Persönlichkeiten der modernen amerikanischen Architektur ein Mann von derart bemerkenswerter Vielseitigkeit ist. Ein Kritiker, der 1993 Johnsons Glass House in New Canaan besuchte, kam in seinem Artikel den gleichen Fragen sehr nahe, die auch schon an Gehrys Bauwerk am Prager Rasinufer gerichtet wurden. Er bezog sich auf Johnsons »hysterischen Exhibitionismus« und kam zu der Schlußfolgerung, daß »der Trugschluß des Formalismus nicht darin liegt, Architektur als Kunst zu betrachten, sondern in der Annahme, man diene

nisme continuent à être créées sous différentes formes par des architectes qui vont des plus jeunes stars de la scène internationale aux vieux maîtres. Les trois exemples suivants concernent de vastes bâtiments rectangulaires et montrent à quel point peuvent différer les approches d'une forme aussi basique.

Le néo-modernisme pratiqué par de jeunes architectes comme Herzog et de Meuron en Europe, ou Kazuyo Sejima au Japon, n'a pas encore pris racine aux États-Unis, mais l'agence de Miami, Arquitectonica, animée par Bernardo Fort-Brescia, d'origine péruvienne, et Laurinda Spear, a remporté récemment de grand succès avec des plans modernistes qui rappellent la discrète neutralité de certains de leurs confrères européens. Ce sont des réalisations que l'on ne peut que remarquer, comme la nouvelle ambassade américaine de Lima (Pérou). Il faut noter que la forme rectangulaire de ce bâtiment ne vient pas tant des architectes que d'une exigence de sécurité. Les formes complexes et les retraits peuvent en effet multiplier les effets du souffle d'une bombe, tandis qu'une forme carrée ou rectangulaire à petites ouvertures résiste mieux à ce type de risque. Ceci dit, un revêtement coloré et des motifs décoratifs géométriques donnent à cette forteresse une allure très contemporaine.

Situé dans la Casa de la Caritat, une ancienne enclave monastique en plein centre ancien de Barcelone, le nouveau musée d'art contemporain (MACBA) se dresse comme un phare de perfection immaculée. Bien qu'il s'agisse également d'un bloc rectangulaire de 36 x 122 m, il est marqué d'articulations complexes qui sont autant d'éléments de la «signature» Meier. Selon le descriptif de son agence: «La nature labyrinthique des passages et voies existantes sur le site se reflète dans l'organisation du bâtiment», mais certains ont ouvertement critiqué le manque d'intégration contextuelle. L'architecte Peter Buchanan écrit ainsi dans la revue «Architecture»: «L'implantation de l'entrée, du passage, et de la cafétéria sont les seules prises en compte du site par le bâtiment. La nouvelle plaza est traitée comme un vide duquel on peut voir cette hautaine nouvelle construction, non contaminée par le contexte, ou les bonnes manières urbaines – point de départ surprenant dans un site si chargé d'histoire.»[10]

have been outspoken in their criticism of Meier's lack of contextual integration. The architect Peter Buchanan, writing in the magazine *Architecture,* said, "The locations of the entrance, passage, and café constitute the building's sole recognition of its setting... the new plaza is treated as a void from which to view the haughty new building, which is uncontaminated by context, or good urban manners – a startling departure in a setting so heavy with history."[10] Undoubtedly rendered more complex by the lack of a collection or a director during the planning and construction, this structure is, according to Richard Meier, one of his favorite buildings. Despite the argument over whether such a modern white building does truly react and correspond with its environment, there has also been the suggestion that this classical Meier building is just that, too classical. "Paradoxically," writes Joseph Giovannini, "Meier's Modernism is Classical and traditional. Inevitably, the Turk has become the Dean, and it seems that something has been lost in the transition. At the recent dedication of the new museum in Barcelona, a speaker called it 'the most beautiful contemporary building in Spain.' Possibly. Even probably. One can hardly imagine a more generous design: Every opportunity for architectural richness has been explored and built within a cogent, but not simplistic structure. Urbanistically, this magnificent creature opens up a dark and congested district and enlightens it with order. The disappointment is that the Barcelona Museum of Contemporary Art no longer surprises the way the Douglas House once did. We have grown to expect a Meier from Meier."[11]

The new San Francisco Public Library designed by James Ingo Freed of Pei Cobb Freed is another almost perfect rectangle, at least along its outer boundaries. Covering slightly more than one hectare in an area bounded by Fulton and Grove Streets near City Hall (Bakewell and Brown, 1915), the Library is indeed deceptively traditional from the outside. Because it is in an historic zone inspired by the 1905 Burnham/Bennett plan, the Library was required by city officials to fit in with the classical vocabulary of neighboring buildings. As James Freed, the author of the Washington Holocaust Museum, has said, this structure

der Kunst, wenn man sie aus ihrem sozialen Kontext herauslöst.«[9] Ist es möglich, daß die von Persönlichkeiten wie Johnson, Gehry oder Eisenman erkämpfte Freiheit der zeitgenössischen Architektur – die Freiheit, ein Bauwerk als ästhetische, skulpturale oder formale Komposition zu betrachten – als Thema heute der Vergangenheit angehört?

Die Verwandlung der Kastenform

Die geometrische Kastenform ist die Ikone der modernen Architektur – sei es in Mies van der Rohes Barcelona Pavillon (1929) oder in Philip Johnsons Glass House (1949). Johnson sagt heute dazu: »Im Bereich der Architektur besitzen der Klassizismus, die Moderne und alle Spielarten dazwischen die gleiche Wertigkeit.« Überraschenderweise werden Varianten der größtenteils gradlinigen Geometrie der Moderne nach wie vor in einer Reihe unterschiedlicher Stilrichtungen verwendet – und zwar sowohl von den jüngsten Stars als auch von den alten Meistern der internationalen Architekturszene. Drei Beispiele zeigen jedoch, auf welch unterschiedliche Weise man sich dieser Grundform nähern kann.

Die von jüngeren Architekten wie Herzog & de Meuron in Europa oder Kazuyo Sejima in Japan praktizierte Neo-Moderne hat die USA noch nicht erreicht, aber die in Miami ansässige Architektengruppe Arquitectonica, die von dem Peruaner Bernardo Fort-Brescia und von Laurinda Spear geleitet wird, konnte vor kurzem einen großen Erfolg mit modernistischen Entwürfen verzeichnen, die die langweilige Zurückhaltung einiger ihrer europäischen Gegenstücke vermeiden. Dabei handelt es sich um Bauten, die man einfach nicht übersehen kann, wie etwa das neue Gebäude der amerikanischen Botschaft in Lima. Allerdings war die streng rechtwinklige Form dieses Gebäudes weniger eine Idee der Architekten als vielmehr eine Frage der Sicherheitsanforderungen: Einbuchtungen oder komplexe Formen vergrößern offensichtlich die Wirkung einer Bombenexplosion, während eine quadratische oder rechteckige Form mit kleinen Fenstern besser gegen eine solch verhängnisvolle Möglichkeit gewappnet ist. Wie dem auch sei – die farbenfrohe Fassadenverkleidung

Richard Meier, Museum of Contemporary Art, Barcelona, Spain, 1987–95. A photograph showing the shining white presence of the building in its otherwise dark setting, and a drawing showing the museum and the Plaça dels Angels.

Richard Meier, Museum für Zeitgenössische Kunst, Barcelona, Spanien, 1987–95. Die Fotografie zeigt das strahlend weiße Erscheinungsbild des Gebäudes in einer ansonsten dunklen Umgebung, während die Zeichnung die Lage des Museums und des Plaça dels Angels veranschaulicht.

Richard Meier, Musée d'art contemporain, Barcelone, Espagne, 1987–95. Étincelante présence de ce bâtiment dans un environnement plutôt sombre, et dessin montrant le musée sur la Plaça dels Angels.

Si la construction de cet ensemble a été rendue encore plus délicate par l'absence d'une collection et d'un directeur lors de la mise au point du programme et de la construction, elle n'en est pas moins l'une des réalisations que préfère Richard Meier. Malgré l'argument de savoir si un bâtiment blanc aussi moderne s'intègre, ne serait-ce que par réaction, à son environnement, on trouve également la suggestion que cette réalisation si classiquement «Meier» est justement trop classique. «Paradoxalement», écrit Joseph Giovannini, «le modernisme de Meier est classique et traditionnel. Le rebelle s'est embourgeoisé, et quelque chose s'est perdu au cours de cette évolution. Lors de la récente inauguration du nouveau musée, un intervenant l'a qualifié de ‹plus belle réalisation architecturale contemporaine en Espagne.› C'est possible, et même probable. On pourrait même difficilement imaginer une conception plus généreuse: tout ce qui pouvait accroître l'effet de richesse architecturale a été exploré et mis à profit dans le cadre d'une structure puissante, sans être pour autant simpliste. Urbanistiquement, ce magnifique objet éclaire un quartier dense et congestionné et l'illumine d'un ordre différent. La déception est que ce musée de Barcelone ne nous surprend plus de la façon dont la Douglas House avait su le faire. Nous avons fini par attendre un Meier de Meier.»[11]

La nouvelle Bibliothèque publique de San Francisco conçue par James Ingo Freed, de Pei Cobb Freed, est un autre de ces rectangles quasiment parfaits, du moins en ce qui concerne sa forme extérieure. Recouvrant une surface d'un peu plus d'un hectare dans un quartier délimité par Fulton et Grove Street près de l'hôtel de ville (Bakewell et Brown, 1915), elle semble bien traditionnelle vue de l'extérieur. Parce qu'elle se trouve dans une zone historique répondant au plan Burnham/Bennett de 1905, les autorités municipales ont voulu qu'elle s'inspire du classicisme des bâtiments voisins. Comme l'indique James Freed, signataire par ailleurs du musée de l'Holocauste de Washington, cette construction est en fait ce qu'il appelle un «bâtiment hybride, qui répond spécifiquement à toute une série de forces préexistantes diverses, mais néanmoins conserve sa lecture

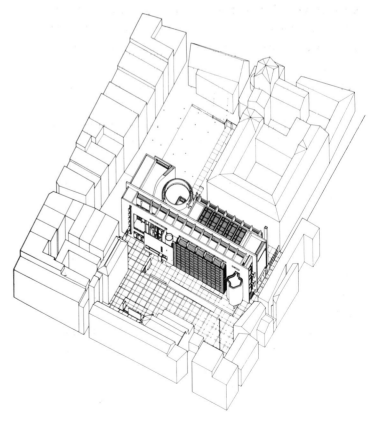

is in fact what he calls a "hybrid building... one that responds specifically to a variety of preexisting forces but nevertheless retains its reading as a singular work of architecture – part barrier – part gate – part tower – part slab – part new – part old. Hybrid buildings require a sober approach in order to retain the sense of the 'new' with the intention of augmenting rather than destroying an urban fabric of great value." Within the building, such formal constraints of course apply less, and Freed has created a spectacular 24.4 meter high cylindrical atrium. Surprisingly, four stories up into this light-filled space, an angle of the magazine reading room juts out into space. The message here may be that beyond the limits imposed by what can now be considered classical modernism, geometry can be turned to new purposes. Although Freed employs circular or spiral patterns, his design consists largely of rectangles, but he suddenly rotates the periodicals room or the compact stacks vis-à-vis the main volume, generating spatial tensions that are not typical of an earlier modernism, which would also have had difficulty being as respectful of the past as is the architect in this instance.

Bending The Rules
Clearly, some architects have found that it is profitable to develop their work on the basis of modernist thought. Others have sought sources of inspiration further afield, and some have entirely rejected the operating mechanisms of contemporary architecture to imagine, if only on paper, a "better" world. Two built projects, and one that is not likely to ever be built, illustrate these trends, which must certainly be considered more than marginal.

Born in Albuquerque, New Mexico, Bart Prince worked as an assistant to Bruce Goff from 1968 to 1973, establishing his credentials as the most legitimate representative of a strong regional tradition of organic architecture. The Hight Residence, which he completed in 1995 in Mendocino, California, is indicative of his unusual style, with its cedar-shingled undulating roof. As Prince says, "The Hights spent a good deal of time looking for an architect and interviewed several. They selected me after

und die geometrischen Muster verleihen dieser Festung ein ausgesprochen zeitgenössisches Erscheinungsbild.

Richard Meiers neues Museum für Zeitgenössische Kunst in der Casa de la Caritat, einer ehemaligen klösterlichen Enklave in der Altstadt von Barcelona, ragt in seiner weißen Perfektion wie ein Leuchtturm aus seiner Umgebung heraus. Obwohl es sich bei diesem Bauwerk ebenfalls um einen rechtwinkligen Block mit einer Kantenlänge von 36 x 122 m handelt, zeichnet es sich durch eine komplexe Formensprache aus, die gleichermaßen zu Meiers prägnantem Stil gehört. Laut Angaben seiner Firma »kommt die labyrinthartige Wegführung des Geländes in der Organisation des Gebäudes zum Ausdruck«, aber es wurde auch Kritik bezüglich des mangelnden Integrationsvermögens in die bebaute Umgebung laut. Peter Buchanan schrieb in der Zeitschrift »Architecture«, »Die Lage des Eingangs, der Passage und des Cafés bilden die einzigen Bezüge des Gebäudes zu seiner Umgebung... der neue Platz wird als leerer Raum behandelt, von dem aus man das überhebliche, von keinem Umfeld oder guten urbanen Sitten angekränkelte, neue Bauwerk betrachten kann – eine erschreckende Entgleisung in einer derart historischen Umgebung.«[10] Richard Meier zählt dieses Gebäude zu seinen Lieblingsbauwerken, da es aufgrund der fehlenden Sammlung und des noch nicht ernannten Direktors während der Planungs- und Bauphase besonders komplex gestaltet werden konnte. Ungeachtet der Frage, ob und inwiefern ein solch modernes, weißes Gebäude tatsächlich auf seine bebaute Umgebung eingeht, wurde auch die These geäußert, daß dieses klassische Meier-Bauwerk genau das sei – nämlich allzu klassisch. Joseph Giovannini schrieb: »Paradoxerweise ist Meiers Moderne zugleich klassisch und traditionell. Der Rebell wurde zwangsläufig zum ehrenwerten Bürger, und offensichtlich ist bei dieser Verwandlung etwas verlorengegangen. Bei der Einweihungsfeier bezeichnete ein Sprecher das neue Museum als ›das schönste zeitgenössische Bauwerk Spaniens. Möglich. Sogar wahrscheinlich. Man kann sich kaum einen großzügigeren Entwurf vorstellen: Jede Gelegenheit zu architektonischer Pracht wurde genutzt und in eine überzeugende, aber nicht vereinfachende Konstruktion

d'œuvre d'architecture singulière – en partie barrière, en partie porte, en partie tour, en partie bloc, en partie nouvelle, en partie ancienne. Les bâtiments hybrides exigent une approche sobre pour maintenir un sens de «nouveauté» avec l'intention d'enrichir plutôt que de détruire un tissu urbain de grande valeur». À l'intérieur, ces contraintes formelles s'appliquent moins, et Freed a créé un atrium cylindrique spectaculaire de 24, 4 m de haut. Curieusement, à la hauteur du quatrième niveau, un angle de la salle de lecture des magazines fait irruption dans ce lumineux volume. Le message est peut-être ici qu'au-delà des limites imposées par ce qui peut aujourd'hui être considéré comme un modernisme classique, la géométrie peut poursuivre d'autres objectifs. Bien que Freed emploie des modèles circulaires ou spiralés, ses plans font largement appel aux rectangles, mais il fait brusquement pivoter la salle des périodiques ou les rangements par rapport au volume principal, générant des tensions spatiales rares chez les modernistes précédents, qui auraient également rencontré des difficultés à être aussi respectueux du passé que l'a été l'architecte dans ce cas.

Distordre les règles

Il est évident que certains architectes ont trouvé confortable de développer leur travail sur les bases de la pensée moderniste. D'autres ont recherché des sources d'inspiration encore plus anciennes, et certains ont entièrement rejeté les mécanismes opératoires de l'architecture contemporaine pour imaginer, ne serait-ce que sur le papier, un monde «meilleur». Deux projets construits, et un troisième qui semble ne devoir jamais l'être, illustrent ces tendances qui ne doivent pas être considérées comme purement marginales.

Né à Albuquerque, Nouveau-Mexique, Bart Prince a travaillé comme assistant auprès de Bruce Goff de 1968 à 1973, ce qui lui donne le titre de l'un des représentants les plus légitimes de la solide tradition régionale d'architecture organique. La Hight Residence, qu'il a achevée en 1995 à Mendocino, Californie, avec son toit ondulé recouvert d'un bardage de cèdre, est représentative de ce style inhabituel. Il précise: «Les Hight ont passé beau-

Pei Cobb Freed, San Francisco Public Library, San Francisco, California, 1992–96. A view of the spectacular central atrium, with the periodicals room jutting out to the left.

Pei Cobb Freed, San Francisco Public Library, San Francisco, Kalifornien, 1992–96. Innenansicht des aufsehenerregenden, zylindrischen Atriums. Auf der linken Seite ragt eine Ecke des Zeitschriftenlesesaals in den Raum hinein.

Pei Cobb Freed, San Francisco Public Library, San Francisco, Californie, 1992–96. Vue du spectaculaire atrium central, avec l'avancée de la salle des périodiques sur la gauche.

Bart Prince, Hight Residence, Mendocino County, California, 1994–95. In the organic tradition of architects like Bruce Goff, the house stands in its setting almost like a natural object.

Bart Prince, Hight Residence, Mendocino County, Kalifornien, 1994–95. Das Haus, das in der organischen Bautradition eines Bruce Goff gehalten ist, wirkt in seiner Umgebung fast wie ein natürliches Objekt.

Bart Prince, Hight Residence, Mendocino County, Californie, 1994–95. Dans la tradition organique d'architectes comme Bruce Goff, la maison est posée comme un objet dans son environnement naturel.

seeing several of my buildings and talking with me. They were very interested in architecture and liked the work of Charles (1868–1957) and Henry Greene (1870-1954) as well as that of Frank Lloyd Wright." The reference to Wright or the Greene brothers is no coincidence, nor could the "natural" styles of architecture that they represent be considered in any way eccentric. And yet this has little to do with the sculptural forms even of architects like Frank O. Gehry. Its formal source of inspiration is not art but nature.

Although a different set of ideas is at work in the new Los Angeles International Airport Control Tower designed by Siegel Diamond Architects, they too make reference to natural phenomena or, more precisely, the "organic imagery of the high tech tree" in describing their design. This 78 meter high tower, which they also call "an adult tree-house," is located directly next to the Los Angeles International Airport Theme building (Luckman, Pereira, Becket and Williams, 1960), a "futurist" design, which resembles a stabile by Alexander Calder. It is interesting to note that despite its apparent modernity, Los Angeles is plagued with one of the more inadequate airports in the United States. The master plan for the airport by William Pereira, Paul Williams and Welton Becket dates from the mid 1950s. When jet service began in 1962, some seven million people a year went through the LAX terminal. In 1991, the airport handled 657,436 takeoffs and landings and 45,688,204 passengers, making it the world's third busiest airport. It was high time that this important hub of transportation found a symbol a bit more in the spirit of the times than the "flying saucer" Theme Building. Commissioned by the Federal Aviation Administration as a prototypical air control tower, this structure incorporates a reference to its neighbor and to its situation within the airport, a figurative design element that marks its distance from the abstraction implicit in much modern architecture. According to the architects, "the paraboloid arches of the Theme Building Restaurant are evolved into flattened arches, which express the themes of wings/ flight/aircraft."

Lebbeus Woods is a figure apart in the world of contemporary

umgesetzt. Unter städtebaulichen Aspekten öffnet dieses phantastische Gebilde einen dunklen und übervölkerten Bezirk und erhellt ihn mit Ordnung. Die eigentliche Enttäuschung liegt jedoch darin, daß das Museum für Zeitgenössische Kunst in Barcelona uns nicht mehr überrascht, wie es etwa das Douglas House vermochte. Wir haben uns daran gewöhnt, von Meier einen Meier zu erwarten.«[11]

Die von James Ingo Freed (einem Teilhaber der Firma Pei Cobb Freed) entworfene San Francisco Public Library stellt ein weiteres, nahezu perfektes Rechteck dar – zumindest in Bezug auf ihr äußeres Erscheinungsbild. Die auf einem kaum 1 ha großen Gelände zwischen der Fulton und der Grove Street gelegene Bibliothek wirkt in der Tat von außen täuschend traditionell. Da es sich um ein historisches, von Burnham/Bennetts Bebauungsplan aus dem Jahre 1905 stark geprägtes Gebiet handelt, verlangte die Stadt, daß sich die Bibliothek in die klassische Formensprache der umliegenden Gebäude einpaßt. James Freed, der Schöpfer des Washington Holocaust Museum, bezeichnete dieses Bauwerk als »Hybridgebäude... das auf die Vielzahl bereits existierender Kräfte eingeht, aber nichtsdestotrotz seine Deutung als eigenständiges Werk der Architektur bewahrt – teils Mauer – teils Tor – teils Turm – teils Sockel – teils neu – teils alt. Hybridgebäude erfordern eine nüchterne Vorgehensweise, damit das Neue eine Erweiterung darstellt und nicht urbanes Gewebe von großem Wert zerstört.« Innerhalb des Gebäudes sind solche formalen Beschränkungen natürlich von geringerer Bedeutung, und Freed schuf ein aufsehenerregendes, 24,4 m hohes, zylindrisches Atrium. Auf Höhe des vierten Geschosses ragt eine Ecke des Lesesaals überraschend in den lichtgefüllten Raum hinein. Die Botschaft dahinter könnte lauten, daß die Geometrie jenseits der Grenzen, die ihr die heute als klassische Moderne bezeichnete Stilrichtung auferlegt, neuen Zielen zugeführt werden kann. Obwohl Freed runde oder spiralförmige Muster verwendet, besteht sein Entwurf größtenteils aus Rechtecken. Aber plötzlich verschwenkt er den Zeitschriftenraum oder die kompakten Magazine gegenüber dem Hauptbaukörper und erzeugt so räumliche Spannungen, die für die frühere Moderne keines-

coup de temps à chercher un architecte et en ont interrogé plusieurs. Ils m'ont choisi après avoir vu plusieurs de mes réalisations et discuté avec moi. Ils étaient très intéressés par l'architecture et aimaient le travail de Charles (1868–1957) et Henry Greene (1870–1954) aussi bien que celui de Frank Lloyd Wright.» La référence à Wright ou aux frères Greene n'est pas une coïncidence, et les styles «naturels» d'architecture qu'ils représentent ne peuvent être considérés en aucune façon excentriques, sans qu'ils n'aient cependant de rapport avec des formes sculpturales, même celles d'architectes comme Frank O. Gehry. Leur source d'inspiration n'est pas l'art, mais la nature.

C'est un corpus de concepts différents qui se trouve à l'œuvre dans la nouvelle tour de contrôle de l'aéroport international de Los Angeles, due aux architectes Siegel Diamond, qui font cependant également référence aux phénomènes naturels, ou plus précisément à «l'imagerie organique de l'arbre high-tech». Cette tour de 78 m de haut, qu'ils décrivent également comme «une maison dans l'arbre pour adultes», se dresse juste à côté du Los Angeles International Airport «Theme Building» (Luckman, Pereira, Becket and Williams, 1960), bâtiment «futuriste» qui fait penser à un stabile d'Alexander Calder. Il est curieux de noter que malgré sa modernité apparente, Los Angeles possède l'un des aéroports les moins bien conçus des États-Unis. Le plan de masse de William Pereira, Paul Williams et Welton Becket date du milieu des années 50. Lorsque les avions à réaction sont entrés en service en 1962, sept millions de voyageurs utilisaient chaque année l'aérogare. En 1991, l'aéroport gérait 657 436 atterrissages et décollages et 45 688 204 passagers, devenant du coup le troisième aéroport du monde. Il était plus que temps que cet important noyau de transports se trouve un symbole un peu plus actuel que la «soucoupe volante» du «Theme Building». Commandé par l'Administration fédérale de l'aviation, ce prototype de tour de contrôle fait référence à son voisin et à sa situation à l'intérieur de l'aéroport, élément de design figuratif qui marque ses distances par rapport à l'abstraction implicite de tant de réalisations contemporaines. Selon les architectes: «Les arches en forme de parabole du restaurant du

American architecture. Born in 1940 in Lansing, Michigan, he was educated at Purdue University School of Engineering and the University of Illinois School of Architecture. Having worked with the firm of Kevin Roche and John Dinkeloo on the Ford Foundation Building (New York, 1966–67) and on other projects up to 1972, he decided to make a break with what appeared to be a promising career. As he says, "I had all the standard training, the beginnings of a career in corporate architecture back in the 1960s. Obviously, I was in enough of a crisis that I had to begin to experiment, primarily through my work." The experimentation that he has gone toward consists of drawings of highly unusual and complex buildings, which seem to obey none of the known stylistic rules, and yet which, thanks to his knowledge of architecture and engineering, would be structurally viable. He has participated in several projects organized by Peter Noever, Director of the Österreichisches Museum für Angewandte Kunst in Vienna. The most recent of these, the International Conference on Contemporary Architecture, held in Havana, Cuba in January 1995, gave rise to his Havana Project, which is a proposal for a dynamic reassessment of the architectural needs of this city. The drawings of Lebbeus Woods, together with proposals on the same theme by Coop Himmelblau, Zaha Hadid, Steven Holl, Thom Mayne, Eric Owen Moss, and Carme Pinós, were conceived for an exhibition whose theme would be the movement toward "architecture that comprises complexity, sensitivity, and dynamics; architecture that focuses on the human being and withstands commercial definitions; architecture that copes with new tasks as well as the old traditional ones – an everyday architecture that yet contains the claim of universality and topicality – architecture as a universal and unifying metaphor of space, time and body." The point of view of Lebbeus Woods about this project, and about the need for experimental architecture, which may never be built, provides a fitting conclusion to this evocation of mostly completed buildings.

Philip Jodidio: *Why are you interested in cities like Havana or Sarajevo where you went previously?*

Lebbeus Woods: This whole idea of experimental architecture

wegs typisch wären. Sie hätte ihrerseits Schwierigkeiten gehabt, so respektvoll mit der Vergangenheit umzugehen, wie es der Architekt in diesem Fall tat.

Jenseits der Regeln

Einige Architekten sind ganz offensichtlich zu der Überzeugung gelangt, daß es sich lohnt, ihre Arbeiten auf dem Fundament der Theorien der Moderne aufzubauen; andere Architekten suchten auf völlig anderen Gebieten eine Quelle der Inspiration, und wieder andere lehnen die Vorgehensweise zeitgenössischer Architektur entschieden ab und weigern sich, eine »bessere« Welt zu erschaffen – und sei es auch nur auf dem Papier. Drei Bauprojekte illustrieren diesen Trend, der keineswegs nur als marginal eingestuft werden darf.

Der in Albuquerque, New Mexico, geborene Bart Prince hat durch seine Arbeit als Assistent von Bruce Goff (1968–73) bewiesen, daß er unter den rechtmäßigen Vertretern einer starken regionalen Tradition organischer Architektur führend ist. Die 1995 fertiggestellte Hight Residence in Mendocino, Kalifornien, mit ihrem gewellten Holzschindeldach ist typisch für seinen ungewöhnlichen Baustil. Prince erklärte dazu: »Die Hights investierten sehr viel Zeit in die Suche nach einem Architekten und führten viele Vorgespräche. Ihre Wahl fiel auf mich, nachdem sie einige meiner Bauwerke gesehen und mit mir gesprochen hatten. Sie interessierten sich wirklich sehr für Architektur und schätzen die Arbeit von Charles (1868–1957) und Henry Greene (1870–1954) ebenso wie die Werke von Frank Lloyd Wright.« Der Verweis auf Wright oder die Gebrüder Greene ist kein Zufall, und genauso wenig kann der »natürliche« Architekturstil, den sie repräsentieren, in irgendeiner Form als exzentrisch gelten. Dennoch besteht hier kaum ein Zusammenhang zu den skulpturalen Formen selbst solcher Architekten wie Frank O. Gehry. Die formale Inspirationsquelle ist hier nicht die Kunst, sondern die Natur.

Obwohl dem neuen Los Angeles International Airport Control Tower der Architekten Siegel Diamond ein ganz anderer theoretischer Unterbau zugrundeliegt, beziehen sich auch diese Archi-

Theme Building ont évolué en arches aplaties qui expriment le thème ailes/vol/avion.»

Lebbeus Woods est un personnage à part dans le monde de l'architecture contemporaine américaine. Né en 1940 à Lansing, Michigan, il a étudié à la Purdue University School of Engineering et à l'University of Illinois School of Architecture. Après avoir travaillé avec l'agence de Kevin Roche et John Dinkeloo sur l'immeuble de la Ford Foundation (New York, 1966–67) et d'autres projets jusqu'en 1972, il a décidé de faire une pause dans ce qui s'annonçait comme une carrière prometteuse: «J'avais reçu la formation standard, et fais mes débuts dans une carrière vouée à l'architecture pour grandes entreprises, dès les années 60. Il est certain que je me trouvais suffisamment en crise pour commencer à me lancer dans des expériences nouvelles, tout d'abord à travers mon travail.» Ces expériences consistent en dessins de constructions très curieuses et très complexes qui semblent n'obéir à aucune règle stylistique connue, et qui cependant, grâce à sa connaissance de l'architecture et de l'ingénierie, sont structurellement réalisables. Il a participé à plusieurs projets lancés par Peter Noever, directeur de l'Österreichisches Museum für Angewandte Kunst de Vienne. Le plus récent est la Conférence Internationale sur l'architecture contemporaine qui s'est tenue à La Havane, à Cuba, en janvier 1995, et a donné naissance à son Havana Project, proposition pour une réévaluation dynamique des besoins architecturaux de cette ville. Les dessins de Lebbeus Woods, ainsi que les propositions sur le même thème de Coop Himmelblau, Zaha Hadid, Steven Holl, Thom Mayne, Eric Owen Moss, Carme Pinós ont été conçus pour une exposition dont le thème serait l'orientation de l'architecture vers «une architecture qui intègre la complexité, la sensibilité, et la dynamique; une architecture qui se concentre sur l'être humain, et résiste aux définitions commerciales; une architecture qui se préoccupe aussi bien de tâches nouvelles que traditionnelles, une architecture au quotidien qui conserve cependant ses prétentions à l'universalité et à l'actualité – une architecture métaphore universelle et unificatrice de l'espace, du temps et du corps». Le point de vue de Lebbeus

Siegel Diamond Architects (Architectural Design Consultant), Holmes & Narver (Architect of Record), LAX Control Tower, Los Angeles, California, 1993–95. A ground-level view showing one of the arches inspired by the nearby Theme Building.

Siegel Diamond Architects (Architectural Design Consultant), Holmes & Narver (Architect of Record), LAX Control Tower, Los Angeles, Kalifornien, 1993–95. Ansicht des Erdgeschosses mit Blick auf einen der Bögen, für die das nahegelegene Theme Building als Inspirationsquelle diente.

Siegel Diamond Architects (Architectural Design Consultant), Holmes & Narver (Architect of Record), LAX Control Tower, Los Angeles, Californie, 1993–95. Vue au niveau du sol montrant l'une des arches inspirées par le Theme Building voisin.

Lebbeus Woods, Havana Project, Havana, Cuba, 1995. An effort to analyze the real needs of a city that has suffered from a long period of inattention.

Lebbeus Woods, Havana Project, Havanna, Kuba, 1995. Der Versuch, die wahren Bedürfnisse einer über lange Zeit vernachlässigten Stadt zu analysieren.

Lebbeus Woods, Havana Project, La Havane, Cuba, 1995. Effort d'analyse des besoins concrets d'une ville qui souffre d'une longue période d'abandon.

is not that it is an answer for everyone. It is more of an architecture for those people who are in some state of crisis. That is why I felt I could go to Sarajevo. In that city, experimentation is necessary for survival. Creativity and invention is not just an option, it is a necessity, because the old systems have broken down completely. It is the logical place for experimental architecture.

Philip Jodidio: *Would you actually consider building the structures you draw?*

Lebbeus Woods: Of course I would build them. I spend a lot of time thinking about them. I have asked a few people why I haven't more of a chance to build. It is just that people think I am really crazy, and maybe they are right, or there is something in the way I present my work which seems not to ask for its realization. I haven't been out trying to hustle work. I do not participate in competitions because I am not interested in the type of buildings that competitions call for. I am not interested in finding a new form for an old program. I am interested in a new program for architecture. A new spatial program, a new type of habitation. I am interested in those conditions which are new, at least historically new in our period.

Philip Jodidio: *Your work seems to be closely connected to the concept of war and destruction.*

Lebbeus Woods: That is only one aspect of it. The forms are fractured and broken, but that relates to an idea of a different spatial configuration. I call them free spaces. The relation we have to the physical has everything to do with our way of life. The second idea has to do with methods of construction. I respect that aspect of architecture very much. In my work now, even though the forms are not the forms of our industrial society, they are nevertheless related to how one might make things with certain materials, and labor-intensive methods, as opposed to mass-production. I would not expect that these forms would be built exactly as I draw them. I do not see design as an attempt to control completely. The design is experimental too. So the drawings and models are basically guides for the builders.

Philip Jodidio: *You seem to be constantly challenging esthetic assumptions. Are you seeking an aggressive image?*

tekten auf Naturphänomene, oder genauer gesagt auf »die organische Metaphorik des High-Tech-Baums« – wie sie ihren eigenen Entwurf beschreiben. Dieser 78 m hohe Turm, den Siegel Diamond als »Baumhaus für Erwachsene« bezeichnen, steht direkt neben dem Los Angeles International Airport Theme Building (Luckman, Pereira, Becket und Williams, 1960), einem »futuristischen« Design, das einer abstrakten Freiplastik von Alexander Calder ähnelt. Interessanterweise gehört der Flughafen von Los Angeles trotz seiner scheinbaren Modernität zu den unzulänglichsten Flughäfen der USA. Der Bebauungsplan für diesen von William Pereira, Paul Williams und Welton Becket entworfenen Flughafen stammt aus der Mitte der 50er Jahre. Als der Flugverkehr 1962 aufgenommen wurde, nutzten jährlich sieben Millionen Passagiere das LAX Terminal. 1991 verzeichnete der Flughafen jedoch bereits 675 436 Starts und Landungen, bei denen 45 688 204 Passagiere transportiert wurden – was ihn in Punkto Passagieraufkommen zum drittgrößten Flughafen der Welt macht. Es wurde höchste Zeit, daß dieser wichtige Verkehrsknotenpunkt ein Symbol erhält, das mehr dem Zeitgeist entspricht als das einer »fliegenden Untertasse« ähnelnde Theme Building. Der von der Federal Aviation Administration in Auftrag gegebene Tower soll als Prototyp zukünftiger Kontrolltürme dienen und enthält Bezüge zu seinem Nachbargebäude sowie zu seiner Lage auf dem Flughafengelände – ein symbolträchtiges Designelement, das seine Distanz zu der Abstraktion, die moderner Architektur häufig eigen ist, deutlich zum Ausdruck bringt. Laut Aussage der Architekten »wurden die paraboloiden Bögen des Theme Building Restaurant zu abgeflachten Bögen weiterentwickelt, die die Themen Flügel/Flug/Flugzeug symbolisieren.«

Lebbeus Woods ist in der zeitgenössischen amerikanischen Architektenschaft eine Klasse für sich. Er wurde 1940 in Lansing, Michigan, geboren und studierte an der Purdue University School of Engineering sowie an der University of Illinois School of Architecture. Nach seiner Tätigkeit für Kevin Roche und John Dinkeloo, für die er an verschiedenen Projekten mitarbeitete, entschloß sich Wood 1972 zum Abbruch einer vielversprechen-

Woods sur ce projet et la nécessité d'une architecture expérimentale, qui ne sera peut-être jamais construite, offre une excelente conclusion à cette évocation de bâtiments pour la plupart construits:

Philip Jodidio: *Pourquoi vous intéressez-vous à des villes comme La Havane ou Sarajevo où vous vous êtes rendu récemment?*

Lebbeus Woods: L'idée globale de l'architecture expérimentale n'est pas qu'il s'agit d'une réponse valable pour chacun. Il s'agit davantage d'une architecture pour ceux qui se trouvent dans un état de crise. C'est pourquoi j'ai senti que je pouvais aller à Sarajevo où l'expérimentation est nécessaire si l'on veut survivre. La créativité et l'invention ne sont pas simplement des options, mais une nécessité, parce que l'ancien système s'est effondré. C'est le lieu logique pour une architecture expérimentale.

Philip Jodidio: *Pensez-vous réellement construire un jour les projets que vous dessinez?*

Lebbeus Woods: Bien entendu. Je passe beaucoup de temps à y réfléchir. J'ai demandé à quelques personnes pourquoi je n'avais cependant guère de chances de construire. Eh bien les gens pensent que je suis réellement fou, et peut-être ont-ils raison, ou peut-être y a-t-il dans la manière dont je présente mon travail quelque chose qui semble décourager la réalisation. Je n'ai pas essayé de précipiter les choses. Je ne participe pas à des concours parce que je ne m'intéresse pas au type de bâtiment qui fait l'objet de concours. Je ne suis pas préoccupé par la recherche de formes nouvelles sur des programmes anciens. Je m'intéresse à de nouveaux programmes pour l'architecture. Un nouveau programme spatial, un nouveau type d'habitat. Je m'intéresse à des conditions qui sont nouvelles, au moins historiquement pour la période où nous vivons.

Philip Jodidio: *Votre travail semble étroitement lié au concept de guerre et de destruction.*

Lebbeus Woods: Ce n'est qu'un de ses aspects. Les formes sont fracturées et brisées, mais ceci est en rapport avec une idée de configuration spatiale différente. Je les appelle des «espaces libres». La relation que nous avons avec ce qui est physique est intégralement en rapport avec notre façon de vivre. La seconde

Lebbeus Woods: To be honest, it is not something I set out to do. In many ways, I consider myself very traditional. My ethics of materials and function are modernist. I may have a different definition of function than other architects. My program is radically different. I am trying to do away with the idea of building types and with the idea of spatial types. At least I am trying to challenge it. Not everywhere. I am just interested in introducing this type of free space as an expansion of the possibilities of the city. So that the city is not pre-designed, pre-lived in. There is a potential which does not exist in the city as it is.

Philip Jodidio: *Your vision is apocalyptic, though, isn't it?*

Lebbeus Woods: Apocalyptic only in the sense that I think that it is important to face things as they are. To see the ugly, to see the troublesome.

Philip Jodidio: *By embracing it?*

Lebbeus Woods: By having a dialogue with it. By embracing it, or engaging it. If that means some aspects of my work are difficult, that does not mean we should retreat from it. We need difficulty too. I am not interested in creating peaceful places.[12]

Notes | Anmerkungen

1 Johnson, Philip and Mark Wigley: *Deconstructivist Architecture.* Museum of Modern Art, New York, 1988.
2 Collins, Brad (compiled by): *Eric Owen Moss, Buildings and Projects 2.* Rizzoli, New York, 1996.
3 Edelman, Gerald: "The Wordless Metaphor: Visual Art and the Brain", in: *1995 Biennial Exhibition.* Whitney Museum of American Art, New York, 1995.
4 Muschamp, Herbert: "To a Neuroscientist's Liking: Calm, yet Complex", *The New York Times*, October 22, 1995.
5 Filler, Martin: "Husbands and Wives", *Architecture,* June 1996.
6 Muschamp, Herbert: "Viñoly's Vision for Tokyo and for the Identity of Japan," *The New York Times,* July 16, 1993.
7 Ghiradro, Diane: "Eisenman's Bogus Avant-Garde", *Progressive Architecture,* November 1994.
8 Interview with Peter Eisenman, New York, Monday, May 15, 1995.
9 Muschamp, Herbert: "A Man Who Lives in Glass Houses", *The New York Times,* October 17, 1993.
10 Buchanan, Peter: "Aloof Abstraction", *Architecture,* February 1996.
11 Giovannini, Joseph: "Is Richard Meier Really Modern?" *Architecture,* February 1996.
12 Interview with Lebbeus Woods, New York, May 18, 1995.

den Karriere. Er erklärte dazu: »Ich hatte die klassische Architekturausbildung und somit alle Voraussetzungen für eine Karriere als Firmenarchitekt während der 60er Jahre. Aber offensichtlich befand ich mich in einer solchen Krise, daß ich einfach beginnen mußte zu experimentieren – hauptsächlich durch meine Arbeit.« Die Experimente bestanden aus Zeichnungen von ausgesprochen ungewöhnlichen und komplexen Gebäuden, die keiner der bekannten stilistischen Regeln zu folgen schienen und die dennoch – dank seiner Kenntnisse der Architektur und des Bauwesens – konstruktionstechnisch realisierbar gewesen wären. Woods nahm an mehreren Projekten teil, die Peter Noever, der Direktor des Österreichischen Museums für Angewandte Kunst in Wien, organisiert hatte. Die aktuellste dieser Veranstaltungen, die Internationale Konferenz für Zeitgenössische Architektur, fand im Januar 1995 in Havanna statt; dabei entstand sein »Havana Project«, das als Vorschlag für eine dynamische Neubeurteilung der architektonischen Bedürfnisse dieser Stadt konzipiert ist. Zusammen mit Beiträgen zum gleichen Thema von Coop Himmelblau, Zaha Hadid, Steven Holl, Thom Mayne, Eric Owen Moss und Carme Pinós wurden Lebbeus Woods Zeichnungen für eine Ausstellung entworfen, deren Thema die Entwicklung einer Architektur sein sollte, »die Komplexität, Sensibilität und Dynamik umfaßt; eine Architektur, die sich auf den Menschen konzentriert und kommerziellen Definitionen widersteht; eine Architektur, die die neuen Aufgaben ebenso meistert wie die alten, traditionellen – eine alltägliche Architektur, die dennoch den Anspruch auf Universalität und Aktualität erhebt – Architektur als universelle und vereinigende Metapher von Raum, Zeit und Gesellschaft.« Lebbeus Woods persönliche Meinung zu diesem Thema und seinem Bedürfnis nach experimenteller Architektur, die möglicherweise nie gebaut wird, liefert ein passendes Schlußwort zu dieser Darstellung überwiegend fertiggestellter Bauwerke.

Philip Jodidio: *Warum interessieren Sie sich für Städte wie Havanna oder Sarajewo, wo Sie vor kurzem waren?*

Lebbeus Woods: Die Idee der experimentellen Architektur versteht sich nicht als Antwort auf alle Fragen. Es handelt sich eher

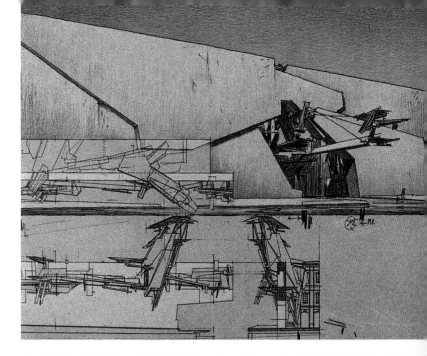

idée est liée aux méthodes de construction. Je respecte beaucoup cet aspect de l'architecture. Dans mon travail, même si les formes ne sont pas celles de notre société industrielle, elles sont néanmoins en connexion avec la façon dont on peut faire certaines choses avec certains matériaux, et des méthodes de travail intensif, en tant qu'opposée à la production de masse. Je n'attends pas que ces formes soient construites exactement comme je les ai dessinées. Je ne vois pas le dessin comme une tentative de tout contrôler. Le dessin, lui aussi, est expérimental. Les dessins et maquettes sont des guides pour les constructeurs.

Philip Jodidio: *Vous semblez défier en permanence les certitudes esthétiques. Êtes-vous à la recherche d'une image agressive?*

Lebbeus Woods: Pour être honnête, ce n'est pas quelque chose qui me tente. À de nombreux égards, je me considère comme très traditionnaliste. Mon éthique des matériaux et des fonctions est moderniste. Je peux avoir une définition de fonction différente de celle d'autres architectes. Mon programme, lui, est radicalement différent. J'essaie de me défaire de l'idée de type de construction et de types spatiaux. Au moins j'essaie de les remettre en question. Pas partout. La seule chose qui m'intéresse est d'introduire ce type d'espace libre comme expansion des possibilités de la cité. Afin que la ville ne soit pas pré-dessinée, pré-vécue. Il existe un potentiel que l'on ne retrouve pas dans la ville telle qu'elle est. Je veux juste étendre les possibilités.

Philip Jodidio: *Votre vision est apocalyptique, cependant...*

Lebbeus Woods: Seulement dans le sens où je pense qu'il est important de faire face aux choses telles qu'elles sont. Voir ce qui est laid, voir ce qui pose des problèmes.

Philip Jodidio: *En y participant?*

Lebbeus Woods: En dialoguant avec. En le comprenant, ou en le prenant en charge. Si cela signifie que certains aspects de mon travail sont difficiles, cela ne veut pas dire que nous devons nous en détourner. Nous avons aussi besoin de la difficulté. Créer des lieux paisibles ne m'intéresse pas.[12]

um eine Architektur für Menschen, die sich in einer Art Krise befinden. Aus diesem Grunde hatte ich das Gefühl, daß ich Sarajewo besuchen sollte. In dieser Stadt ist das Experimentieren überlebenswichtig geworden. Kreativität und Erfindungsgabe sind nicht nur eine Möglichkeit, sondern eine absolute Notwendigkeit, da das alte System vollständig zusammengebrochen ist. Diese Stadt ist der logische Platz für experimentelle Architektur.

Philip Jodidio: *Würden Sie die Gebäude, die Sie entwerfen, auch tatsächlich bauen wollen?*

Lebbeus Woods: Natürlich würde ich sie bauen. Ich beschäftigte mich intensiv mit ihnen. Aber ich habe mich bei einigen Leuten erkundigt, warum ich so wenig Gelegenheit erhalte, meine Entwürfe zu verwirklichen. Es ist einfach so, daß mich manche Leute für verrückt halten, und vielleicht haben sie sogar recht, oder es liegt an der Art und Weise, wie ich meine Werke präsentiere. Ich habe weder versucht, mich um Arbeit zu bemühen, noch nehme ich an Wettbewerben teil, da mich die Art von Gebäuden, die solche Ausschreibungen verlangen, nicht interessiert. Mir liegt nichts daran, eine neue Form für ein altes Programm zu finden. Mich interessiert vielmehr ein neues Programm für die Architektur. Ein neues räumliches Programm, eine neue Form des Wohnens. Ich interessiere mich für diese neuen, zumindest in unserer Zeit historisch neuen Bedingungen.

Philip Jodidio: *Ihre Arbeit scheint in engem Zusammenhang zum Konzept des Krieges und der Zerstörung zu stehen.*

Lebbeus Woods: Das ist nur ein Aspekt. Die Formen sind fragmentiert und zerbrochen, aber das bezieht sich auf die Idee einer anderen räumlichen Konfiguration. Ich nenne sie »freie Räume«. Unser Verhältnis zum Physikalischen steht in engem Zusammenhang mit unserem Lebensstil. In zweiter Linie geht es um Konstruktionsmethoden. Ich respektiere diesen Aspekt der Architektur sehr. In meiner jetzigen Arbeit stehen die Formen, auch wenn es sich nicht um die Formen unserer Industriegesellschaft handelt, nichtsdestoweniger in Bezug zu der Art und Weise, wie man Dinge aus bestimmten Materialien bauen könnte, und zu arbeitsintensiven Verfahren – ganz im Gegensatz

zur Massenproduktion. Ich erwarte nicht, daß diese Formen genauso verwirklicht werden könnten, wie ich sie zeichne, und betrachte den Entwurf nicht als Versuch der völligen Kontrolle. Auch das Design ist experimentell. Daher sind die Zeichnungen und Modelle nur Richtlinien für die Erbauer.

Philip Jodidio: Sie scheinen die ästhetischen Grundsätze ständig herauszufordern. Streben Sie ein aggressives Image an?

Lebbeus Woods: Ehrlich gesagt, strebe ich das keineswegs an. In vielerlei Hinsicht bin ich Traditionalist. Meine Ethik der Materialien und Funktionen ist modernistisch. Möglicherweise unterscheidet sich meine Auffassung von Funktion von der anderer Architekten. Mein Programm ist völlig unterschiedlich. Ich versuche, die Vorstellung von Gebäudetypen und Raumtypen zu eliminieren. Zumindest bemühe ich mich, sie in Frage zu stellen. Nicht überall. Ich interessiere mich nur für die Einführung dieser Art von freiem Raum als Erweiterung zu den Möglichkeiten der Stadt – so daß die Stadt nicht vor-entworfen, vor-gelebt ist. Ich meine ein Potential, das die Stadt, so wie sie ist, nicht besitzt. Ich möchte lediglich die Möglichkeiten erweitern.

Philip Jodidio: Könnte man Ihre Vision als apokalyptisch bezeichnen?

Lebbeus Woods: Apokalyptisch nur insofern, als daß ich der Ansicht bin, daß es wichtig ist, die Dinge so zu sehen, wie sie sind. Das Häßliche und das Unangenehme zu sehen.

Philip Jodidio: Indem Sie es sich zu eigen machen?

Lebbeus Woods: Indem ich einen Dialog mit ihm führe; indem ich es mir zu eigen mache oder es involviere. Wenn das bedeutet, daß einige Teile meiner Arbeit schwierig sind, heißt das nicht, daß wir uns von ihr zurückziehen sollten. Wir brauchen auch die Schwierigkeiten. Mir ist nicht an der Schaffung friedlicher Orte gelegen.[12]

Arquitectonica

Both the reticence of clients who normally trust only well-established designers with major projects, and the construction time of large buildings, usually imply that important figures in the world of architecture emerge only after the age of 50. Despite being in their mid-forties, the couple Bernardo Fort-Brescia/Laurinda Spear have succeeded in breaking this rule, and in establishing themselves as much more than flamboyant local architects. In fact the shift of architectural fashion away from the post-modernism of the 1970s has placed their own brand of spectacular modernism firmly in the mainstream. This position was confirmed when the firm was chosen to build its first European project in Luxembourg, and its first tower in New York, in both instances by powerful figures in the banking and corporate sectors. Their most recent commission is for a complete reconstruction of the Miami International Airport, and the firm has substantial projects under way in Asia (Hong Kong, Jakarta, Singapore), as well as in Latin America.

Die Zurückhaltung vieler Auftraggeber, die ihre Großprojekte meist nur an etablierte Firmen vergeben, sowie die Bauzeit großer Gebäude haben im allgemeinen zur Folge, daß Architekten erst nach ihrem fünfzigsten Geburtstag als bedeutende Persönlichkeiten bekannt werden. Obwohl sie beide erst Mitte Vierzig sind, ist es Bernardo Fort-Brescia und Laurinda Spear gelungen, diese Regel zu durchbrechen und den Status regional bekannter, extravaganter Architekten hinter sich zu lassen. Die Abkehr der Architekturströmungen von der Postmoderne der 70er Jahre hat dafür gesorgt, daß Arquitectonicas persönliche Spielart eines spektakulären Modernismus heute fest im Mainstream verankert ist. Ihre Position wurde zusätzlich gefestigt, als man die Gruppe bat, ihr erstes Projekt auf europäischem Boden (in Luxemburg) und ihr erstes Hochhaus in New York zu bauen, wobei es sich in beiden Fällen um bedeutende Auftraggeber aus dem Finanz- bzw. Firmensektor handelt. Zu den aktuellsten Bauaufträgen Arquitectonicas zählen die grundlegende Neugestaltung des Miami International Airport sowie weitere Projekte in Asien (Hongkong, Djakarta, Singapur) und Lateinamerika.

Les timidités de clients qui ne font confiance qu'à des architectes établis, et la durée de construction de certains grands projets, expliquent qu'il est rare qu'un architecte soit reconnu avant l'âge de 50 ans. Et pourtant, le couple Bernardo Fort-Brescia et Laurinda Spear, qui n'ont que 45 ans, a réussi à bousculer cette règle et à se donner une image qui va bien au-delà de celle de flamboyants praticiens «locaux». En fait, la fin de la mode postmoderniste des années 70 a placé sous les projecteurs leur version personnelle et spectaculaire de modernisme. Leur position s'est vu confirmée par l'obtention de leur première commande en Europe, le siège de la Banque de Luxembourg, et de leur première tour à New York, sur Times Square. Ils ont récemment été chargés de la reconstruction complète de l'aéroport international de Miami, et travaillent à de vastes projets en Asie (Hongkong, Djakarta, Singapour), et en Amérique latine.

United States Embassy, Lima, Peru, 1993–95. A view of the main entrance.

Gebäude der amerikanischen Botschaft, Lima, Peru, 1993–95. Ansicht des Haupteinganges.

Ambassade américaine, Lima, Pérou, 1993–95. Vue de l'entrée principale.

United States Embassy

Lima, Peru, 1993–1995

This 11,000 square meter office building, a five-story chancery which consolidates Embassy functions, is not the first large building completed in Lima by Arquitectonica. Their Banco de Crédito was inaugurated in the same city in 1988. It should be noted that Arquitectonica principal Bernardo Fort-Brescia is of Peruvian origin, a fact that has permitted the firm to be involved in the booming development of the capital city. The new building is the first phase of a 27 acre master plan for the U.S. Embassy compound, located on the site of the former Lima Polo Club. Given the risk of potential attacks against the structure, the U.S. State Department insisted on a rectangular structure known to resist bomb blasts better than more complex designs. Window size was also strictly limited for the same reason. Using these rigorous constraints to its advantage, Arquitectonica has given what could easily have been a grim fortress a joyous exterior, which calls on geometric designs and materials that are inspired by the patterns of pre-Columbian textiles. The structure was built under budget for a total of $41 million.

Dieses 11 000 m² große fünfgeschossige Bürogebäude, in dem sämtliche Funktionen der Botschaft untergebracht sind, ist nicht das erste große Bauprojekt des Architekturbüros Arquitectonica in Lima: Bereits 1988 wurde hier ihre Banco de Crédito eröffnet. Da der Leiter von Arquitectonica, Bernardo Fort-Brescia, aus Peru stammt, gelang es der Firma, an der rasanten Entwicklung der Hauptstadt teilzuhaben. Das neue Gebäude, das für Gesamtkosten in Höhe von 41 Millionen Dollar entstand, bildet die erste Bauphase eines knapp 11 ha umfassenden Bebauungsplans für die gesamte amerikanische Botschaft auf dem Gelände des ehemaligen Lima Polo Club. Aufgrund der Sorge vor möglichen Anschlägen bestand das U.S. State Department auf einer rechtwinkligen Konstruktion, die Bombenattentaten größeren Widerstand bietet als komplexere Entwürfe. Aus dem gleichen Grunde wurde auch die Größe der Fenster stark eingeschränkt. Arquitectonica gelang es jedoch, die strengen Auflagen zu ihrem Vorteil zu nutzen und dem Botschaftsgebäude – das leicht einer grimmigen Festungsanlage hätte ähneln können – ein erfreuliches Erscheinungsbild zu verleihen, das aufgrund seiner geometrischen Aufteilung und der verwendeten Materialien an die attraktiven Muster präkolumbinanischer Stoffe erinnert.

Cette chancellerie de 11 000 m² et cinq étages réunit les différents services de l'ambassade. Elle n'est pas le premier bâtiment important construit par Arquitectonica à Lima, puisque leur Banco de Crédito y a été inauguré en 1988. L'origine péruvienne du dirigeant d'Arquitectonica, Bernardo Fort-Brescia, explique sa participation à l'essor urbain considérable de la capitale. Ce nouvel immeuble est la première phase du plan de masse de réinstallation de l'ambassade américaine sur les 11 ha des anciens terrains du club de polo de Lima. Prenant en compte les risques d'attentats, le département d'État a insisté pour que la construction soit de forme rectangulaire, censée mieux résister au souffle de bombes éventuelles qu'un plan plus complexe. La taille des ouvertures a été strictement limitée pour les mêmes raisons. Tournant ces contraintes à son avantage, Arquitectonica a donné à ce qui aurait pu avoir l'air d'une austère forteresse une façade presque joyeuse grâce à des matériaux bien choisis et à des motifs inspirés par les textiles pré-colombiens. L'ensemble a été construit pour un budget de 41 millions de $.

An aerial view showing the bulk of the Embassy building and the surrounding green areas as they are integrated into the city.

Eine Luftaufnahme zeigt die Integration des massiven Gebäudekomplexes der Botschaft und der umliegenden Grünflächen in die urbane Umgebung.

Vue aérienne montrant la masse du bâtiment de l'ambassade et l'intégration à la ville des espaces verts environnants.

Despite strict security requirements, the building gives
an impression of brightness and playful decoration.

Ungeachtet strenger Sicherheitsvorkehrungen vermittelt
das Gebäude ein strahlendes und verspieltes Erscheinungsbild.

Malgré les strictes exigences requises pour sa sécurité, le
bâtiment et son ornementation ludique donnent une
impression de luminosité.

Centerbrook

Mark Simon

Centerbrook began its existence as the New Haven firm of Charles Moore. Moore left Berkeley in 1965 to chair Yale's department of architecture, and brought Moore Lyndon Turnbull Whitaker with him. Mark Simon, currently one of five partners in Centerbrook, had Charles Moore as a teacher at Yale before joining Charles Moore Associates in 1974. Simon became a partner in Moore Grover Harper (now Centerbrook) in 1978. Tired of the urban environment in New Haven, Moore's firm purchased an abandoned 1874 auger bit factory on the banks of the Falls River, in the village of Centerbrook, part of the town of Essex, 35 miles east of New Haven. Having built numerous private houses in a variety of different styles, as well as the Hood Museum of Art (Dartmouth College, Hanover, New Hampshire, 1985), and the Williams College Museum of Art (Williamstown, Massachusetts, 1986), the firm is now working on the University of Colorado Health Sciences Center and Campus Center (Denver, Colorado, 2002), and a Chemistry Building at University of Connecticut, 1997.

Centerbrook wurde 1965 in New Haven von Charles Moore gegründet. Moore hatte im gleichen Jahr die University of California in Berkeley verlassen, um künftig den Fachbereich Architektur an der Yale University zu leiten und dabei Moore Lyndon Turnbull Whitaker mitgebracht. Mark Simon, der heute zu den fünf Partnern von Centerbrook gehört, lernte Charles Moore als Dozenten in Yale kennen, bevor er 1974 zu Charles Moore Associates kam. 1978 wurde Simon Partner bei Moore Grover Harper, dem heutigen Centerbrook. Der städtischen Umgebung New Havens müde, erwarb Moores Firma im Ort Centerbrook am Ufer des Falls River eine verlassene Bohreisenfabrik aus dem Jahre 1874 (Centerbrook gehört zur Stadt Essex, etwa 50 km östlich von New Haven). Nach dem Bau zahlreicher Privathäuser in einer Vielfalt unterschiedlicher Stile und den Entwürfen für das Hood Museum of Art (Dartmouth College, Hanover, New Hampshire, 1985) sowie das Williams College Museum of Art (Williamstown, Massachusetts, 1986) arbeitet die Firma zur Zeit am University of Colorado Health Sciences Center and Campus Center (Denver, Colorado, 2002) und an einem Gebäude für die chemische Fakultät der University of Connecticut.

Centerbrook est à l'origine l'agence de New Haven de Charles Moore. Moore quitte Berkeley en 1965 pour présider le département d'architecture de Yale, et y transplante Moore Lyndon Turnbull Whitaker. Mark Simon, l'un des cinq associés actuels de Centerbrook, a eu Moore comme enseignant à Yale avant de rejoindre l'agence Charles Moore Associates en 1974, et de devenir associé de Moore Grover Harper (aujourd'hui Centerbrook) en 1978. Lassé de l'environnement urbain de New Haven, l'agence achète une fabrique abandonnée datant de 1874 sur les rives de la Falls River dans le village de Centerbrook, commune d'Essex, à 35 miles à l'est de New Haven. Après avoir construit de nombreuses résidences privées dans des styles divers, le Hood Museum of Art (Dartmouth College, Hanover, New Hampshire, 1985), le Museum of Art de Williams College (Williamstown, Massachusetts, 1986), l'agence travaille actuellement sur l'université du Colorado Health Sciences Center et le campus (Denver, Colorado, 2002), et le bâtiment de la chimie à l'université du Connecticut.

Nauticus, National Maritime Center, Norfolk, Virginia, 1988–94.

Nauticus, National Maritime Center, Norfolk, Virginia, 1988–94.

Nauticus, National Maritime Center, Norfolk, Virginie, 1988–94.

Nauticus, National Maritime Center
Norfolk, Virginia, 1988–1994

This 11,200 square meter building was built for a cost of $ 22 million. Housing interactive maritime science exhibits, an aquarium, research labs, a wide screen theater and the Hampton Roads Naval Museum, it is intended as a "national landmark to draw visitors and herald the Hampton Roads' pre-eminence in marine technology." According to the firm, the structure is intended to recall a number of different maritime objects, including a "21st century aircraft carrier," without becoming a literal representation of any one type of vessel. Together with the building itself, Centerbrook was called on to rebuild the waterfront to permit large naval ships, research vessels and sailing ships to dock there. The total cost of the project, including the waterfront and exhibits, designed by Ralph Appelbaum Associates of New York, was $50 million. Exemplary of a new type of museum that mixes education and entertainment (edutainment), the Nauticus National Maritime Center calls on an architectural vocabulary that is inspired by the sleek, blank surfaces of contemporary low radar profile warships, an impression reinforced by its gray coloring. It escapes Disney-style literalism and succeeds in imposing itself, much as the architects' brief requested, as a landmark.

Die Baukosten für dieses 11 200 m² große Bauwerk beliefen sich auf 22 Millionen Dollar. Das Center umfaßt eine interaktive Ausstellung zum Thema Marinewissenschaft, ein Aquarium, Forschungslabors, ein Breitwandkino sowie das Hampton Roads Naval Museum und soll sich zu einem »nationalen Wahrzeichen« entwickeln, »das Besucher anzieht und Hampton Roads Vorherrschaft im Bereich der Marinetechnologie verkündet«. Laut Angaben des Architekturbüros erinnert die Konstruktion an eine Reihe verschiedener Marineobjekte, einschließlich eines »Flugzeugträgers des 21. Jahrhunderts«, ohne jedoch irgendeinen dieser Schiffstypen exakt zu repräsentieren. Neben dem Auftrag für die Errichtung des Gebäudes wurde Centerbrook mit der Neugestaltung der Kaianlagen beauftragt, damit dort große Kriegsschiffe, Forschungsschiffe und Segelschiffe anlegen können. Die Gesamtkosten für dieses Projekt, einschließlich der Kaianlagen und der von Ralph Appelbaum Associates of New York entworfenen Ausstellung, betrugen 50 Millionen Dollar. Exemplarisch für einen neuen Museumstypus, der seinen Bildungsauftrag mit Unterhaltung verknüpft (dem sogenannten »Edutainment«), spielt das Nauticus National Maritime Center mit einer architektonischen Formensprache, der die glatten, eleganten Oberflächen moderner, auf dem Radarschirm kaum zu erkennender Kriegsschiffe als Inspirationsquelle dienten. Dieser Eindruck wird durch den grauen Anstrich zusätzlich verstärkt. Dabei verzichteten die Architekten auf eine allzu wörtliche Auslegung im Disney-Stil, so daß sich ihr Gebäude – wie geplant – als Wahrzeichen darstellt.

Ce bâtiment de 11 200 m² a été édifié pour un budget de 22 millions de $. Abritant des expositions interactives sur les sciences de la mer, un aquarium, des laboratoires de recherche, une salle à écran géant, et le Hampton Roads Naval Museum, il se veut «un monument national qui attire les visiteurs et affiche la prééminence d'Hampton Roads dans le domaine des technologies de la mer». Selon l'agence, la construction évoque un certain nombre de navires, dont un «porte-avions du XXIe siècle». Parallèlement, Centerbrook s'est vu demandé la reconstruction du quai pour permettre aux grands navires de guerre, aux bateaux de recherche et aux voiliers d'y accoster. Le coût total du projet, y compris le quai et les expositions, conçues par Ralph Appelbaum Associates de New York, s'est élevé à 50 millions de $. Exemplaire de ce nouveau type de musée qui associe éducation et divertissement (les Américains parlent de *edutainment*) le Nauticus National Maritime Center fait appel à un langage architectural inspiré par les surfaces lisses et neutres des nouveaux bateaux de guerre furtifs, impression renforcée par sa couleur grise. Il échappe ainsi au littéralisme de style Disney, et impose sa puissante monumentalité, comme l'avaient souhaité ses créateurs.

Pages 68–69: The lengthy profile of the Center, recalling the sleek lines of the Aegis-class Navy cruisers that occasionally dock here.

Seite 68–69: Die langgestreckte Seitenansicht des Centers, das an die elegante Linienführung der manchmal hier anlegenden Marinekreuzer der Aegis-Klasse erinnert.

Pages 68–69: Le profil allongé du Centre rappelle les lignes profilées des croiseurs de classe Aegis de la marine américaine, qui y accostent parfois.

A light gray finish emphasizes the maritime function of the Center, while its massing is reminiscent not only of ships, but also of port-side facilities.

Der hellgraue Anstrich betont die maritime Funktion des Centers, während sein massives Erscheinungsbild nicht nur an Schiffe erinnert, sondern auch an mächtige Kais und Hafenanlagen.

Une couleur gris léger met en évidence la fonction maritime du Centre, tandis que sa masse évoque à la fois les navires et les équipements portuaires.

The 4,600 square meter third floor is filled with
interactive displays and multimedia exhibits.

*Das dritte Geschoß bietet auf einer Gesamtfläche
von 4 600 m² die Möglichkeit zu einem interaktiven,
multimedialen Ausflug in die Welt der Marine.*

*Les 4 600 m² du troisième niveau accueillent de
multiples présentations interactives et multimédias.*

Below: The 55 meter long "people-mover" which brings visitors from the lobby to the third floor.
Bottom: A plan shows the center with a Navy cruiser docked in front.

Mitte: Das 55 m lange »Laufband«, das die Besucher vom Eingangsbereich bis in den dritten Stock bringt.
Unten: Der Grundriß zeigt das Center mit einem angedockten Marinekreuzer.

Ci-dessous: Le trottoir roulant de 55 m de long qui emmène les visiteurs du hall d'entrée vers le troisième niveau. *En bas:* Plan du Centre, avec un croiseur à quai.

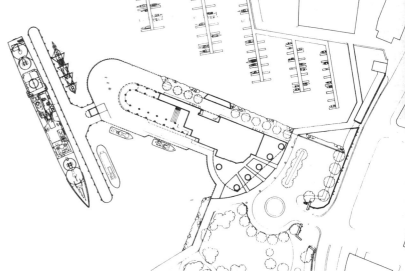

Centerbrook: Nauticus, National Maritime Center, 1988–94 **73**

Steven Ehrlich

Fifty-year-old Steven Ehrlich has an unusual variety of experiences. Born and educated on the East Coast, and now established in California, he uses ideas developed while he worked in North and West Africa and Japan to create a personal style intended to blend Los Angeles tradition and architectural innovation. His homes have often included courtyards that bring nature into his architecture, creating an environment that he sees as a "cleansing from the outside world." In the 1990s he has branched out into larger projects, with the 1991 Shatto Recreation Center, which *Newsweek* called a "graceful example of defensive architecture," and the Sony Music Campus (Santa Monica, 1993), a 9,500 square meter complex blending indoor and outdoor space. With two new projects for Sony, the Game Show Network, and a Child Care Center, he is making his mark in the ongoing renovation of the industrial or warehouse area of Culver City.

Der fünfzigjährige Steven Ehrlich kann auf einen ungewöhnlichen Erfahrungsschatz zurückgreifen. Ehrlich, der an der Ostküste der USA geboren und ausgebildet wurde und heute in Kalifornien lebt, verwendet Ideen, die er während seiner Aufenthalte in Nord- und Westafrika sowie in Japan entwickelte, und verbindet sie zu einem persönlichen Stil, bei dem die Tradition der Stadt Los Angeles und architektonische Innovation miteinander verschmelzen. Seine Häuser besitzen häufig einen Innenhof, durch den die Natur in die Architektur einbezogen wird. Damit schafft Ehrlich eine Umgebung, die er als »Ort der spirituellen Reinigung von der Außenwelt« bezeichnet. Seit Beginn der 90er Jahre beschäftigt sich Ehrlich mit größeren Projekten wie etwa dem Shatto Recreation Center (1991), das »Newsweek« ein »anmutiges Beispiel defensiver Architektur« nannte, und dem Sony Music Campus (Santa Monica, 1993), einem 9500 m² großen Komplex, der Außen- und Innenräume miteinander verbindet. Mit zwei weiteren Projekten für Sony, dem Game Show Network und dem Child Care Center (einer Kindertagesstätte), drückt Ehrlich der momentanen Neugestaltung des ehemaligen Industrie- und Lagerhausgebietes in Culver City seinen Stempel auf.

À 50 ans, Steven Ehrlich peut se targuer d'une expérience étonnamment variée. Né et formé sur la Côte Est, et aujourd'hui établi en Californie, il a mis à profit des idées développées lors de séjours en Afrique du Nord et de l'Ouest ainsi qu'au Japon pour créer un style personnel qui associe innovation architecturale et tradition de Los Angeles. Ses maisons possèdent souvent des cours fermées qui introduisent la nature dans son architecture, créant un environnement qu'il voit comme une «épuration du monde extérieur.» Dans les années 90, il s'est lancé dans des projets plus importants, comme le Shatto Recreation Center (1991) que «Newsweek» a qualifié de «gracieux exemple d'architecture défensive», et le Sony Music Campus (Santa Monica, 1993), complexe de 9500 m² associant espaces intérieurs et extérieurs. Avec deux nouveaux projets pour Sony, le Game Show Network et le Child Care Center, il affirme sa présence dans la rénovation de la zone des anciens entrepôts de Culver City.

Game Show Network, Culver City, California, 1995.
Game Show Network, Culver City, Kalifornien, 1995.
Game Show Network, Culver City, Californie, 1995.

Game Show Network

Culver City, California, 1995

Part of a large scale-renovation of a site taken over by Sony from MGM, this transformation of a 1930s garage leaves little of the appearance of the original structure intact, aside from its external contours. Measuring about 1,200 square meters, the building includes three major elements. The first, baptized the "tech core" is a glass-enclosed studio where programming for this twenty-four hour a day all-digital cable network is assembled; the second is a studio where automated cameras film original programs; and finally, the conference room that is another glass box. Although the renovation of this building was extensive enough for the architect to admit that it might have been less expensive to build an entirely new structure, the pattern of urban renewal that is taking shape in Culver City thanks to clients like Sony is an example of what can be done in urban areas with underutilized space. The Game Show Network building is located next to the Child Care Center, a new facility, also built by Steven Ehrlich for Sony Pictures Entertainment (1992–94). Ehrlich was also the architect of the Sony Music Entertainment headquarters (Santa Monica, 1991–92) – a new three-building complex.

Als Teil eines großen Sanierungsplans für ein durch Sony übernommes, ehemaliges Gelände von MGM besitzt diese Neugestaltung einer Autowerkstatt aus den 30er Jahren – abgesehen von der äußeren Form – nur noch wenig Ähnlichkeit mit dem ursprünglichen Gebäude. Das 1200 m² große Bauwerk setzt sich aus drei Hauptkomponenten zusammen. Bei der ersten, »tech core« genannten Komponente handelt es sich um ein verglastes Studio, in dem das Programm für diesen rund um die Uhr ausstrahlenden digitalen Kabelsender zusammengestellt wird. Die zweite Komponente umfaßt ein Studio mit automatischen Kameras, die neue Programme aufzeichnen, während eine weitere verglaste Kastenform – die dritte Komponente – einen Konferenzraum beherbergt. Obwohl sich die Kosten für die Sanierung des Gebäudes auf eine derart hohe Summe beliefen, daß der Architekt eingestand, der Bau eines völlig neuen Gebäudes wäre sicher kostengünstiger gewesen, handelt es sich hierbei um eine beispielhafte Stadterneuerung, die dank solcher Auftraggeber wie Sony in Culver City langsam Gestalt annimmt und zeigt, was sich mit wenig genutzten Flächen in urbaner Umgebung bewerkstelligen läßt. Das Game Show Network Building befindet sich direkt neben dem Child Care Center, einer ebenfalls von Steven Ehrlich konzipierten Einrichtung für Sony Pictures Entertainment (1992–94). Darüber hinaus zeichnete Ehrlich auch als Architekt für die Zentrale von Sony Music Entertainment verantwortlich (Santa Monica, 1991–92), einem neuen, aus drei Gebäuden bestehenden Komplex.

Faisant partie de la rénovation d'un vaste site acheté à la MGM par Sony, cette transformation d'un garage des années 30 n'a presque rien conservé d'intact de l'ancienne structure, si ce n'est son apparence extérieure. Avec ses 1200 m² environ, le bâtiment comprend trois éléments principaux. Le premier, baptisé «tech core» (cœur technique) est un studio aux parois de verre, réservé à la programmation d'une chaîne de télévision par câble émettant jour et nuit; le second est un studio de réalisation de programmes télévisés; le troisième une salle de conférence, également entourée de murs de verre. Si cette rénovation s'est révélée coûteuse au point où l'architecte admet qu'il aurait peut-être été plus économique de la reconstruire entièrement à neuf, l'exercice modèle de rénovation urbaine qui prend forme à Culver City grâce à des clients comme Sony montre ce que l'on peut tirer d'espaces urbains sous-employés. L'immeuble du Game Show Network Building est situé près du Child Care Center, un nouvel équipement social également construit par Steven Ehrlich pour Sony Pictures Entertainment (1992–94). Ehrlich a également été l'architecte du siège de Sony Music Entertainment (Santa Monica, 1991–92), un ensemble de trois immeubles.

Aside from the lower, square mass, very little of the original garage structure is visible. The skylight is set up on four angled steel columns, which follow the original angle of the roof.

Bis auf den unteren, quadratischen Baukörper erinnert nur noch wenig an die ehemalige Autowerkstatt. Das Oberlicht ruht auf vier angewinkelten Stahlstützen, die der Neigung des ursprünglichen Daches folgen.

Il reste peu de chose de la structure originale du garage en dehors de sa partie inférieure, carrée. La verrière est montée sur quatre colonnes d'angle en acier, qui reprennent la forme d'origine du toit.

Steven Ehrlich: Game Show Network, 1995 **77**

Despite the very thorough renovation of the building,
something of its original spirit remains, undoubtedly
justifying in the minds of the architect and the client
the extra expense incurred.

Trotz der sorgfältigen Sanierung des Gebäudes blieb
ein Teil der Werkstattatmosphäre erhalten, was nach
Ansicht des Architekten und des Bauherren die
zusätzlichen Kosten zweifellos rechtfertigt.

Malgré une rénovation en profondeur, quelque chose de
l'esprit du bâtiment d'origine subsiste, ce qui justifie
pour l'architecte et le client les coûts supplémentaires
entraînés par cette opération.

Peter Eisenman

Peter Eisenman takes some pride in being one of the most controversial figures in contemporary architecture. Having established his reputation as a theorist, he came into view first as a member of the "New York Five" with Meier, Hejduk, Gwathmey and Stern, and more recently as the author of the very visible Wexner Center for the Visual Arts (Ohio State University, Columbus Ohio, 1982–89). Although his sources of inspiration vary from the theories of deconstruction formulated by Jacques Derrida to the shapes of plate tectonics or sound waves, and more recently to the "morphing" capacity of the computer, he retains a declared desire to create an architecture that disturbs, which even makes its users uncomfortable. He has achieved this through the unexpected geometries of his buildings, where right angles and truly vertical or horizontal surfaces are rare. Although this architecture is clearly more intellectual than it is sensual, Eisenman's need to disturb does correspond to trends in contemporary art, which have not often found their way into the world of architecture.

Peter Eisenman legt großen Wert darauf, zu den umstrittensten Persönlichkeiten der zeitgenössischen Architektur zu zählen. Nachdem er sich einen Ruf als bedeutender Theoretiker erworben hatte, wurde er als Mitglied der »New York Five« (zusammen mit Meier, Hejduk, Gwathmey und Stern) und durch seinen Entwurf für das vor kurzem fertiggestellte, aufsehenerregende Wexner Center for the Visual Arts (Ohio State University, Columbus, Ohio, 1982–89) einem größeren Publikum bekannt. Obwohl Eisenmans Inspirationsquellen von den von Jacques Derrida formulierten Theorien des Dekonstruktivismus über die Formen von Plattentektonik und Klangwellen bis hin zu den »Morphing«-Fähigkeiten des Computers reichen, gilt sein erklärtes Interesse immer noch dem Entwurf einer Architektur, die beunruhigt und deren Benutzer sich unwohl fühlen. Dieses Ziel erreicht er durch die ungewöhnliche Geometrie seiner Gebäude, in denen rechte Winkel und horizontale oder vertikale Flächen nur selten vorkommen. Obwohl seine Architektur deutlich eher intellektuell als sinnlich ausgerichtet ist, deckt sich Eisenmans Wunsch nach Beunruhigung mit Entwicklungen in der zeitgenössischen Kunst, die nicht oft ihren Weg in die Architektur finden.

Peter Eisenman aime à être l'une des figures les plus controversées de l'architecture contemporaine. Théoricien établi, il se fait initialement connaître par sa participation aux «New York Five», avec Meier, Hejduk, Gwathmey et Stern, et plus récemment comme auteur du très remarqué Wexner Center for the Visual Arts (Ohio State University, Columbus, Ohio, 1982–89). Avec des sources d'inspiration allant des théories de la déconstruction de Jacques Derrida aux formes des plaques tectoniques ou des ondes sonores, en passant récemment par les techniques de *morphing* par ordinateur, il maintient le souhait de créer une architecture qui dérange, au point de mettre ses usagers mal à l'aise. Il y réussit à travers des compositions géométriques inattendues, dans lesquelles les angles droits et les surfaces vraiment horizontales ou verticales sont rares. Bien que cette architecture soit clairement plus intellectuelle que sensuelle, le besoin de déranger d'Eisenman fait écho à certaines tendances de l'art contemporain qui ne trouvent pas souvent leur place dans l'univers de l'architecture.

Aronoff Center for Design and Art, University of Cincinnati, Cincinnati, Ohio, 1988–96.

Aronoff Center for Design and Art, University of Cincinnati, Cincinnati, Ohio, 1988–96.

Aronoff Center for Design and Art, université de Cincinnati, Cincinnati, Ohio, 1988–96.

82 Peter Eisenman: Aronoff Center for Design and Art, 1988–96

Aronoff Center for Design and Art

Cincinnati, Ohio, 1988–1996

Part of a campus master plan including projects by Frank O. Gehry, Michael Graves, Pei Cobb Freed and Venturi, Scott Brown, the University of Cincinnati College of Design, Architecture, and Planning's Aronoff Center for Design and Art is one of the larger completed buildings by Peter Eisenman, measuring a total of 25,000 square meters, with an estimated cost of $35 million, of which 12,000 square meters is new construction. In this section, there are exhibition, library, theater, studio and office space. As the architect says, «The project is designed to challenge and change the mode by which we educate people. We can no longer train people to design the superficial and the inconsequential; design disciplines must assume far more important roles in our media-dominated age of information than ever before.» The unusual shapes of the new structure are related to the curvature of land forms and the chevron-like shapes of the existing buildings. Given the relatively long delay between the initial design and the completed project, this structure may not represent the current state of Peter Eisenman's design thinking, but it does put his theories of an architecture that does not necessarily make its users comfortable to the test.

The New York Times dubbed the exterior of this building "a tumbling stack of candy-colored slabs," and the inside "a stunning feat of interior decoration."

Die »New York Times« bezeichnete das Gebäude hinsichtlich seiner Außenfassade als »wirren Haufen bonbonfarbener Platten« und als »ein verblüffendes Meisterstück der Innenarchitektur«.

«The New York Times» a parlé au sujet de l'extérieur de ce bâtiment d'une «pile vacillante de dalles couleur de sucre d'orge», et d'un «étonnant festin de décoration intérieure».

Das ingesamt 25 000 m² große Aronoff Center for Design and Art des College of Design, Architecture and Planning der University of Cincinnati ist Teil eines Campusbebauungsplans, der auch Projekte von Frank O. Gehry, Michael Graves, Pei Cobb Freed und Venturi, Scott Brown umfaßt. Die Kosten für dieses Gebäude – eines der größten, die Peter Eisenman je fertigstellte – belaufen sich schätzungsweise auf 35 Millionen Dollar, womit unter anderem 12 000 m² Neubaufläche mit Ausstellungs-, Bibliotheks-, Theater-, Studio- und Büroräumen finanziert wurden. Der Architekt beschrieb das Gebäude so: »Das Projekt wurde entworfen, um die Art und Weise in Frage zu stellen und zu verändern, in der wir Menschen unterrichten. Wir können den Menschen nicht länger beibringen, Oberflächliches und Inkonsequentes zu entwerfen; die Designerausbildung muß in unserer, von den Medien beherrschten Zeit eine wesentlich wichtigere Rolle spielen.« Die ungewöhnlichen Formen des Neubaus leiten sich von den Krümmungen der Landformen und den Zickzackformen des bestehenden Gebäudes ab. Angesichts der relativ langen Bauzeit – zwischen den ursprünglichen Entwürfen und der Fertigstellung des Gebäudes vergingen acht Jahre – ist diese Konstruktion möglicherweise nicht mehr repräsentativ für Peter Eisenmans aktuelle Designansichten, aber sie stellt seine Theorie einer Architektur, in der sich die Nutzer nicht notwendigerweise wohlfühlen, auf die Probe.

Élément prévu par le plan de masse du campus qui regroupe des projets de Frank O. Gehry, Michael Graves, Pei Cobb Freed et Venturi, Scott Brown, l'Aronoff Center for Design and Art du collège de design, architecture et urbanisme de l'université de Cincinnati est l'une des plus importantes réalisations de Peter Eisenman à ce jour. Ses 25 000 m², dont 12 000 de construction neuve, coûteront environ 35 millions de $. La partie nouvelle accueille une galerie d'exposition, une bibliothèque, une salle de spectacle, un atelier, et des bureaux. Pour l'architecte, «le projet est un défi à la façon dont nous éduquons les étudiants, et se propose de la changer. Nous ne pouvons plus former des gens pour concevoir du superficiel et de l'inconséquent; à notre époque dominée par les médias, les disciplines créatives doivent assumer un rôle beaucoup plus important». L'aspect curieux de cette nouvelle construction reprend les courbes du terrain et les formes en chevron des bâtiments préexistants. Étant donné le délai relativement long entre le plan initial et l'achèvement du projet, cette réalisation ne représente peut-être pas l'état actuel de la pensée créative d'Eisenman, mais illustre bien ses théories architecturales qui n'ont pas nécessairement pour objectif le confort des utilisateurs.

Designed to accommodate 240 graduate students
and 1,500 undergraduates, the facility is arranged
around a 245 meter long below grade passageway.

Die für 240 Absolventen und 1500 Studenten
konzipierte Einrichtung erstreckt sich entlang eines
245 m langen, unter Erdgeschoßniveau verlaufenden
Verbindungsganges.

Conçu pour 240 étudiants diplômés et 1500 en cours
d'études, ce centre s'articule autour d'un passage
souterrain de 245 m de long.

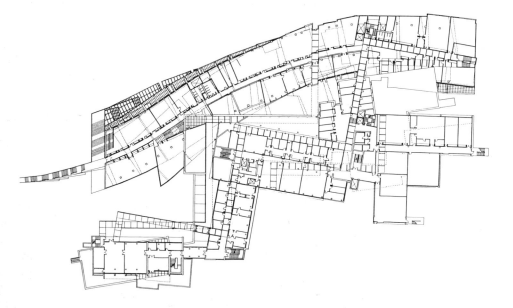

Frank O. Gehry

Born in Toronto, Canada in 1929, Frank O. Gehry was named one of "America's twenty-five Most Influential People" by *Time Magazine* (June 17, 1996). Not only has he successfully called into question the forms that modern architecture has taken for granted, but he has done the same for materials of construction. Reaching out to the inspiration provided by California artists of his generation, Gehry has made it possible for younger architects to explore new directions and not be afraid to imagine sculptural forms. His recent American Center in Paris met with considerable criticism over the design, and his largest project to date, the Disney Concert Hall in Los Angeles, has been halted for the moment for budgetary reasons. With the Nationale-Nederlanden Building (Prague, Czech Republic, 1994–96), or the new Minden-Ravensberg Electric Company Offices (Bad Oeynhausen, Germany, 1991–95), together with the Guggenheim Bilbao Museum (under construction, Bilbao, Spain), it would almost seem that his true influence has spread more to Europe than it has been exerted, at least in built form, in the United States.

Der 1929 in Toronto, Kanada geborene Architekt Frank O. Gehry wird von »Time Magazine« (17. Juni 1996) zu den »25 einflußreichsten Menschen Amerikas« gezählt. Gehry ist es gelungen, nicht nur die Formen, sondern auch die Baumaterialien in Frage zu stellen, die die moderne Architektur als selbstverständlich voraussetzte. Indem er die Arbeiten kalifornischer Künstler seiner Generation als Inspirationsquelle nutzte, ermöglichte er es jüngeren Architekten, neue Richtungen zu erforschen und dabei ohne Angst skulpturale Formen zu verwenden. Allerdings sah sich das von Gehry entworfene American Center in Paris starker Kritik ausgesetzt, und bei seinem bisher größten Projekt, der Disney Concert Hall In Los Angeles, erfolgte aus budgettechnischen Gründen ein Baustopp. Anscheinend hat sich Gehrys Tätigkeitsfeld mit dem Gebäude der Nationale-Nederlanden (Prag, Tschechien, 1994–96), dem neuen Bürogebäude des Elektrizitätswerks Minden-Ravensberg (Bad Oeynhausen, Deutschland, 1991–95) und dem Bau des Guggenheim Bilbao Museum (Bilbao, Spanien, im Bau befindlich) mehr nach Europa verlagert, wo er einen stärkeren Einfluß ausübt, als ihm dies – zumindest in gebauter Form – in den Vereinigten Staaten gelungen ist.

Né en 1929 à Toronto au Canada, Frank O. Gehry a été nommé l'un des «25 Américains les plus influents» par «Time Magazine» (17 juin 1996). Non seulement il a remis en question avec succès des formes que l'architecture moderne considérait acquises, mais a fait de même avec les matériaux de construction. Sensible à l'inspiration apportée par les artistes californiens de sa génération, il a permis à des architectes plus jeunes d'explorer de nouvelles directions sans craindre d'explorer la sculpturalité. Son récent American Center de Paris a été très critiqué, et son plus important projet à ce jour, le Disney Concert Hall à Los Angeles, est arrêté pour des raisons budgétaires. Avec le Nationale-Nederlanden Building (Prague, République Tchèque, 1994–96), ou le nouvel immeuble de bureaux de la compagnie d'électricité Minden-Ravensberg (Bad Oeynhausen, Allemagne, 1991–95) et le Guggenheim Museum de Bilbao (en construction en Espagne), on pourrait presque penser que son influence s'étend davantage en Europe qu'aux États-Unis, du moins pour ses œuvres construites.

Minden-Ravensberg Electric Company Offices, Bad Oeynhausen, Germany, 1991–95.

Bürogebäude des Elektrizitätswerks Minden-Ravensberg, Bad Oeynhausen, Deutschland, 1991–95.

Bureaux de la compagnie d'électricité Minden-Ravensberg, Bad Oeynhausen, Allemagne, 1991–95.

Minden-Ravensberg Electric Company Offices
Bad Oeynhausen, Germany, 1991–1995

Located between Hanover and Osnabrück, Bad Oeynhausen is an old spa town whose most spectacular building is certainly this new "gateway into the community", which was intended to update the public image of an electrical company. The 4,300 square meter, 19 million DM facility contains a network control center for regional power distribution, an office wing, a small conference center, and an exhibition hall with working models intended to demonstrate energy use and conservation. This display was designed by the California architects Craig Hodgetts and Ming Fung. As is frequently the case in many Gehry buildings, external volumes are clad in a variety of materials such as stucco, glass, zinc and copper. Energy efficiency is a highlight of the building, including an array of roof-mounted photovoltaic cells, which apparently produce 80% of the facility's electricity. Maximum use is made of daylight and natural ventilation, as well as heat flows generated by heavy concrete walls. Inspired by Frank O. Gehry's Vitra Museum in Weil am Rhein, one of the directors of the Minden-Ravensberg Electric Company chose the architect for this new building without consulting any other designers.

Bad Oeynhausen zwischen Hannover und Osnabrück ist ein traditionsreicher Kurort, dessen aufsehenerregendstes Gebäude zweifellos das neue »Tor zur Gemeinde« ist, welches das öffentliche Bild des Elektrizitätswerks aufpolieren soll. Das 4300 m² große und 19 Millionen DM teure Gebäude umfaßt ein Netzwerkkontrollzentrum für die regionale Stromversorgung, einen Flügel mit Büroräumen, ein kleines Konferenzzentrum und eine von den kalifornischen Architekten Craig Hodgetts und Ming Fung gestaltete Ausstellungshalle mit funktionsfähigen Modellen zu den Themen Energieverbrauch und -einsparung. Wie bei vielen von Gehrys Entwürfen sind die Fassaden seiner Gebäude mit einer Vielzahl von Materialien verkleidet, wie etwa Glattputz, Glas, Zink und Kupfer. Energieeinsparung ist eines der wichtigsten Merkmale dieses Bauwerks, was durch zahlreiche auf dem Dach montierte Solarzellen zum Ausdruck kommt, die 80% des Strombedarfs des Elektrizitätswerkes decken. Darüber hinaus zeichnet sich das Gebäude durch ein Maximum an Tageslicht und natürlicher Be- und Entlüftung sowie durch einen Wärmefluß aus, der durch die Schwerbetonwände erzeugt wird. Inspiriert von Frank O. Gehrys Vitra-Museum in Weil am Rhein erteilte einer der Direktoren des Elektrizitätswerks Frank O. Gehry den Auftrag für dieses Gebäude, ohne weitere Architekten zu Rate zu ziehen.

Entre Hanovre et Osnabrück, Bad Oeynhausen est une ancienne ville thermale dont le bâtiment le plus spectaculaire est maintenant cette nouvelle «porte communautaire» chargée de renouveler l'image d'une compagnie d'électricité. Les 4300 m² de cette réalisation de 19 millions de DM abritent un centre de contrôle de réseau pour la distribution régionale d'électricité, une aile pour les bureaux, un petit centre de conférences, et un hall d'exposition avec maquettes animées illustrant l'usage et la conservation de l'énergie, et conçues par les architectes californiens Craig Hodgetts et Ming Fung. Comme dans beaucoup des bâtiments construits par Gehry, les volumes extérieurs sont recouverts de toutes sortes de matériaux comme le stuc, le verre, le zinc, et le cuivre. Cet immeuble aux panneaux de cellules photovoltaïques montés sur le toit, qui produisent 80% de l'énergie consommée sur le site, est d'esprit écologique. La lumière et la ventilation naturelles sont exploitées au maximum, ainsi que la récupération de la chaleur générée par d'épais murs de béton. C'est après avoir vu le Vitra Museum conçu par Gehry à Weil am Rhein que l'un des directeurs de Minden-Ravensberg a choisi l'architecte, sans autre consultation.

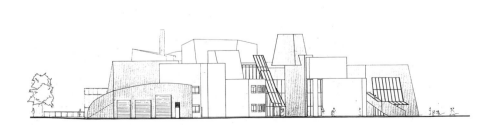

According to the architect, "the building program is distributed on the site in a manner which responds to the urban context of the buildings fronting Mindener Strasse."

Nach Aussage des Architekten »bildet die Anordnung der Bauten auf dem Gelände eine Antwort auf den urbanen Kontext der Gebäude an der Mindener Straße«.

Selon l'architecte, «le programme de construction est distribué sur le site d'une façon qui répond au contexte urbain des immeubles bordant la Mindener Straße».

Frank O. Gehry: Minden-Ravensberg Electric Company Offices, 1991–95 **89**

Stucco, glass, zinc and copper are the major exterior cladding materials. "We tried to let the energy question generate the form," says Gehry, "but we failed. In this sense, the building does not have the clarity we would have liked."

Glattputz, Glas, Zink und Kupfer bilden die Hauptbestandteile der Fassadenverkleidung. »Die Frage der Energieversorgung sollte ursprünglich die Form bestimmen«, erklärte Gehry. »Dies ist uns jedoch nicht gelungen. In dieser Hinsicht besitzt das Gebäude also nicht die Klarheit, die wir uns gewünscht hätten.«

Stuc, verre, zinc et cuivre sont les principaux matériaux utilisés pour l'extérieur. «Nous avons essayé de laisser l'énergie générer la forme», précise Gehry, «mais nous avons échoué. À cet égard, le bâtiment ne présente pas l'évidence que nous aurions aimée».

Frank O. Gehry: Minden-Ravensberg Electric Company Offices, 1991–95 **91**

The exhibition hall (bottom left) has a display designed by the California couple Hodgetts + Fung. One unexpected feature of the building (bottom right), is the willful display of the technical spaces through a glass wall.

Die Ausstellungshalle (links unten) zeigt ein von dem kalifornischen Paar Hodgetts + Fung entworfenes Objekt. Ein überraschendes Detail des Gebäudes sind die durch eine Glaswand sichtbaren Räume mit den technischen Anlagen (rechts unten).

Dans le hall d'exposition (en bas à gauche) on aperçoit un élément dessiné par le couple californien Hodgetts + Fung. Une caractéristique surprenante de l'immeuble est la vision des espaces techniques à travers un mur de verre (en bas à droite).

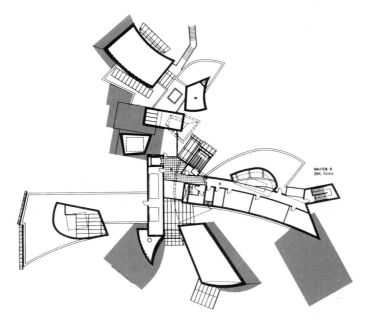

A plan of the building reveals that it has no readily discernible geometric pattern, unless reference is made to an underlying spiral. Rather, the different functions are pieced into a whole whose style can be described as vintage Gehry.

Der Grundriß des Gebäudes zeigt kein auf den ersten Blick erkennbares geometrisches Muster außer wenn man eine Spirale zugrundelegt. Die Einzelteile mit den unterschiedlichen Funktionsbereichen bilden ein Ganzes, dessen Stil als klassisches Gehry-Design bezeichnet werden kann.

Le plan révèle que sa géométrie n'est pas facilement compréhensible, même si l'on peut penser à une spirale. Les différentes fonctions sont réunies en un ensemble dont le style est classiquement Gehry.

Philip Johnson

Born in Cleveland, Ohio (1906), Philip Johnson turned ninety with more projects under way than most well-known architects who are half his age. Founder and Director of the Department of Architecture at the Museum of Modern Art in New York, he wrote *The International Style* with Henry-Russell Hitchcock (1932) on the occasion of landmark exhibit at MoMA. He arranged the first visits to the United States of both Gropius and Mies van der Rohe. Winner of the 1979 Pritzker Prize, he also organized the 1988 exhibition "Deconstructivist Architecture" at MoMA with Mark Wigley. From the strict modernism of his 1949 Glass House (New Canaan, Connecticut), to the post-modern flourish that adorns his AT&T Headquarters Building, New York (1979), and finally to the indeterminate lines of his Gate House (New Canaan, 1995), Johnson has led or at least confirmed almost every major trend in contemporary architecture for the past sixty years. Only the organic modernity of a Frank Lloyd Wright seems to be lacking in his palette. Today, with forms inspired by the Gate House, which themselves resemble drawings by the German artist Hermann Finsterlin, Johnson is designing the 2,000 seat Cathedral of Hope for the Universal Fellowship of Metropolitan Community Churches in Dallas, Texas.

Als der 1906 in Cleveland, Ohio geborene Philip Johnson seinen neunzigsten Geburtstag feierte, hatte er mehr Projekte in Planung als viele bekannte Architekten, die nur halb so alt waren wie er. Als Gründer und erster Direktor des Department of Architecture am New Yorker Museum of Modern Art schrieb er 1932 zusammen mit Henry-Russell Hitchcock »The International Style«, das im Rahmen der gleichnamigen, bahnbrechenden Ausstellung am MoMA erschien. Johnson organisierte die ersten Besuche von Gropius und Mies van der Rohe in den Vereinigten Staaten; 1979 gewann er den Pritzker Preis und veranstaltete 1988 zusammen mit Mark Wigley die Ausstellung »Deconstructivist Architecture« am New Yorker MoMA. Im Laufe der letzten 60 Jahre hat Johnson nahezu jede größere Entwicklung in der zeitgenössischen Architektur eingeleitet oder zumindest bestätigt – vom strengen Modernismus seines 1949 entstandenen Glass House über die postmodernen Schnörkel, die sein 1979 erbautes AT&T Headquarters Building in New York zieren, bis hin zu den nicht genau definierten Linien des Gate House (New Canaan, 1995). Nur die organische Moderne eines Frank Lloyd Wright scheint in seinem Repertoire zu fehlen. Im Augenblick arbeitet Philip Johnson in Dallas, Texas, an der 2 000 Plätze umfassenden Cathedral of Hope für die Universal Fellowship of Metropolitan Community Churches; die Formen dieses Kirchengebäudes sind von Johnsons Gate House inspiriert, das wiederum Zeichnungen des deutschen Künstlers Hermann Finsterlin ähnelt.

Né à Cleveland, Ohio, en 1906, Philip Johnson a abordé sa quatre-vingt-dixième année avec plus de projets en cours que bien des architectes de la moitié de son âge. Fondateur et directeur du département d'architecture du Museum of Modern Art de New York, il rédige le catalogue «International Style» avec Henry-Russell Hitchcock (1932) à l'occasion de l'exposition fondatrice du même nom au MoMA. Il organise les premiers séjours aux U.S.A. de Gropius et de Mies van der Rohe. Lauréat du Prix Pritzker 1979, il organise également l'exposition «Deconstructivist Architecture» au MoMA, avec Mark Wigley. Du strict modernisme de sa Maison de verre de 1949 (New Canaan, Connecticut) au postmodernisme provocant de son siège pour AT&T à New York (1979), et pour finir aux lignes indéterminées de sa Gate House (New Canaan, 1995), Johnson a animé, ou appuyé, la plupart des grandes tendances de l'architecture de ces soixante dernières années. Seule la modernité organique de Frank Lloyd Wright semble manquer à sa palette. Aujourd'hui, avec des formes inspirées de celles de sa Gate House – qui font penser aux dessins de l'artiste allemand Hermann Finsterlin – Johnson travaille aux plans de la Cathédrale de l'espoir (2 000 places) pour l'Universal Fellowship of Metropolitan Community Churches, à Dallas, Texas.

Gate House, New Canaan, Connecticut, 1995. Interior view.

Gate House, New Canaan, Connecticut, 1995. Innenansicht.

Gate House, New Canaan, Connecticut, 1995. Vue intérieure.

Gate House

New Canaan, Connecticut, 1995

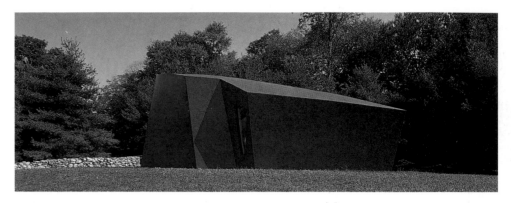

"The purpose of this building," says Philip Johnson, "is to serve as a reception for tourists to see a film and wait their turn for the tour (of the estate) to begin. The real purpose, however," he confides, "is to test out my new theory of architecture without right angles, without verticals, made more like a piece of sculpture." Made with prefabricated panels of structural wire mesh around an insulating urethane foam core, cut and bent to shape and then sprayed with concrete, the pavilion measures about 84 square meters. Perhaps the last of a series of garden "follies" built by Johnson on his New Canaan estate since he designed the 1949 Glass House, the pavilion is also intended as the ninety-year-old architect's homage to the "kids" who practice deconstructivist architecture. Fundamentally, as Johnson himself admits, it is the sculptural qualities of the building that dominate. "I am delighted with the results," he says. "It is a very emotional space to be in and to observe."

»Das Gebäude« erklärt Philip Johnson, »dient als Empfangsraum für Touristen, die hier einen Film sehen, während sie auf ihre Führung (über das Anwesen) warten. Der wahre Zweck« gesteht er, »besteht jedoch darin, meine neue Architekturtheorie auszuprobieren, die weder rechte Winkel noch Senkrechte aufweist und eher einer Skulptur ähnelt.« Der 84 m² große Besucherpavillon entstand aus vorgefertigten Paneelen einer tragenden Maschendrahtkonstruktion, die zunächst rund um einen isolierenden Kern aus Urethanschaum gebogen, danach zugeschnitten und schließlich mit Beton besprüht wurden, und stellt wahrscheinlich die letzte einer Reihe von architektonischen »Spielereien« dar, die Johnson seit dem 1949 konzipierten Glass House auf seinem Anwesen in New Canaan entwickelte. Darüber hinaus stellt der Pavillon eine Hommage des 90jährigen Architekten an die »Kids« dar, die den Dekonstruktivismus propagieren. Im Grunde, so gesteht Johnson, ist die skulpturale Ausdruckskraft des Gebäudes vorherrschend: »Ich bin sehr zufrieden mit dem Ergebnis. Es handelt sich um einen Raum, der sowohl beim Betrachten als auch beim Betreten starke Emotionen hervorruft.«

«L'objectif de cette construction», dit Philip Johnson, «est de servir d'espace d'accueil pour les touristes. Ils y regarderont un film en attendant le départ de la visite (du domaine). Le but réel, cependant», ajoute-t-il, «est de tester ma nouvelle théorie d'architecture sans angle droit, sans verticale, davantage conçue comme une sculpture». Réalisé en panneaux préfabriqués de fers à béton autour d'une âme en mousse d'uréthane, coupés et mis en formes puis recouverts de béton projeté, le pavillon mesure 84 m². C'est peut-être la dernière de ces «folies» de jardin édifiées par Johnson sur son domaine de New Canaan depuis sa première Glass House (1949). Il s'agit également d'un hommage de l'architecte âgé de 90 ans aux «gamins» qui pratiquent une architecture déconstructiviste. Fondamentalement, comme il l'admet lui-même, ce sont les qualités sculpturales du bâtiment qui dominent. «Je suis ravi du résultat. C'est un lieu plein d'émotion, à parcourir ou à observer.»

The New Canaan Gate House can best be described as an inhabited sculpture. Its basic form has already served to inspire the architect to design a much larger church, the Cathedral of Hope, to be built in Dallas, Texas.

Das Gate House läßt sich am besten als begehbare Skulptur beschreiben. Seine Grundform diente dem Architekten bereits als Inspirationsquelle für einen wesentlich größeren Bau, der Cathedral of Hope, die in Dallas, Texas, entstehen soll.

Ce nouveau pavillon d'entrée de New Canaan est une sculpture habitée. Sa forme a déjà inspiré l'architecte pour la conception d'une vaste église, la Cathédrale de l'espoir, qui sera construite à Dallas, Texas.

Philip Johnson: Gate House, 1995 **97**

Richard Meier

A member of the "New York Five," Richard Meier has been an architect whose consistent, some would even say obsessional use of modernist white forms has become a universally recognizable signature style. Influenced by Le Corbusier, Meier has proven that a gridded, geometrical vocabulary is capable of an astonishing variety of types of expression, up to and including the massive Getty Center, located on a hilltop in Los Angeles and due to be opened to the public in the fall of 1997. Initially on a small scale, for numerous private residences, and later in progressively larger commissions, office buildings, museums or housing, Richard Meier has evolved toward more complex floor plans, rotated axes and a layering of space, modulated by a masterful use of bright, natural light. A large amount of light is of course not ideal for the preservation of works of art, and Richard Meier's latest white masterwork, the Barcelona Museum of Contemporary Art, is situated in a particularly dark quarter of the old city. Despite these potential shortcomings, the Barcelona building shows once again just how much the architect is appreciated in Europe.

Die konsequente, von einigen auch als »besessen« bezeichnete Verwendung weißer Baukörper gilt als das Markenzeichen Richard Meiers, einem Mitglied der »New York Five«. Der von Le Corbusier beeinflußte Architekt hat bewiesen, daß auch gerasterte geometrische Baukörper vielfältige Ausdrucksmöglichkeiten bieten – bis hin zum Bau des gewaltigen Getty Center, das auf einem Hügel über Los Angeles liegt und im Herbst 1997 für die Öffentlichkeit freigegeben werden soll. Meier begann in kleinem Rahmen mit zahlreichen Privathäusern und entwickelte später bei größeren Aufträgen für Verwaltungsgebäude, Museen oder Wohnanlagen immer kompliziertere Grundrisse, Achsenverschwenkungen und schichtweise Anordnungen des Raums, der durch den meisterhaften Einsatz von hellem Tageslicht moduliert wird. Allerdings sind große Lichtmengen für die Erhaltung von Kunstwerken nicht besonders geeignet, und darüber hinaus liegt Richard Meiers neuestes weißes Meisterwerk, das Museum für zeitgenössische Kunst in Barcelona, in einem besonders dunklen Viertel der Altstadt. Aber trotz dieser potentiellen Unzulänglichkeiten zeigt Meiers Bauwerk in Barcelona wieder einmal, wie sehr dieser Architekt in Europa geschätzt wird.

Membre des «New York Five», Richard Meier est un architecte dont le style moderniste et l'usage de la couleur blanche, que certains jugent obsessionnel, sont devenus une signature internationalement reconnue. Influencé par Le Corbusier, il a prouvé qu'un vocabulaire à base de trame géométrique permet une étonnante variété d'expression, y compris le massif Getty Center situé au sommet d'une colline de Los Angeles et qui devrait ouvrir au public à l'automne 1997. Travaillant initialement à petite échelle, pour de nombreuses résidences privées, puis sur des commandes de plus en plus importantes, des immeubles de bureaux ou de logement, et des musées, Meier a évolué vers une complexité grandissante, faisant pivoter les axes, stratifiant l'espace, et le modulant par une grande maîtrise de l'éclairage naturel. L'abondance de lumière naturelle n'est pas idéale pour la conservation des œuvres d'art, ce qui peut se révéler un problème pour sa dernière réalisation, le musée d'art contemporain de Barcelone, situé en plein cœur de la vieille ville. Ce chef-d'œuvre montre néanmoins à quel point l'architecte est apprécié en Europe.

Museum of Contemporary Art, Barcelona, Spain, 1987–95.

Museum für Zeitgenössische Kunst, Barcelona, Spanien, 1987–95.

Musée d'art contemporain, Barcelone, Espagne, 1987–95.

Museum of Contemporary Art

Barcelona, Spain, 1987–1995

Richard Meier considers this to be one of his most successful projects. Indeed, the three-story 13,800 square meter structure contains all of the hallmarks of his mature style, confronted here with a particularly dense and dark urban environment. A new public square in front of the museum, the Plaça dels Angels permits visitors to appreciate the sweeping white facade of the 23 meter high building. Although all critics do not agree with the architect's claim that he has privileged a "low profile and contextual harmony," it is true that the impact of the white metal panel and stucco exterior is all the stronger because of the almost medieval character of the rest of the area. Next to the new museum, which the architect was obliged to design in the absence not only of a director, but also of a real collection, the converted Casa de Caritat, a former 19th century hospital building, has now become a Center of Contemporary Culture, creating a new hub for visitors interested in recent art. With its jewel-like precision, Meier's Barcelona Museum of Contemporary Art harkens back in many ways to the ambitions of the founders of modern architecture who saw a bright future in the new era. Though other contemporary architects have set aside this almost utopian approach, Richard Meier makes a strong case for the continued validity of the modern ideal.

Richard Meier selbst zählt das neue Museum zu seinen erfolgreichsten Projekten. Und tatsächlich trägt das dreigeschossige, 13 800 m² große Gebäude in einer besonders dicht bebauten und dunklen urbanen Umgebung alle Kennzeichen Meiers späten Stils. Ein neuangelegter öffentlicher Platz vor dem Museum, der Plaça dels Angels, ermöglicht den Besuchern eine ausgiebige Würdigung der geschwungenen weißen Fassade des 23 m hohen Bauwerks. Und obwohl keiner der Kritiker mit dem Architekten darin übereinstimmt, daß er eine »zurückhaltende und der Umgebung entsprechende Harmonie« bevorzugt habe, kommt die Ausdruckskraft der mit weißen Metallpaneelen und mit Putz gestalteten Fassade besonders gut zur Geltung – nicht zuletzt aufgrund der Tatsache, daß der Rest des Areals von nahezu mittelalterlichem Charakter ist. Neben dem neuen Museum, das Meier zu einem Zeitpunkt entwarf, als weder der Museumsdirektor noch eine Sammlung feststanden, befindet sich die neugestaltete Casa de Caritat – ein ehemaliges Hospital aus dem 19. Jahrhundert, das zu einem Zentrum für zeitgenössische Kultur umgewandelt wurde und ebenfalls viele, an moderner Kunst interessierte Besucher anzieht. Mit seiner edelsteinartigen Präzision greift Meiers Museum für Zeitgenössische Kunst in vielerlei Hinsicht auf die Ziele der Gründer moderner Architektur zurück, die einer strahlenden Zukunft in der neuen Ära entgegenblickten. Obwohl sich andere Architekten von diesem nahezu utopischen Ansatz gelöst haben, dokumentiert Richard Meier hiermit die unveränderte Gültigkeit des modernen Ideals.

Richard Meier considère qu'il s'agit de son projet le plus réussi. Confronté à un environnement urbain particulièrement dense, ce bâtiment de 13 800 m² reprend en effet toutes les caractéristiques du style de sa maturité. Une nouvelle place publique devant le musée, la Plaça dels Angels, permet aux visiteurs d'apprécier la vaste façade blanche immaculée de 23 m de haut. Si les critiques ne sont pas tous d'accord avec la revendication de l'architecte d'avoir privilégié «un profil bas et l'harmonie contextuelle», il est vrai que l'impact des panneaux de métal blanc et de stuc est d'autant plus fort qu'il s'oppose au caractère ancien et même médiéval du reste du quartier. Proche de ce nouveau musée que l'architecte a été obligé de concevoir en l'absence non seulement d'un directeur mais aussi d'une collection, la Casa de Caritat, ancien hôpital du XIXᵉ siècle, a été transformée en Centre de culture contemporaine, nouveau pôle d'attraction pour les visiteurs sensibles à l'art d'aujourd'hui. Avec sa précision de joyau, le musée de Meier ramène à de nombreux égards aux ambitions des fondateurs de l'architecture moderne convaincus d'un avenir radieux. Bien que d'autres architectes actuels aient abandonné cette approche utopique, Richard Meier défend encore avec brio la permanence de la validité de l'idéal moderniste.

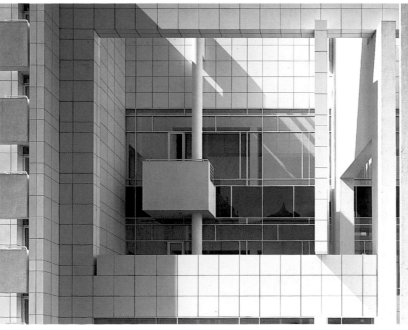

Above: A view toward the Museum from the newly created Plaça dels Angels.
Left: A typically articulated facade shows Meier's signature style.

Oben: Blick auf das Museum vom nahegelegenen Plaça dels Angels aus.
Links: Die charakteristisch gegliederte Fassade trägt eindeutig die Handschrift Richard Meiers.

Ci-dessus: Vue du musée prise de la nouvelle Plaça dels Angels.
À gauche: L'articulation de la façade est caractéristique du style Meier.

Page 103: *The majestic sweep of the facade with its sun screens recalls other Meier buildings, and does not necessarily announce, at least from this angle, the function of the structure.*

Seite 103: *Die majestätische Krümmung der Fassade mit ihren Sonnenblenden erinnert an andere Bauwerke Richard Meiers und läßt – zumindest aus dieser Perspektive – nicht sofort Rückschlüsse auf die eigentliche Funktion des Gebäudes zu.*

Page 103: *La majestueuse envolée de la façade, avec ses pare-soleil, rappelle d'autres œuvres de Meier, et n'annonce pas clairement, au moins sous cet angle, la fonction du bâtiment.*

Although some critics have found that natural light levels are too high in the Museum, light is one of the hallmarks of Richard Meier's architecture, accentuated here by the bright local sun.

Licht zählt zu den typischen Kennzeichen in Richard Meiers Architektur – ein Aspekt, der hier durch die strahlende Sonne Spaniens besonders zum Ausdruck kommt. Allerdings bemängelten einige Kritiker, daß das Museum einen zu hohen Anteil an Tageslicht erhält.

Même si certains critiques trouvent que le niveau de l'éclairage naturel à l'intérieur du bâtiment est trop élevé, le traitement de la lumière est un des signes de reconnaissance des réalisations de Richard Meier, accentué ici par l'éclat du soleil local.

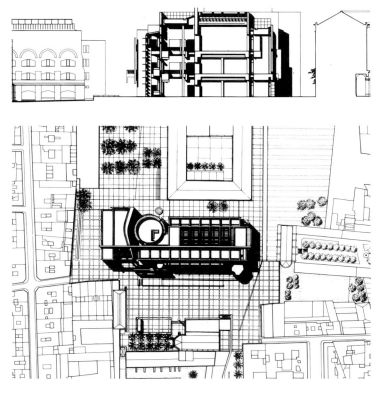

Eric Owen Moss

Unexpected, poetic at times, Eric Owen Moss was dubbed the "jeweler of junk" by Philip Johnson, but he might just as well have been named the "dreamer of Culver City." Rarely has such a talented architect concentrated most of his built work in such a narrow area of a given city. His rehabilitation projects and new construction in this Los Angeles area where the movie industry got its start are directly connected to the land holdings of the developer Frederick Norton Smith, who has consistently called on Moss to create environments that attract new tenants to formerly abandoned or underused spaces. In this respect, the importance and interest of the work of Eric Owen Moss extends far beyond Los Angeles. With his sculptural approach, very clearly visible in his latest building, Samitaur, Moss will certainly influence and encourage other rehabilitation projects, and help to redefine the role of the architect in difficult economic times.

Philip Johnson nannte Eric Owen Moss zwar den »Juwelier des Schrotts«, aber dieser ungewöhnliche und manchmal poetische Architekt könnte ebenso gut auch als »Träumer von Culver City« bezeichnet werden. Es kommt äußerst selten vor, daß ein talentierter Architekt den größten Teil seiner gebauten Arbeiten auf einen derart kleinen Bereich einer bestimmten Stadt konzentriert. Moss' Sanierungsprojekte und Neubauten in einem Stadtbezirk von Los Angeles, in dem die Filmindustrie ihre Ursprünge hatte, sind untrennbar mit dem Grundstücksbesitz des Bauunternehmers Frederick Norton Smith verbunden, der Moss regelmäßig mit der Schaffung von Baukomplexen beauftragt, um so neue Mieter für zuvor leerstehende oder ungenutzte Räume gewinnen zu können. In dieser Hinsicht erstrecken sich die Bedeutung und der Reiz der Arbeiten von Eric Owen Moss weit über die Grenzen von Los Angeles hinaus. Mit seinem skulpturalen Ansatz – der in seinem letztem Projekt, Samitaur, besonders deutlich zutage tritt – wird Moss mit Sicherheit andere Sanierungsprojekte fördern und beeinflussen sowie dazu beitragen, die Rolle des Architekten in wirtschaftlich schwierigen Zeiten neu zu definieren.

Inattendu, poétique parfois, Eric Owen Moss a été surnommé le «joaillier de la ferraille» par Philip Johnson, mais aurait pu également être appelé «le rêveur de Culver City». Rarement un architecte d'un tel talent a concentré autant d'efforts sur une zone urbaine aussi limitée. Ses projets de réhabilitation et de constructions nouvelles dans cette communauté de Los Angeles qui a vu les débuts de l'industrie du cinéma sont directement liés aux investissements immobiliers du promoteur Frederick Norton Smith, qui fait systématiquement appel à Moss pour créer des environnements susceptibles d'attirer de nouveaux occupants vers ces constructions abandonnées ou sous-utilisées. L'importance et l'intérêt de l'œuvre d'Eric Owen Moss dépassent largement Los Angeles. À travers son approche sculpturale, particulièrement affirmée dans sa dernière réalisation, Samitaur, Moss va certainement influencer et encourager d'autres projets de réhabilitation, et contribuer à redéfinir le rôle de l'architecte en période de difficultés économiques.

Samitaur, Culver City, California, 1990–96.
Samitaur, Culver City, Kalifornien, 1990–96.
Samitaur, Culver City, Californie, 1990–96.

Samitaur
Culver City, California, 1990–1996

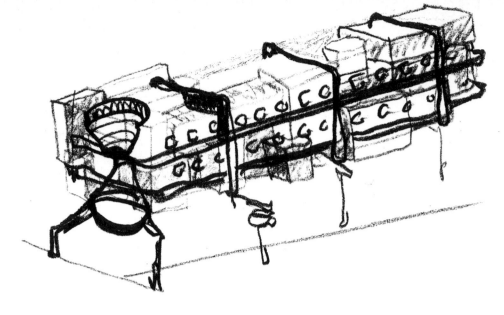

It was in 1989 that the developer Frederick Norton Smith first spoke to Eric Owen Moss about the project that was to become Samitaur. Smith had a client who needed more space, and Moss proposed that air rights be used to build a block 100 meters long above an existing road. Zoning regulations limited the height to 14.5 meters, and the fire department did not permit construction over the existing building. Furthermore, a 4.5 meter high passage had to be provided below the new block for truck clearance. Within these constraints, Eric Owen Moss has once again innovated in the conversion or new use of existing warehouse or office space in Culver City. Moss compares its most sculptural element, the "entry piece," alternately to a cone, a cylinder, a pumpkin or an hour-glass. A planned second phase building, called "The Hook," would be granted a zoning variance to reach a total height of 38 meters, adding even more credence to Moss's own appreciation of the project: "The area isn't sacrosanct, but still has residual meaning; the new changes the old, but doesn't blot it out."

The enigmatic skin of the Samitaur building certainly recalls earlier projects of Moss, which were more specifically rehabilitation jobs. Here, he creates a structure that nonetheless seems to retain an intimate relation to its location.

Die rätselhafte Fassade des Samitaur-Gebäudes erinnert zweifellos an frühere Projekte von Moss, bei denen es sich um spezielle Sanierungsaufträge handelte. Hier schuf er ein Bauwerk, das einen engen Bezug zu seiner Umgebung zu besitzen scheint.

La «peau» énigmatique de Samitaur rappelle certains projets antérieurs de Moss, qui étaient essentiellement des travaux de réhabilitation. Ici, il crée une structure qui semble néanmoins entretenir une relation intime avec son site.

Bereits 1989 wandte sich der Bauunternehmer Frederick Norton Smith an Eric Owen Moss bezüglich eines Projektes, aus dem das Samitaur-Gebäude entstehen sollte. Da ein Kunde mehr Raum benötigte, schlug Moss die Nutzung des Luftraumrechtes vor, um über einer bereits existierenden Straße eine 100 m lange Konstruktion zu errichten. Aufgrund des Flächennutzungsplans war dessen Höhe auf 14,5 m beschränkt, während feuerpolizeiliche Bestimmungen eine Bebauung über dem bereits vorhandenen Gebäude untersagten. Darüber hinaus mußte unter dem neuen Bauwerk eine 4,5 m hohe Passage für den LKW-Verkehr freigehalten werden. Trotz dieser Auflagen gelang es Eric Owen Moss wieder einmal, bei der Umwandlung oder Wiederverwendung eines bereits bestehenden Lager- oder Bürohauses in Culver City neue Maßstäbe zu setzen. Moss vergleicht das skulpturalste Element des Gebäudes, den »Eingangsbereich«, abwechselnd mit einem Kegel, einem Zylinder, einem Kürbis oder einem Stundenglas. Für die geplante zweite Bauphase namens »The Hook« (Der Haken) wurde eine Änderung des Flächennutzungsplans zugunsten einer Höhe von 38 m zugesagt – was Moss' eigener Einschätzung des Projekts noch mehr Glaubwürdigkeit verleiht: »Dieses Gebiet ist zwar nicht unantastbar, besitzt aber noch einen Rest von Charakter; das Neue verändert das Alte, löscht es aber nicht aus.«

C'est en 1989 que le promoteur Frederick Norton Smith a parlé pour la première fois du projet qui allait devenir Samitaur. Smith avait un client qui voulait développer ses installations, et Moss proposa que l'on se serve des *air rights* (droits de construire en hauteur) pour construire un bloc de 100 m de long au-dessus d'une route existante. La réglementation d'urbanisme limitait la hauteur à 14,5 m, les pompiers interdisaient la construction au-dessus d'un immeuble existant, et un passage de 4,5 m de haut devait être aménagé sous le nouveau bloc pour l'entrée des camions. Malgré ces contraintes, Eric Owen Moss a une fois de plus réussi à innover en transformant dans ses reconversions d'entrepôts ou de bureaux à Culver City. L'architecte compare l'élément le plus sculptural, l'entrée, à un cône, un cylindre, une citrouille ou un sablier. Un second bâtiment prévu, «The Hook» devrait bénéficier d'une dérogation pour atteindre les 38 m de haut, donnant encore plus de pertinence au jugement que Moss lui-même porte sur son projet: «L'endroit n'est pas sacro-saint, mais il possède encore une sorte de sens résiduel; la nouveauté change l'ancien, mais ne l'efface pas.»

3457
LA CIENEGA

Because it is lifted up above ground level, Samitaur seems related to the concept of motion, whether it be a mechanical crawling forward or a train or boat metaphor.

Da es sich über dem Boden erhebt, läßt das Gebäude an Bewegung denken: Es erinnert an etwas mechanisch vorwärts Kriechendes bzw. an eine Zug- oder Schiffs- metapher.

Parce qu'il est surélevé, Samitaur semble se rattacher à une idée de mouvement, que ce soit une reptation mécanique ou une métaphore de train, voire de bateau.

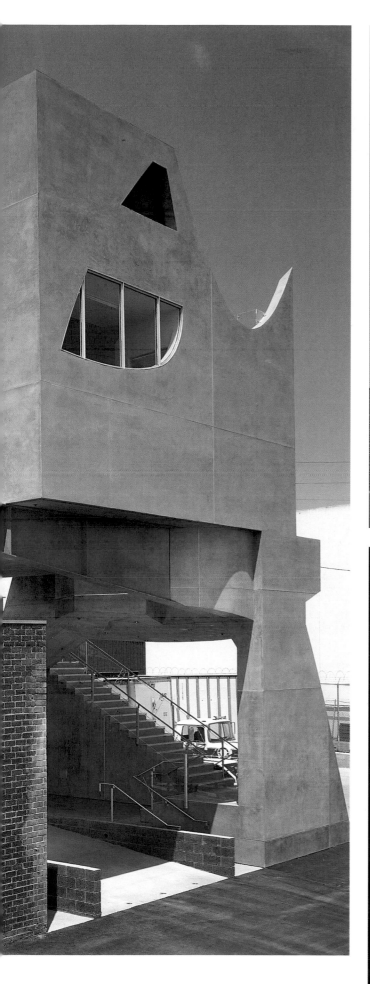

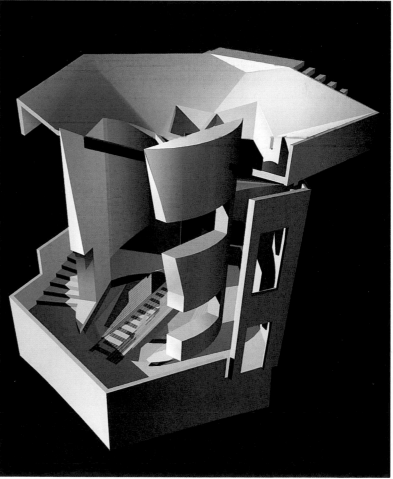

Touching down as lightly as possible on a lower brick structure, Samitaur is replete with sculptural detailing, which challenges traditional assumptions about space and motion.

Das auf der niedrigen Ziegelsteinkonstruktion nur leicht aufliegende Samitaur-Gebäude ist übersät mit skulpturalen Details, die traditionelle Auffassungen von Raum und Bewegung in Frage stellen.

S'appuyant aussi légèrement que possible sur une structure de brique, Samitaur est chargé de détails architecturaux qui narguent les idées reçues sur l'espace et le mouvement.

Pei Cobb Freed

James Ingo Freed

The firm Pei Cobb Freed has often been identified with the most famous of its partners, I.M. Pei, to the extent that the accomplishments of Harry Cobb and James Ingo Freed have on occasion been misrepresented or even ignored. That situation is now changing with the relative independence taken on by Pei, and the greater visibility of his partners. James Ingo Freed, who has completed such significant structures as the Jacob Javits Convention Center (New York, 1986), or the United States Holocaust Memorial Museum (Washington, D.C., 1993), was the partner in charge of the design of the new San Francisco Public Library. Although he shares with Pei a sense of dramatic contemporary spaces, such as the atrium of the Library, it may be that Freed has evolved toward a more complex approach to building in an historic environment. This was particularly evident in the Holocaust Memorial, where the facades of the structure correspond to the neighboring official Washington architecture, while creating a transition toward an inner complexity and unease for the visitor that is very much in keeping with the subject matter of the museum.

Die Firma Pei Cobb Freed wird häufig mit dem berühmtesten der drei Partner, I.M. Pei, identifiziert – was gelegentlich dazu führt, daß die Leistungen von Harry Cobb und James Ingo Freed entweder falsch dargestellt oder sogar ignoriert werden. Diese Situation beginnt sich nun zu ändern – zum einen wegen der immer größeren Unabhängigkeit Peis, aber auch aufgrund des immer höheren Bekanntheitsgrades seiner Partner. James Ingo Freed, der solch bedeutende Bauten wie das Jacob Javits Convention Center (New York, 1986) oder das United States Holocaust Memorial Museum (Washington, D.C., 1993) fertigstellte, zeichnet für den Entwurf der neuen San Francisco Public Library verantwortlich. Obwohl ihn mit Pei ein Gefühl für aufsehenerregende zeitgenössische Räume verbindet – wie das Atrium der neuen Bücherei beweist –, entwickelte Freed in Bezug auf das Bauen in historischer Umgebung einen komplexeren Ansatz. Dies wird besonders beim Holocaust Memorial deutlich: Während die Außenfassaden des Gebäudes Bezüge zur benachbarten offiziellen Washingtoner Architektur aufweisen, erzeugen sie gleichzeitig einen Übergang zu einer inneren Komplexität und ein Gefühl der Unbehaglichkeit beim Besucher, das dem Thema des Museums durchaus angemessen ist.

L'agence Pei Cobb Freed a souvent été confondue avec le plus célèbre de ses associés, I.M. Pei, au point où les réussites de Harry Cobb et de James Ingo Freed ont à l'occasion été mal présentées où même ignorées. Cette situation est en train de changer avec l'indépendance relative prise par Pei, et la visibilité plus grande laissée à ses partenaires. C'est James Ingo Freed, auteur de projets aussi importants que le Jacob Javits Convention Center (New York, 1986) ou l'United States Holocaust Memorial Museum (Washington D.C., 1993), qui a été chargé de la conception de la nouvelle bibliothèque publique de San Francisco. Bien qu'il partage avec Pei un sens spectaculaire et contemporain de l'espace, comme le montre l'atrium de cette bibliothèque, il se peut qu'il ait évolué vers une approche plus complexe de l'intégration d'un bâtiment dans son environnement historique. C'est particulièrement évident dans le mémorial de l'Holocauste, dont les façades s'intègrent à l'architecture officielle de Washington, tout en créant une transition vers une complexité interne et une certaine gêne du visiteur, appropriée au thème de ce musée.

San Francisco Public Library, San Francisco, California, 1992–96. The central atrium.

San Francisco Public Library, San Francisco, Kalifornien, 1992–96. Das zentrale Atrium.

San Francisco Public Library, San Francisco, Californie, 1992–96. L'atrium central.

San Francisco Public Library
San Francisco, California, 1992–1996

Despite an external bow to neighboring official architecture, which was in part mandated by local authorities, the San Francisco Public Library is a resolutely contemporary structure. With 1.5 million volumes arranged in 50 linear kilometers of closed and open stacks, the Library is a large (34,893 square meters) structure, which occupies more than 1 hectare of land. With six stories above grade and one below, it reaches a height of 24.4 meters, with the central atrium penetrating the entire volume. Clad in Sierra White granite-faced concrete panels, the exterior does betray its contemporary nature with the steel columns of the west facade, or the affirmed grid based on a 3 foot module. Built for a cost of $94 million, the Library includes 300 terminals for consultation of the on-line catalogue, and 500 data ports for Internet connection located in the reader tables. By accepting the constraints of external contextual harmony, James Ingo Freed here further develops his own very successful approach to the design of a contemporary building in an historic environment, as seen already in his 1993 Holocaust Memorial in Washington, D.C.

Ungeachtet ihrer äußerlichen Reverenz an die benachbarte formelle Architektur, die teilweise auf Drängen der örtlichen Behörden zustandekam, ist die San Francisco Public Library ein entschieden zeitgenössisches Bauwerk. Die Bibliothek nimmt über 1 ha Land ein und beherbergt auf einer Gesamtfläche von 34 893 m² 1,5 Millionen Bände in zahlreichen offenen und geschlossenen Regalen, die zusammen eine Länge von 50 km ergeben. Mit seinen sechs Ober- und einem Untergeschoß besitzt das Gebäude eine Höhe von 24,4 m, wobei sich das zentrale Atrium durch den gesamten Baukörper zieht. Die Fassade mit ihren mit weißem Granit verblendeten Betonplatten offenbart ihren zeitgenössischen Charakter durch die Stahlsäulen auf der Westseite oder das auf einem etwa 1 m großen Grundmaß basierende Raster. Die mit einem Budget von 94 Millionen Dollar errichtete Bibliothek umfaßt 300 Terminals für die Online-Abfrage des Katalogs sowie 500 Internetzugänge, die sich in den Lesetischen befinden. Dank seiner Akzeptanz der durch die bebaute Umgebung auferlegten Beschränkungen gelang James Ingo Freed eine Weiterentwicklung seines eigenen, sehr erfolgreichen Designansatzes für zeitgenössische Bauwerke in einem historischen Umfeld – der bereits in seinem Holocaust Memorial in Washington, D.C. (1993) zum Ausdruck kam.

Malgré l'hommage rendu par ses façades à l'architecture officielle avoisinante – exigé en partie par les autorités locales – la San Francisco Public Library est un bâtiment résolument moderne. Avec 1,5 million de volumes sur 50 km de rayons tant fermés qu'ouverts, cette bibliothèque est une vaste construction de 34 893 m² qui recouvre plus de 1 ha de terrain. Haute de 24,4 m, elle compte sept niveaux dont un souterrain, et son atrium central occupe toute sa hauteur. Recouvert de panneaux en béton plaqués de granit «Sierra White», l'extérieur affiche sa nature contemporaine à travers des colonnes d'acier sur la façade ouest et une trame modulaire de 1 m de côté. Construite pour un coût de 94 millions de $, la bibliothèque est équipée de 300 terminaux informatiques pour la consultation du catalogue, et de 500 prises pour se brancher sur Internet, directement disposées aux places de lecture. En acceptant les contraintes de l'harmonie du contexte urbain, James Ingo Freed pousse encore plus loin son approche personnelle très réussie de l'intégration d'un immeuble contemporain dans un environnement historique, comme le montrait déjà son mémorial de l'Holocauste à Washington D.C.

Its apparently traditional facade punctuated by four large steel columns, the Library is located to the left of the dome of City Hall.

Die Bibliothek mit ihrer eindeutig traditionellen, durch vier große Stahlsäulen akzentuierten Fassade befindet sich links von der Kuppel des Rathauses.

La façade apparemment traditionnelle est marquée par quatre grandes colonnes d'acier. La bibliothèque est située à gauche du dôme de l'hôtel de ville.

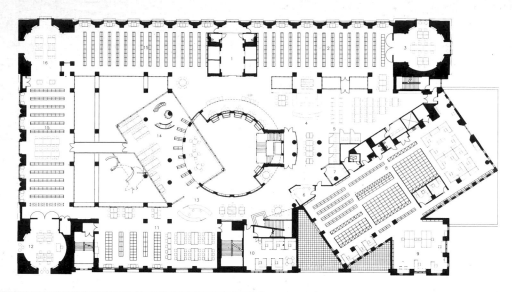

Like Freed's Holocaust Memorial in Washington, D.C., the Library is made up of contrasts. Its rectilinear or traditional aspect is constantly questioned by surprising intrusions, which nonetheless correspond naturally to the functioning of the institution.

Genau wie Freeds Holocaust Memorial in Washington, D.C., besteht auch diese Bibliothek aus Kontrasten. Ihre geradlinige oder traditionelle Ausstrahlung wird permanent durch überraschend in den Raum hineinragende und dennoch funkionale Bauteile in Frage gestellt.

Comme l'Holocaust Memorial de Freed à Washington D.C., la bibliothèque cultive les contrastes. Son aspect rectiligne est constamment remis en question par des intrusions surprenantes, qui correspondent néanmoins toujours à des fonctions du bâtiment.

Page 116 top: *A plan shows the basic rectangular layout of the building, with the rotated volumes of the periodicals room or stacks interacting with the central circular atrium.*

Seite 116 oben: *Der Grundriß zeigt die im Grunde rechtwinklige Anlage des Gebäudes, wobei die verschwenkten Baukörper des Zeitschriftenlesesaals und der Magazine mit dem zentralen runden Atrium korrespondieren.*

Page 116 en haut: *Le plan reprend simplement une forme extérieure de rectangle, les volumes pivotés de la salle des périodiques et des réserves jouant avec l'atrium circulaire.*

Cesar Pelli

Cesar Pelli, born in Tucuman, Argentina in 1926, is one of the outstanding figures of contemporary American architecture. He emigrated to the United States, and worked for ten years in the office of Eero Saarinen. The major buildings designed by Pelli with his different firms – DMJM, Gruen Associates, and Cesar Pelli & Associates – amount to one of the most prestigious lists of any practicing architect today. These include the famous Pacific Design Center in Los Angeles (1975), the tower expansion of the Museum of Modern Art in New York (1977), the World Financial Center in New York (1980–88), and the Canary Wharf Tower in London (1987–91). The Petronas Twin Towers in Kuala Lumpur published here mark his significant Asian presence, also evidenced by two Japanese projects completed in 1995, the thirty-story NTT Shinjuku Headquarters Office (Tokyo), and the thirty-six-story Sea Hawk Hotel & Resort in Fukuoka. Recipient of the 1995 AIA Gold Medal, Pelli recently won a competition to design the Performing Arts Center of Greater Miami.

Der 1926 in Tucuman, Argentinien geborene Cesar Pelli zählt zu den herausragendsten Figuren der zeitgenössischen amerikanischen Architektur. Nach seiner Einwanderung in die Vereinigten Staaten arbeitete er 10 Jahre für das Büro von Eero Saarinen. Zu den bekanntesten von Pelli und seinen verschiedenen Firmen – DMJM, Gruen Associates und Cesar Pelli & Associates – entworfenen Gebäuden zählen das Pacific Design Center in Los Angeles (1975), die Erweiterung des Museum of Modern Art in New York (1977), das World Financial Center in New York (1980–88) sowie der Canary Wharf Tower in London (1987–91). Die hier vorgestellten Petronas Twin Towers stehen stellvertretend für Pellis großen Einfluß in Asien, der sich auch in zwei 1995 in Japan fertiggestellten Gebäuden manifestiert, dem 30-stöckigen NTT Shinjuku Headquarters Building in Tokyo und dem 36 Stockwerke hohen Sea Hawk Hotel & Resort in Fukuoka. Ebenfalls 1995 erhielt Pelli die Goldmedaille der AIA und gewann den Wettbewerb für den Bau des 139 Millionen Dollar teuren Performing Arts Center in Groß-Miami.

Né en 1926 à Tucuman, Argentine, Cesar Pelli est l'une des grandes figures de l'architecture américaine contemporaine. Il émigre aux États-Unis et travaille pendant 10 ans dans l'agence d'Eero Saarinen. Les grandes réalisations conçues par Pelli pour ses différentes agences – DMJM, Gruen Associates, et Cesar Pelli & Associates – représentent l'une des plus prestigieuses listes de clients du moment. Il a ainsi construit le Pacific Design Center à Los Angeles (1975), la tour de l'extension du Museum of Modern Art de New York (1977), le World Financial Center de New York (1980–88), et la Canary Wharf Tower à Londres (1987–91). Les tours Petronas à Kuala Lumpur marquent sa présence en Asie, ainsi que deux autres projets au Japon achevés en 1995, une tour de 30 étages pour le siège de NTT à Tokyo, et le Sea Hawk Hotel & Resort (36 étages) à Fujuoka. Lauréat de la médaille d'or 1995 de l'AIA, Pelli a récemment remporté le concours pour le Performing Arts Center dans le grand Miami.

Petronas Twin Towers, Kuala Lumpur, Malaysia, 1991–97.
Facade detail.

Petronas Twin Towers, Kuala Lumpur, Malaysia, 1991–97.
Fassadendetail.

Petronas Twin Towers, Kuala Lumpur, Malaisie, 1991–97.
Détail de la façade.

Petronas Twin Towers
Kuala Lumpur, Malaysia, 1991–1997

With GDP growth of 8.4% in 1994, Malaysia is one of the fastest-expanding economies in the world, and the ultra-modern downtown area of the capital city Kuala Lumpur clearly shows this prosperity. Winner of an invited international competition for Phase One of the Kuala Lumpur City Centre project, Cesar Pelli has just completed the twin 452 meter high Petronas Twin Towers, named after the national oil company. Set in a development area of some 45 hectares, formerly the site of the Selangor Turf Club in the heart of the commercial district or "Golden Triangle," the towers are eighty-eight stories high, and are linked at the 41st and 42nd floors by a 58 meter skybridge. The floor area of each tower is 214,000 square meters. The symmetrical disposition of the structures emphasizes their role as a symbolic gateway, not only to the city but also to the "infinite," as the architect says. An exterior cladding of horizontal ribbons of vision glass and stainless steel spandrel panels makes these monumental buildings stand out against the skyline of Kuala Lumpur. Although some local figures have contested the need for such high buildings, especially designed by a foreign architect, Pelli points out that the plan of the buildings is based on the geometry of two interlocked squares, a typical Islamic design. Despite its large Chinese minority (32% of the population), Malaysia is a Muslim country.

Top: *An aerial view, showing the massive Kuala Lumpur City Centre construction site. The Petronas Twin Towers are located to the right.*
Bottom: *A plan that indicates the situation of the two towers vis-à-vis each other.*

Oben: *Ein Luftbild des Baugeländes des Kuala Lumpur City Center, rechts die Petronas Twin Towers.*
Unten: *Der Grundriß zeigt den Standort der beiden einander gegenüberliegenden Türme.*

En haut: *Vue aérienne, montrant le chantier du centre-ville. Les tours Petronas sont à droite.*
En bas: *Plan de la situation respective des tours.*

Mit einer Wachstumsrate des Bruttoinlandsproduktes von 8,4% zählt Malaysia zu den am stärksten expandierenden Volkswirtschaften; der steigende Wohlstand des Landes zeigt sich inbesondere in der ultramodernen Innenstadt der Hauptstadt Kuala Lumpur. Als Gewinner einer geschlossenen internationalen Ausschreibung für die Phase Eins des Kuala Lumpur City Centre-Projektes konnte Cesar Pelli kürzlich die Fertigstellung der 452 m hohen Zwillingstürme der Petronas Towers feiern, die nach der nationalen Ölgesellschaft benannt wurden. Das inmitten eines gewaltigen, etwa 45 ha großen Erschließungsgebietes gelegene Bauwerk befindet sich auf dem Gelände des ehemaligen Selangor Turf Club im Herzen des Finanzviertels oder »Goldenen Dreiecks«. Die beiden Türme verfügen über je 88 Geschosse; sie sind im 41. und 42. Stock durch eine 58 m lange Fußgängerbrücke miteinander verbunden und weisen jeder eine Gesamtfläche von 214 000 m² auf. Die symmetrische Anordnung unterstreicht ihre Rolle als symbolisches Tor nicht nur zur Stadt, sondern zum »Unendlichen«, wie der Architekt es formuliert. Dank der Fassadenverkleidung mit ihren horizontalen Bändern aus Klarglas und Edelstahlbrüstungsplatten hebt sich dieses monumentale Gebäude vor der Silhouette Kuala Lumpurs ab. Obwohl einige ortsansässige Kritiker den Sinn eines solch hohen Bauwerks – noch dazu von einem ausländischen Architekten – bezweifelten, erklärt Pelli, der Gebäudegrundriß basiere auf der Geometrie zweier ineinandergreifender Quadrate – einem typisch islamischen Motiv. Denn ungeachtet seiner großen chinesischen Minderheit (mit einem Bevölkerungsanteil von 32%) ist Malaysia ein islamischer Staat.

Avec un taux de croissance de 8,4% en 1994, la Malaisie possède l'une des économies les plus dynamiques au monde, et le centre-ville de Kuala Lumpur affiche clairement cette prospérité. Appelé par concours international à réaliser la phase I du projet de rénovation du centre de la capitale, Cesar Pelli vient d'achever les tours jumelles «Petronas» de 452 m de haut qui portent le nom de la société nationale des pétroles. Situées dans une zone de 45 ha au cœur du quartier commercial du « Triangle d'or», ces tours de 214 000 m² chacune, et de 88 étages, sont reliées au 41e et au 42e par une passerelle aérienne de 58 m de long. Leur disposition symétrique accentue leur rôle de «porte» non seulement de la ville, mais également vers l'infini, comme l'a écrit Pelli. Le dessin des façades en rubans horizontaux de baies de verre et de panneaux d'acier inoxydable fait ressortir ces monuments sur le panorama de la ville. Certaines personnalités locales ont contesté le besoin d'immeubles de grande hauteur, de plus dessinés par un étranger. C. Pelli fait remarquer que le plan de chaque tour repose sur un motif de deux carrés superposés, typique de l'art islamique. Malgré son importante communauté chinoise (32% de la population), la Malaisie est en effet un pays musulman.

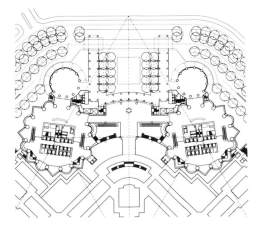

Below: A photo taken during construction (mid-1996).
Right: The model of the completed buildings with the skybridge linking them at the 41st and 42nd floors.

Unten: Eine während der Bauphase (Mitte 1996) angefertigte Fotografie.
Rechts: Ein Modell des Gebäudes mit der »Skybridge«, die den 41. und 42. Stock der beiden Türme miteinander verbindet.

Ci-dessous: Photo prise pendant la construction (mi-96).
À droite: Maquette des bâtiments achevés avec la passerelle aérienne qui les relie au 41e et au 42e étage.

James Stewart Polshek

Polshek and Partners

As Dean of the Graduate School of Architecture at Columbia University in New York from 1972 to 1987, James Stewart Polshek has exerted a considerable influence on his profession. Born in Akron, Ohio in 1930, he has had his own firm in New York since 1963. Despite a thriving practice, it may be difficult for many to identify Polshek with any specific style. The reason for this is explained in his own firm's description: "Since the founding of the firm in 1963, Polshek and Partners' approach to design has evolved according to the belief that style is circumstantial, the configuration of buildings volumes and masses and the articulation of their surfaces emerging from the particular place, program and client requirements rather than from a predetermined or highly personalized design vocabulary. Based on this belief in the importance of context, the firm creates unique and powerful architectural forms for the assertion of institutional identity, the amelioration of contextual dissonances and the reinforcement of a sense of place." Aside from Inventure Place published here, James Stewart Polshek also recently completed the Center for the Arts Theater at Yerba Buena Gardens, San Francisco (1993), which is located next to Mario Botta's San Francisco Museum of Modern Art, and to Fumihiko Maki's Yerba Buena Arts Center.

Als Dekan der Graduate School of Architecture an der New Yorker Columbia University (1972–87) übte James Stewart Polshek einen beträchtlichen Einfluß auf seinen Berufsstand aus. Der 1930 in Akron, Ohio, geborene Polshek gründete bereits 1963 in New York seine eigene Firma. Aber trotz einer regelmäßigen Bautätigkeit ist es für viele Betrachter schwierig, Polshek mit einer speziellen Stilrichtung in Verbindung zu bringen. Die Gründe dafür sind in der Selbstdarstellung der Firma erläutert: »Seit der Gründung 1963 haben sich die architektonischen Vorstellungen der Firma Polshek and Partners dahingehend entwickelt, daß Stil durch den Kontext bedingt ist – die Zusammenstellung von Baukörpern, Massen und der Gliederung ihrer Oberflächen, die eher aus einem bestimmten Ort, einem Programm und den Anforderungen der Auftraggeber heraus entsteht als aus einem vorher festgelegten oder hochgradig personalisierten architektonischen Vokabular. Auf der Basis dieses Glaubens an die Bedeutung des Kontextes schafft die Firma einzigartige und kraftvolle architektonische Formen, die die institutionelle Identität definieren, eventuell aus dem Zusammenhang entstehende Dissonanzen ausgleichen und das Gefühl für einen Ort verstärken sollen.« Neben dem hier vorgestellten Inventure Place beendete James Stewart Polshek ebenfalls vor kurzem die Arbeiten am Center for the Arts Theater in Yerba Buena Gardens, San Francisco (1993), das unmittelbar neben Mario Bottas San Francisco Museum of Modern Art und Fumihiko Makis Yerba Buena Arts Center liegt.

Doyen de la Graduate School of Architecture de Columbia University à New York de 1972 à 1987, James Stewart Polshek a exercé une influence considérable sur sa profession. Né à Akron, Ohio, en 1930, il anime sa propre agence à New York depuis 1963. S'il construit énormément, il est parfois difficile de l'associer à un style précis. Il s'en explique dans la plaquette de présentation de son agence: «Depuis la fondation de l'agence en 1963, l'approche créative de Polshek and Partners a évolué avec la conviction que le style est circonstanciel, la configuration des volumes et masses et l'articulation de leurs surfaces émergeant des particularités du lieu, du programme et des demandes du client, plutôt que d'un langage prédéterminé ou hautement personnalisé. Forte de cette croyance dans l'importance du contexte, l'agence crée des formes puissantes de caractère unique qui affirment une identité institutionnelle, l'amélioration de dissonances contextuelles, et le renforcement d'un sens du lieu.» En dehors d'Inventure Place, reproduit ici, James Stewart Polshek a récemment achevé le Center for the Arts Theater à Yerba Buena Gardens, San Francisco (1993), non loin du musée d'art moderne de San Francisco de Mario Botta, et du Yerba Buena Arts Center de Fumihiko Maki.

Inventure Place, Akron, Ohio, 1993–95. Interior view.

Inventure Place, Akron, Ohio, 1993–95. Innenansicht.

Inventure Place, Akron, Ohio, 1993–95. Vue intérieure.

Inventure Place
Akron, Ohio, 1993–1995

The main purpose of this structure is to provide a Hall of Fame commemorating the United States Patent System. An interactive science museum demonstrates the ideas behind some of the inventions. The total area of the complex is 6,500 square meters, with some 1,950 square meters below grade for the "Inventors Workshop," with its very successful and well-integrated exhibits designed by the firm Hands On!. Above the workshop, there is an open plaza facing the stainless steel, sail-shaped main facade of the building, and a bold "neo-constructivist" sign with red letters, aligned along a curve that echoes those of the facade. The "Hall of the Inventive Mind," an atrium defined by the main arc, rises to a height of over 30 meters, and immediately confers a sense of the soaring space of the external forms on the interior. The Inventors' Hall of Fame itself is located in the floors stacked behind the arc, accessible by elevator and by the stairways cantilevered out into the open space of the hall. Because it blends participatory displays with the often interesting stories of the inventors themselves, Inventure Place is a model for a new type of museum, which in this instance also participates in the reaffirmation of an urban identity.

With its towering sign and sweeping curved facade, Inventure Place stands out, and certainly invites the curious to enter. Through participatory display areas and a sort of Inventors' Hall of Fame, the complex again corresponds to the descriptive term "edutainment."

Mit seiner turmartigen Leuchtreklame und der schwungvollen Fassadenbiegung lädt Inventure Place zum Besuch ein. Dank der interaktiven Ausstellungsbereiche und einer Art »Ruhmeshalle der Erfinder« entspricht der Komplex dem Begriff »Edutainment«.

Avec son signal en forme de tour et sa façade en courbe, Inventure Place marque son territoire et invite le visiteur à la découvrir. À travers des présentations interactives et une salle dédiée aux grands inventeurs, le complexe est une application du nouveau concept d'«edutainment».

Dieses Gebäude mit einer Gesamtfläche von 6 500 m² entstand mit dem Ziel, eine Ruhmeshalle für das United States Patent System und die größten amerikanischen Erfinder zu schaffen, wobei ein interaktives Wissenschaftsmuseum anhand einiger Erfindungen die zugrunde liegenden Ideen veranschaulicht. Im Untergeschoß befindet sich der 1 950 m² große »Inventors Workshop« mit seinen erfolgreichen und passend integrierten Ausstellungsstücken der Firma »Hands On!«. Über dieser Erfinderwerkstatt liegt ein offener Platz mit Blick auf die segelförmige Edelstahlfassade des Gebäudes und auf eine kühne »neo-konstruktivistische« Leuchtreklame mit roten Buchstaben, deren schwungvolle Anordnung die Kurvatur der Fassade noch einmal aufnimmt. Die »Hall of the Inventive Mind«, ein vom Hauptbogen definiertes Atrium, erhebt sich bis zu einer Höhe von 30 m und vermittelt sofort ein Gefühl des erhabenen Raums, das die äußere Form dem Inneren des Gebäudes verleiht. Die »Inventor's Hall of Fame« selbst ist in den Geschossen hinter dem Bogen untergebracht und über Rolltreppen und das in den offenen Raum der Halle hineinragende Treppenhaus zugänglich. Da das Inventure Place interaktive Ausstellungsbereiche mit den häufig interessanten Lebensgeschichten der jeweiligen Erfinder verknüpft, ist dieses Bauwerk ein Modell für einen neuen Museumstypus – der in diesem Fall auch zur Bekräftigung einer urbanen Identität beiträgt.

L'objectif principal de cette réalisation est d'offrir un musée aux grands inventeurs, et de rendre hommage au système de protection de brevet des États-Unis. Un musée scientifique interactif explique les principes qui sont à la base de certaines inventions. La surface totale de l'ensemble est de 6 500 m², dont 1 950 en sous-sol pour l'«Atelier des inventeurs» aux présentations très réussies et bien intégrées, conçues par l'agence Hands On!. Au-dessus de l'atelier se trouve une place ouverte devant la façade principale de ce bâtiment en forme de voile d'acier inoxydable, ainsi qu'une voyante enseigne «néo-constructiviste» en lettres rouges, alignée le long d'une courbe qui fait écho à celle de la façade. Le «Hall de l'esprit d'invention», atrium défini par l'arche principale, s'élève à plus de 30 m, et renvoie un écho immédiat à la grande forme dressée de la façade extérieure. Le «Hall of Fame» des inventeurs est logé dans les différents niveaux derrière l'arche, accessibles par des ascenseurs et des escaliers mécaniques en porte-à-faux dans l'espace ouvert du hall. Parce qu'il sait associer des présentations interactives à l'histoire, souvent intéressante, de la vie des inventeurs, Inventure Place est un modèle de nouveau type de musée qui, ici, participe également à la réaffirmation d'une identité urbaine.

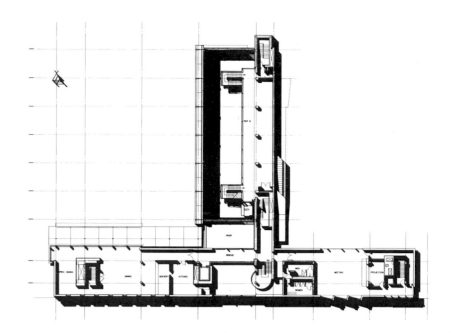

Bart Prince

Born in Albuquerque, New Mexico, Bart Prince worked as an assistant to Bruce Goff from 1968 to 1973, and completed the Pavilion for Japanese Art at the Los Angeles County Museum of Art (1978–89) after Goff's death in 1982, establishing his credentials as the most legitimate representative of a strong regional tradition of organic architecture. His often complex, undulating forms indeed often have a strong natural connotation without being specifically anthropomorphic. It cannot be said that this type of architecture really fits into any international trends, but the indigenous wooden architecture of Hungary for example sometimes calls on similar forms, and it would seem that worldwide interest in ecologically oriented buildings might well extend to houses, often built of wood and inspired by nature. Bart Prince's architecture also calls on a tradition of workmanship and individual design pioneered in California by Charles and Henry Greene. Though architects like the Greenes mainly used wood for their early 20th century houses, Prince has shown his ability to call on modern materials, and even to build on a very low budget, as was the case in his 1994 Mead/Penhall residence (Albuquerque, New Mexico).

Der in Albuquerque, New Mexico, geborene Bart Prince hat durch seine Arbeit als Assistent von Bruce Goff (1968–73) sowie – nach Goffs Tod 1982 – durch die Fertigstellung des Pavillon for Japanese Art im Los Angeles County Museum of Art (1978–89) bewiesen, daß er unter den rechtmäßigen Vertretern einer starken regionalen Tradition organischer Architektur führend ist. Seine vielfach komplexen Wellenformen besitzen häufig starke Bezüge zur Natur, ohne dabei bewußt anthropomorph zu wirken. Zwar liegt Princes Architektur etwas außerhalb der gängigen Architekturtrends, aber er beruft sich teilweise auf ähnliche Formen wie beispielsweise die einheimische Holzarchitektur Ungarns – und es scheint, als ob sich das weltweite Interesse an ökologisch orientierten Bauten auch auf Häuser aus Holz zu erstrecken beginnt, deren Formen von der Natur inspiriert wurden. Darüber hinaus weist seine Architektur Bezüge zu einer Tradition hohen handwerklichen Könnens und individuellen Designs auf, die in Kalifornien von Charles und Henry Greene begründet wurde. Obwohl Architekten wie die Gebrüder Greene zu Beginn des 20. Jahrhunderts für ihre Häuser meist Holz verwandten, hat Prince seine Fähigkeit unter Beweis gestellt, auch mit modernen Materialien und – wie im Falle der Mead/Penhall Residence in Albuquerque, New Mexico – zu einem sehr niedrigen Preis bauen zu können.

Né à Albuquerque, Nouveau-Mexique, en 1947, Bart Prince a été l'assistant de Bruce Goff de 1968 à 1973, et a achevé le Pavilion for Japanese Art du Los Angeles County Museum of Art (1978–89) après le décès de Goff en 1982, reprenant ainsi le titre d'un des représentants les plus légitimes de la tradition architecturale organique californienne. Ses formes ondulées, souvent complexes, présentent en effet de fortes connotations naturalistes, sans être spécifiquement anthropomorphiques. Cette architecture, dont les formes rappellent parfois celles de l'architecture hongroise traditionnelle en bois, s'intègre mal aux grandes tendances internationales du moment. Les maisons de Prince, inspirées par la nature et souvent en bois, présentent des qualités écologiques tout à fait d'actualité. Son architecture s'appuie également sur des traditions artisanales et d'originalité individualiste dont Charles et Henry Greene furent les pionniers californiens du début de ce siècle. Si ces derniers utilisaient surtout le bois, Prince maîtrise les matériaux modernes et sait également construire pour des budgets réduits, comme le montre sa Mead/Penhall Residence (Albuquerque, Nouveau-Mexique, 1994).

Hight Residence, Mendocino County, California, 1994–95. The shingle roof.

Hight Residence, Mendocino County, Kalifornien, 1994–95. Das Schindeldach.

Hight Residence, Mendocino County, Californie, 1994–95. Le toit en bardeaux.

Hight Residence
Mendocino County, California, 1994–1995

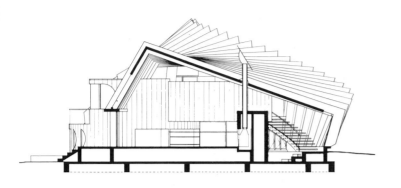

This 325 square meter residence is located on a 1 hectare site, overlooking the Pacific, north of the seaside village of Mendocino. Intended as a weekend house, the residence is cedar shingled, and is built with glue-laminated beams. Its most arresting feature is undoubtedly its undulating shingle roof. The design of the house takes into account the views available to the south and to the southwest, shielding the residents from the winds that come from the north. Within, the roof structure is visible, once again as an undulating surface of wood, copper and glass, "forming a large space visible from one end to the other over the partitions of the bedrooms at each end." As might be evident from the nature of this architecture, Bart Prince says that "The Hights spent a good deal of time looking for an architect and interviewed several." They selected him after seeing a number of his buildings. "They were very interested in architecture, and liked the work of Charles and Henry Greene as well as that of Frank Lloyd Wright," says Prince.

Das 325 m² große Wohnhaus liegt im Norden des Küstenstädtchens Mendocino auf einem 1 ha großen Gelände mit Blick auf den Pazifik. Das ursprünglich als Wochenendhaus geplante Anwesen ist aus Schichtholzbalken errichtet, und zu seinen faszinierendsten Bauelementen zählt zweifellos das geschwungene, mit Zedernholzschindeln gedeckte Dach. Beim Entwurf des Hauses wurde die Aussicht Richtung Süden und Südwesten berücksichtigt, während die Bewohner vor dem kräftigen Nordwind durch die Dachkonstruktion geschützt sind. Diese ist im Inneren des Gebäudes als ebenfalls geschwungene Oberfläche aus Holz, Kupfer und Glas sichtbar, die »einen großen Raum bildet, der von der einen bis zur anderen Seite über die Trennwände der Schlafzimmer am jeweiligen Ende hinaus wahrnehmbar ist. Als wäre es aus der Natur dieser Architektur ersichtlich, erklärt Bart Prince: »Die Hights investierten sehr viel Zeit in die Suche nach einem Architekten und trafen sich mit diversen zu Vorgesprächen.« Ihre Wahl fiel auf ihn, nachdem sie einige seiner Bauwerke gesehen hatten. »Sie interessierten sich wirklich sehr für Architektur und schätzen die Arbeit von Charles und Henry Greene ebenso wie die Werke von Frank Lloyd Wright.«

Cette maison de 325 m² se trouve sur un terrain de 1 ha, qui domine le Pacifique, au nord du village côtier de Mendocino. Maison de week-end, elle est recouverte d'un bardage de cèdre et sa charpente est en poutres de bois lamellé-collé. Sa caractéristique la plus surprenante est certainement son toit ondulé en bardeaux. Le dessin de la maison favorise les vues panoramiques vers le sud et le sud-ouest, et protège les habitants des vents du nord. À l'intérieur, la structure du toit reste visible et présente, là encore, une surface ondulée en bois, cuivre et verre, «formant un vaste espace visible d'un bout à l'autre de la maison, qui passe au-dessus des cloisons des chambres situées à chaque extrémité». Bart Prince explique que «les Hight ont consacré beaucoup de temps à la recherche d'un architecte et en ont interrogé plusieurs». Ils l'ont sélectionné après avoir vu un certain nombre de ses réalisations. «Ils étaient très intéressés par l'architecture, et aimaient l'œuvre de Charles et Henry Green, ainsi que celle de Frank Lloyd Wright.»

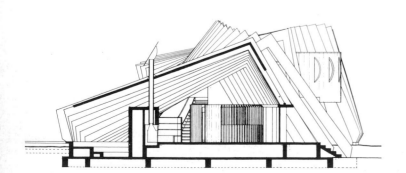

With its shingle roof descending at points to the ground, the Hight Residence is one of Bart Prince's more spectacular buildings, its structure designed to alternately shield from the wind and offer open views toward the outside.

Die Hight Residence zählt mit ihrem teilweise bis zum Boden reichenden Schindeldach, dessen Konstruktionsweise das Gebäude einerseits vor starkem Wind schützt und andererseits den Blick auf die Landschaft freigibt, zu den aufsehenerregendsten Bauwerken von Bart Prince.

Avec son toit recouvert de bardeaux touchant le sol à certains endroits, la Hight Residence est l'une des réalisations les plus spectaculaires de Bart Prince. Sa structure est conçue de façon à protéger du vent et offrir des vues panoramiques vers l'extérieur.

Its interior largely shaped by the complex undulating roof, the Hight Residence offers warm contrasts between wood and stone surfaces, with very little metal in evidence.

Mit dem durch die komplexe Form des gewellten Daches bestimmten Innenraum bietet die Hight Residence einen warmen Kontrast zwischen Holz- und Steinoberflächen, wobei nur wenig Metall- flächen sichtbar sind.

L'intérieur est largement déterminé par le toit de forme complexe et ondulée. Il met en scène de chaleureux contrastes entre le bois et les surfaces en pierre, sans beaucoup de présence de métal.

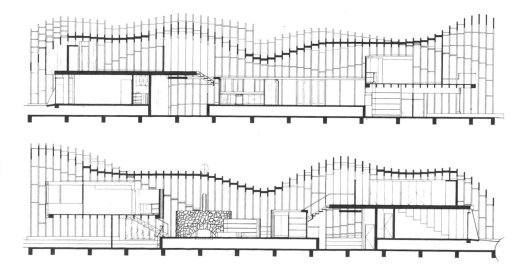

Richard Rauh

Born in Kentucky, Richard Rauh studied art history at Columbia (B.A. 1970); B. Arch., M. Arch., Harvard University GSD, Department of Architecture, 1970–74. A teaching fellow at Harvard and later a research associate, before becoming an assistant professor of architecture at the University of Kentucky (1976–80), he was principal of Carpenter/ Rauh Architects in Lexington, Kentucky (1978–81) before moving to Atlanta (RHPMHR) and finally creating Richard Rauh & Associates in 1984. In the time of his association with Ted and Helen Hatch (RHPMHR), he became quickly involved in a boom of hotel construction in the area. Not wishing to become exclusively a hotel architect, he and Ann Fitzgerald have branched out into office, retail and interior projects, including historic preservation and rehabilitation, as well as a number of treatment centers for head injury victims. Licensed in thirty-one states, Rauh has shown an ability to adapt to differing circumstances, including those of the very low-cost multiplex roadside cinema published here.

Richard Rauh wurde in Kentucky geboren und studierte Kunstgeschichte an der New Yorker Columbia University (Bachelor of Arts 1970), gefolgt von einem Studium in Harvard (1970–74 Bachelor of Architecture, Master of Architecture, Harvard University Graduate School of Design, Department of Architecture). Rauh war zunächst Mitglied des Lehrkörpers, danach Forschungsbeauftragter in Harvard, bis er eine Stelle als Assistenzprofessor für Architektur an der University of Kentucky erhielt (1976–80). Von 1978 bis 1981 leitete Rauh Carpenter/Rauh Architects in Lexington, Kentucky, bevor er nach Atlanta zog (RHPMHR) und schließlich 1984 Richard Rauh & Associates gründete. Während seiner Zusammenarbeit mit Ted und Helen Hatch (RHPMHR) wurde Rauh in einen wahren »Boom« von Hotelbauten hineingezogen, die zu dieser Zeit in der Region entstanden. Da er aber nicht ausschließlich als Hotelarchitekt arbeiten wollte, dehnten Rauh und seine Partnerin Ann Fitzgerald ihr Aufgabengebiet auch auf Büro-, Einzelhandels- und Inneneinrichtungsprojekte aus, wozu neben der Erhaltung und Rekonstruktion historischer Bauten auch eine Reihe von Behandlungszentren für Patienten mit Kopfverletzungen zählen. Der in 31 amerikanischen Bundesstaaten offiziell zugelassene Rauh hat seine Fähigkeit unter Beweis gestellt, sich den unterschiedlichsten Bedingungen anpassen zu können – unter anderem auch beim Entwurf des hier gezeigten Multiplex-Kinos, das mit einem sehr kleinen Budget am Rande von Atlanta entstand.

Né dans le Kentucky, Richard Rauh étudie l'histoire de l'art à Columbia University (B.A. 1970); B. Arch., M. Arch., Harvard University Graduate School of Design, Department of Architecture, 1970–74. Assistant à Harvard puis chercheur, avant de devenir professeur assistant en architecture à l'université du Kentucky (1976–80), il dirige l'agence Carpenter/ Rauh Architects à Lexington, Kentucky (1978–81) avant de s'installer à Atlanta (RHPMHR), et de finalement fonder Richard Rauh & Associates en 1984. Au cours de son association avec Ted et Helen Hatch (RHPMHR), il profite de l'essor de la construction d'hôtels dans la région, ce qui ne l'empêche pas, avec Ann Fitzgerald, de s'intéresser à des projets d'aménagement intérieur de bureaux et de magasins, dont certains dans le cadre de restauration ou de réhabilitation sur des immeubles anciens, ainsi qu'à des centres de traumatologie. Exerçant dans 31 états, Rauh a prouvé sa capacité à s'adapter à des circonstances très diverses, y compris celles d'un cinéma multi-salles à faible budget, illustré ici.

Cinema, Duluth, Georgia, 1994–96.

Multiplex-Kino, Duluth, Georgia, 1994–96.

Cinéma, Duluth, Géorgie, 1994–96.

Cinema

Duluth, Georgia, 1994–1996

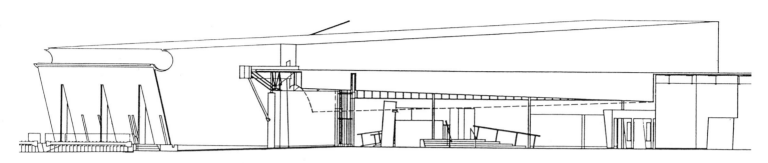

As part of a "remarketing of a distressed nearly vacant ten-year-old minimall," this multiplex cinema for the budget, second-run market is a remarkable success. With it, Richard Rauh shows just how efficiently a talented architect can respond to the extreme price pressures that exist in a competitive low-cost market. Situated next to an interstate highway, the building area is approximately 3,100 square meters, on a site of about 2 hectares. Seating capacity is 1,808, and 666 parking spaces are provided. Built with materials such as galvanized corrugated steel on the outside and galvanized tin on the inside, the cinema respected a very low budget of $55 per square foot, proving that it was not impossible to create a successful blend of inexpensive marketing and good design. Calling on roadside architectural vocabulary with continuous fluorescent billboard lights for example, Richard Rauh's cinema makes a case for the vitality of contemporary American architecture in a changing economic environment.

Dieses Multiplex-Kino entstand als Teil eines »Sanierungsprogramms für ein vernachlässigtes, fast leerstehendes, zehn Jahre altes Einkaufszentrum« – ein Konzept von erstaunlichem Erfolg. Hiermit dokumentierte Richard Rauh, auf welch effiziente Weise ein begabter Architekt auf den extremen Preisdruck im hart umkämpften Billigpreissektor reagieren kann. Das neben einem Interstate Highway auf einem etwa 2 ha großen Gelände gelegene Gebäude besitzt eine Gesamtfläche von schätzungsweise 3100 m² und verfügt über insgesamt 1808 Sitz- sowie 666 Parkplätze. Dank der Verwendung von Materialien wie verzinkten Wellstahlblechen an der Außenfassade und Zinkblech im Inneren konnte das Kino für den extrem günstigen Preis von 592 Dollar pro Quadratmeter erbaut werden und damit unter Beweis stellen, daß eine gelungene Mischung aus preiswerten Materialien und gutem Design nicht unmöglich ist. Richard Rauhs Kinogebäude mit seinen Anspielungen auf die typisch amerikanische Straßenarchitektur mit ständig leuchtenden Reklametafeln spricht für die Lebensfähigkeit zeitgenössischer amerikanischer Architektur in einer starken Veränderungen unterworfenen wirtschaftlichen Lage.

Dans le cadre de «la revitalisation d'un centre commercial en détresse, presque vide et vieux de dix ans», ce cinéma multisalles destiné aux films de seconde exclusivité est une remarquable réussite. Richard Rauh montre ici avec quelle efficacité un architecte de talent peut répondre à des contraintes financières très serrées sur le marché très concurrentiel des constructions économiques. Situé près d'un grand carrefour routier, l'ensemble couvre environ 3100 m², sur un terrain de près de 2 ha, et offre 1808 places assises et 666 emplacements de parking. Construit en matériaux comme l'acier ondulé galvanisé pour l'extérieur et la tôle ondulée pour l'intérieur, ce complexe a respecté le budget très limité de 3000 FF le m², prouvant qu'esprit d'économie et «good design» pouvaient faire bon ménage. Évoquant le vocabulaire architectural des bords de route avec, par exemple, son éclairage fluorescent continu, le cinéma de Richard Rauh prouve la vitalité de l'architecture américaine contemporaine dans un environnement économique en pleine évolution.

Built for the O'Neil Theaters group from Louisiana, this multiplex cinema is located in one of the most densely developed areas around Atlanta, which meant that it had to be visually remarkable in order to be noticed at all.

Dieses für O'Neil Theaters – eine in Lousiana ansässige Firma – errichtete Multiplex-Kino befindet sich in einem sehr dicht besiedelten Stadtteil von Atlanta, wodurch es optisch besonders hervortreten mußte, um überhaupt bemerkt zu werden.

Construit pour la société de Louisiane O'Neil Theaters, cette multisalles est située dans l'une des banlieues les plus densément développées d'Atlanta, d'où la nécessité de trouver une solution visuelle étonnante pour se faire remarquer.

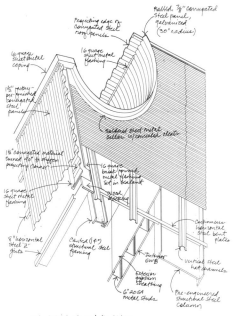

Skin detail at end of open
oversized gutter
Looking up -- reversed plan oblique

Built with a thin triangulated **steel** framework, the cinema's interiors are usually covered with corrugated tin and budget priced carpeting. The auditorium roofs have a 18 meter clear span.

Die Innenräume des auf einer dünnen, dreieckigen Stahlskelettkonstruktion errichteten Kinos sind hauptsächlich mit Wellblech und preiswerter Auslegeware ausgestattet. Die Dachkonstruktionen der Kinosäle weisen eine Spannweite von 18 m auf.

Construites à partir d'une mince ossature d'acier triangulée, les salles sont généralement recouvertes à l'intérieur de tôle ondulée et de moquette bon marché. Les toits des salles ont une portée de 18 m.

The extensive use of corrugated tin within the complex is derived from industrial or agricultural applications, but here takes on another aspect. The architect was obliged to convince workers that such "chicken-coop material" was worthy of their efforts.

Die weitreichende Verwendung von Wellblech bei der Innenraumgestaltung stammt ursprünglich aus der Landwirtschaft und der Industrie, besitzt aber hier eine andere Ausdruckskraft. Dem Architekten gelang es schließlich, die Bauarbeiter davon zu überzeugen, daß dieses »Hühnerfarm-Material« die Mühe durchaus lohne.

L'usage généralisé de la tôle ondulée vient d'applications industrielles ou agricoles, mais prend ici un autre aspect. L'architecte a été obligé de convaincre les ouvriers que ce «matériau de cage à poules» méritait qu'ils le soignent.

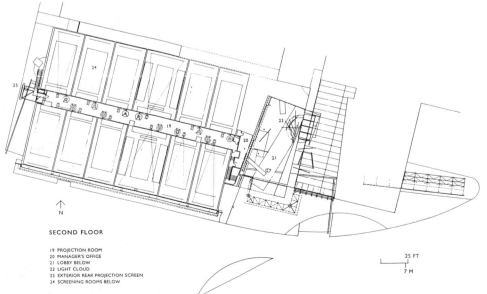

↑
N

SECOND FLOOR

19 PROJECTION ROOM
20 MANAGER'S OFFICE
21 LOBBY BELOW
22 LIGHT CLOUD
23 EXTERIOR REAR PROJECTION SCREEN
24 SCREENING ROOMS BELOW

25 FT
7 M

Siegel Diamond

Katherine Diamond

Born in 1954, in Chicago, Illinois, Katherine Diamond has dual citizenship (USA, Israel), and was a 1st Lieutenant in the Israeli Air Force Engineering Corps. She received her B. Arch. from The Technion, Israel Institute of Technology (1978), and worked on a Masters in Psychology, UCLA (1981–83). She was the first woman president of Los Angeles Chapter of American Institute of Architects (1993–94). Among the projects she has worked on since 1985, there is the design for a new Universal City Metro Red Line Subway Station, Baldwin Park Commuter Rail Station also in Los Angeles, four elevated light rail stations for Los Angeles/Long Beach Metro Blue Line (1989), and the University of California Davis Medical Center Plant with Cogeneration (design architect for the Brown & Caldwell Engineers team). Concentrating on the development of the idea of transport, as the Design Architect for the Holmes & Narver Inc team, she has created one of the more visible landmarks in a city that has few recognizable symbols. As she says, "The design is intended to create a new landmark tower in dialog with the venerable older landmark" Theme Restaurant, "creating a new icon for Los Angeles." "This architecture of metaphor," she says "is not a simple, declarative language. Visitors to LAX will construct their own different stories, and with luck, the ower will become a valued part of the collective memory of Los Angeles."

Die 1954 in Chicago, Illinois geborene Katherine Diamond besitzt zwei Staatsbürgerschaften (Vereinigte Staaten, Israel) und diente als Oberleutnant bei der israelischen Luftwaffe. Sie machte ihren Bachelor of Architecture am Technion, dem Israel Institute of Technology (1978), und studierte von 1981–83 Psychologie an der UCLA in Los Angeles. Von 1993 bis 1994 war sie die erste Präsidentin des Los Angeles Chapter des American Institute of Architects. Zu den Projekten, mit denen sich Katherine Diamond seit 1985 beschäftigt hat, gehören der Entwurf eines Untergrundbahnhofs für die Universal City Metro Red Line, die Baldwin Park Commuter Rail Station in Los Angeles, vier Hochbahnstationen der Los Angeles/Long Beach Metro Blue Line und die University of California Davis Medical Center Plant, zusammen mit Cogeneration (Designarchitekt für Brown & Caldwell Engineers). Durch ihre Konzentration auf die Entwicklung der Vorstellung von Transport und Verkehr schuf Katherine Diamond als Designarchitekt für Holmes & Narver Inc einen auffälligen Orientierungspunkt für eine Stadt, die über nur wenige wiedererkennbare Symbole verfügt. Sie sagt dazu: »Der Tower wurde als neues Kennzeichen konzipiert, das mit dem ehrwürdigen älteren Wahrzeichen des ›Theme Restaurant‹ in Dialog treten soll und so eine neues Wahrzeichen für Los Angeles schafft. Bei dieser metaphorischen Architektur handelt es sich nicht um eine einfache, deklamatorische Sprache. Die Besucher des LAX werden ihre eigenen, unterschiedlichen Geschichten gestalten, und mit etwas Glück entwickelt sich der Tower zu einem hochgeschätzten Teil des kollektiven Gedächtnisses von Los Angeles.«

Née en 1954 à Chicago, Illinois, Katherine Diamond possède la double nationalité américaine et israélienne et a même été lieutenant de l'armée d'Israël. Elle est diplômée en architecture de l'Institut israélien de technologie (1978), et a préparé une maîtrise en psychologie à l'UCLA (1981–83). Elle est la première femme a avoir présidé le chapitre de Los Angeles de l'American Institute of Architects (1993–94). Depuis 1985, elle a travaillé sur la station de métro d'Universal City, la Baldwin Park Commuter Rail Station également à Los Angeles, quatre stations légères sur la ligne bleue du métro Los Angeles/Long Beach (1989), et le Davis Medical Center Plant de l'université de Californie avec Cogeneration (architecte pour Brown & Caldwell Engineers). Réfléchissant à l'évolution de l'idée de transport, en tant qu'architecte-concepteur pour Holmes & Narver Inc elle a créé le plus visible des monuments d'une ville qui ne possède que peu de symboles d'identification. Elle écrit ainsi que «le projet est de créer une nouvelle tour monumentale qui dialogue avec le vénérable monument qu'est le ‹Theme restaurant› en proposant une nouvelle icône pour Los Angeles. Cette architecture de la métaphore n'est pas une simple déclaration d'intention. Les visiteurs de l'aéroport échafauderont à partir d'elle leurs propres histoires, et avec un peu de chance, cette tour deviendra un élément apprécié de la mémoire collective de Los Angeles».

LAX Control Tower, Los Angeles, California, 1993–95.
LAX Control Tower, Los Angeles, Kalifornien, 1993–95.
LAX Control Tower, Los Angeles, Californie, 1993–95.

LAX Control Tower
Los Angeles, California, 1993–1995

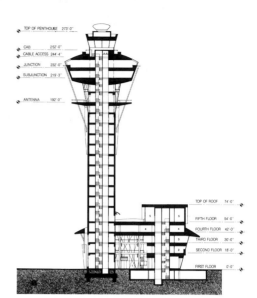

Built for the Federal Aviation Administration on land belonging to Los Angeles, this tower was voluntarily submitted to Los Angeles City Cultural Affairs Commission Design Review, a fact that undoubtedly complicated a concept that already had to deal with such factors as potential seismic activity. Described by the architect as "an adult tree-house," the 78 meter high tower is intended to have the "organic imagery of the high-tech tree." Despite the constraints already mentioned, as well as that of a certain respect for the "flying saucer" design of the nearby Los Angeles International Airport Theme Building (Luckman, Pereira, Becket and Williams, 1960), the originality and powerful presence of the Control Tower make it seem likely that it may well succeed the Theme Building as a symbol of Los Angeles. With a floor area of 1,861 square meters, the tower, built with a steel frame, glass fiber reinforced concrete, metal roofing and blue/green glazing, cost $18.6 million. In a still largely male-dominated profession, it is worth noting that this exceptional tower is the work of a female architect.

Die Tatsache, daß der Entwurf dieses im Auftrag der Federal Aviation Administration errichteten Kontrollturms freiwillig der Los Angeles City Cultural Affairs Commission Design Review zur Begutachtung vorgelegt wurde, verkomplizierte das Konzept zusätzlich, das ohnehin mit solchen Faktoren wie potentiellen Erdbeben zu kämpfen hatte. Der von der Architektin als »Baumhaus für Erwachsene« bezeichnete 78 m hohe Tower soll »die organische Bildsprache eines Hightech-Baums« besitzen. Ungeachtet der bereits erwähnten Baubeschränkungen und einem gewissen Respekt vor dem einer »fliegenden Untertasse« ähnelnden Design des benachbarten Los Angeles International Airport Theme Building (Luckman, Pereira, Becket und Williams, 1960) lassen der originelle Charakter und die kraftvolle Präsenz des Control Towers es als sehr wahrscheinlich erscheinen, daß dieses Bauwerk das Theme Building als Wahrzeichen der Stadt Los Angeles ablösen wird. Die Kosten für den Kontrollturm, der auf einer Gesamtfläche von 1861 m² in Stahlskelettbauweise aus glasfaserverstärktem Beton entstand und ein Metalldach sowie eine blaugrüne Verglasung aufweist, betrugen 18,6 Millionen Dollar. In einem noch stets von Männern beherrschten Berufsfeld ist es um so bemerkenswerter, daß dieses außergewöhnliche Gebäude das Werk einer Architektin darstellt.

Construite pour l'administration fédérale de l'aviation civile sur un terrain appartenant à Los Angeles, cette tour a été volontairement soumise à l'avis de la Commission d'architecture du département des affaires culturelles de la ville, ce qui a sans aucun doute amené à compliquer un projet qui devait déjà tenir compte de facteurs aussi délicats que l'activité sismique. Décrit par l'architecte comme «une maison dans l'arbre pour adultes», la tour de 78 m de haut évoque «l'imagerie organique d'un arbre high-tech». Malgré les contraintes déjà mentionnées et la nécessité de témoigner d'un certain respect pour la «soucoupe volante» toute proche du «Theme Building» de l'aéroport (Luckman, Pereira, Becket and Williams, 1960) l'originalité et la forte présence de cette tour de contrôle font que ce curieux bâtiment a toutes les chances de remplacer l'ancien symbole de la ville. Avec ses 1 861 m², la tour, construite sur ossature d'acier, et en béton renforcé de fibre de verre, avec toit métallique et revêtement bleu-vert, a coûté 18,6 millions de $. Dans une profession encore largement dominée par les hommes, il faut noter que cette tour exceptionnelle est l'œuvre d'une femme.

Above: The LAX Control Tower and the Airport Theme Building.
Left: The lower level of the Control Tower.

Oben: Der LAX Control Tower mit dem Airport Theme Building.
Links: Der untere Bereich des Kontrollturms.

Ci-dessus: La tour de contrôle et le «Theme Building» de l'aéroport.
À gauche: Le rez-de-chaussée de la tour.

Siegel Diamond: LAX Control Tower, 1993–95 **143**

Venturi, Scott Brown

Born in 1925, Robert Venturi may be best known in architectural circles for his seminal 1966 book *Complexity and Contradiction in Architecture,* which has been translated into sixteen languages. With his partner Denise Scott Brown and Steve Izenour, he also wrote *Learning from Las Vegas* (1972), which compared Los Angeles and Las Vegas to the "Rome and Florence" of the United States. After a time of "praise of the ugly and ordinary," Venturi and Scott Brown have completed a number of major buildings, which certainly are neither ugly nor ordinary, including the very widely published and discussed National Gallery Sainsbury Wing (London, 1991). Here the architects resolved the extremely complex contextual problems with a certain mastery, despite being obliged to enter the project after the outspoken remarks of H.R.H. the Prince of Wales about another architect's design. Current projects of this forty-eight person office include student centers at Harvard and the University of Delaware, lab buildings at Princeton, Yale, UCLA and the University of Pennsylvania, and an office building for Disney in Orlando, Florida.

Der 1925 geborene Robert Venturi ist in Architekturkreisen wahrscheinlich am besten für sein 1966 erschienenes, zukunftsweisendes Buch »Complexity and Contradiction in Architecture« bekannt, das in 16 Sprachen übersetzt wurde (dt. Komplexität und Widerspruch in der Architektur). Darüber hinaus veröffentlichte er, zusammen mit seiner Partnerin Denise Scott Brown und Steve Izenour, das Buch »Learning from Las Vegas« (1972, dt. Lernen von Las Vegas), in dem Los Angeles und Las Vegas als »Rom und Florenz« der Vereinigten Staaten bezeichnet werden. Nach einer Phase des »Lobes für alles Häßliche und Gewöhnliche« haben Venturi und Scott Brown eine Reihe von Großprojekten realisiert, die mit Sicherheit weder häßlich noch gewöhnlich genannt werden können, wie etwa den Sainsbury-Flügel der National Gallery (London, 1991), dessen Entwurf großes öffentliches Interesse erregte. In diesem Fall lösten die Architekten die Probleme der extrem komplexen baulichen Umgebung mit großer Meisterschaft, obwohl sie erst für dieses Projekt verpflichtet wurden, nachdem der Prince of Wales den Entwurf eines anderen Architekten unverblümt kritisiert hatte. Zu den aktuellen Projekten des 48 Mitarbeiter starken Architekturbüros gehören Studentenzentren in Harvard und an der University of Delaware, Laborgebäude in Princeton, Yale, an der UCLA und der University of Pennsylvania sowie ein Bürogebäude für Disney in Orlando, Florida.

Né en 1925, Robert Venturi est d'abord connu des cercles architecturaux pour son livre fondamental «Complexité et contradiction en architecture» (1966), traduit en 16 langues. Avec son associée, Denise Scott Brown, et Steve Izenour, il a également écrit «L'enseignement de Las Vegas» (1972), qui voit dans Los Angeles et Las Vegas les Rome et Florence des États-Unis. Après une période «d'éloge du laid et de l'ordinaire», Venturi et Scott Brown ont réalisé un certain nombre d'importants chantiers qui ne sont certainement ni laids ni ordinaires, dont la très souvent reproduite et très discutée aile Sainsbury de la National Gallery de Londres (1991). Les architectes ont résolu à cette occasion avec une certaine maîtrise des problèmes contextuels extrêmement complexes, sans trop se soucier des remarques acerbes du prince de Galles sur les propositions d'un autre architecte. Les projets actuels de leur agence de 48 collaborateurs comprennent des centres pour étudiants à Harvard et à l'université du Delaware, des laboratoires pour Princeton, Yale, UCLA et l'université de Pennsylvanie, et un immeuble de bureaux pour Disney à Orlando, Floride.

Museum of Contemporary Art, San Diego, La Jolla, California, 1986–96.

Museum of Contemporary Art, San Diego, La Jolla, Kalifornien, 1986–96.

Museum of Contemporary Art, San Diego, La Jolla, Californie, 1986–96.

Museum of Contemporary Art

San Diego, La Jolla, California, 1986–1996

Founded in 1941, and located since that date in the 1915 Scripps House designed by Irving Gill, the San Diego Museum of Contemporary Art has a collection of 3,000 works of art, including painting, sculpture, installation art, drawings, prints, photography, video and multimedia. Slowed by fund-raising difficulties, the $9.25 million project doubles the available exhibition space of an institution that also has a location in San Diego itself. Making a coherent whole out of a museum originally intended as a private residence and modified subsequently to fit its new role is a considerable task, which Robert Venturi and Denise Scott Brown seem here to have fulfilled with a sense of contextual harmony. In a much larger project, the Sainsbury Wing of the National Gallery of Art in London, the same pair managed to insert new architecture into a very complex and politically sensitive environment, so their success in La Jolla should come as no surprise. A second phase of the project, not yet under way, would include art storage areas and gallery space in the northwest corner of the site.

Das Museum of Contemporary Art wurde 1941 gegründet und in den Räumen des von Irving Gill 1915 entworfenen Scripps House untergebracht. Es besitzt eine Sammlung von etwa 3 000 Kunstwerken aus den Bereichen Malerei, Bildhauerei, Installationskunst, Zeichnung, Radierung, Fotografie, Video und Multimedia. Das 9,25 Millionen teure Projekt, dessen Bau durch Etatprobleme verzögert wurde, verdoppelt die Ausstellungsfläche einer Einrichtung, die in San Diego über eine Dependance verfügt. Durch die Erweiterung und Neugestaltung eines ursprünglich als Privathaus gedachten Gebäudes zu einem einheitlichen Museum haben Venturi und Brown eine große Aufgabe mit viel Gefühl für den Kontext gemeistert. Aber da es ihnen bereits zuvor bei einem sehr viel größeren Projekt – dem Sainsbury-Flügel der National Gallery of Art in London – gelang, neue Architektur in eine komplexe und politisch sensible Bebauung einzufügen, überrascht ihr Erfolg kaum. Die zweite, noch nicht begonnene Bauphase des Projektes soll im nordwestlichen Teil des Geländes weitere Magazinräume und Ausstellungsflächen zur Verfügung stellen.

Fondé en 1941 et installé dans la Scripps House de Irving Gill (1915), le San Diego Museum of Contemporary Art possède une collection de 3 000 œuvres: peintures, sculptures, installations, dessins, estampes, photographies, vidéo et multimédia. Ralenti par la difficulté de trouver des fonds, le projet actuel (9,25 millions de $) double l'espace d'exposition de cette institution qui possède également une annexe à San Diego. Faire un ensemble cohérent d'un musée installé dans une demeure privée et modifiée pour remplir son nouveau rôle a représenté un travail considérable pour Robert Venturi et Denise Scott Brown. Ils l'ont accompli avec un sens poussé de l'harmonie par rapport au contexte. Dans un projet beaucoup plus important, l'aile Sainsbury de la National Gallery of Art de Londres, ce couple d'architectes avait déjà réussi à insérer une architecture actuelle dans un environnement complexe et politiquement sensible. Leur réussite à La Jolla n'est donc pas surprenante. Une seconde phase de ce projet, qui n'a pas encore été lancée, devrait inclure des espaces de conservation et une nouvelle galerie au nord-ouest du terrain.

Though they once praised the virtues of the "ugly and ordinary" in architecture, Venturi and Scott Brown took great pains to respect the work of Irving Gill, one of the outstanding early modern American architects.

Obwohl sie früher die Tugenden des »Häßlichen und Gewöhnlichen« in der Architektur lobten, unternahmen Venturi und Scott Brown große Anstrengungen, das Werk von Irving Gill – einem der herausragendsten amerikanischen Architekten des späten 19. und frühen 20. Jahrhunderts – mit dem gebührenden Respekt zu behandeln.

Architectes qui louèrent jadis les vertus «de la laideur et de l'ordinaire», Venturi et Scott Brown ont pris le plus grand soin à respecter l'œuvre d'Irving Gill, l'un des plus grands architectes américains modernes.

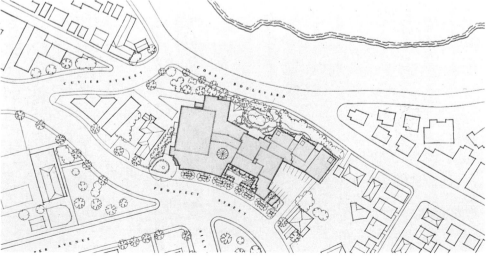

Venturi, Scott Brown: Museum of Contemporary Art, 1986–96 **147**

*One of the intriguing features of this project is that it is
very difficult, at least for the untrained eye, to spot
just where Venturi and Scott Brown intervened, and
where they left some of the original lines of the Irving
Gill house to appear.*

*Einer der faszinierendsten Aspekte dieses Projektes
besteht darin, daß – zumindest für das ungeübte Auge
– schwer zu erkennen ist, an welchen Stellen Venturi
und Scott Brown architektonische Eingriffe vornahmen
und wo sie die ursprüngliche Linienführung von Irving
Gills Gebäude unberührt ließen.*

*L'un des aspects les plus étonnants de ce projet est qu'il
est très difficile, au moins pour un œil non exercé, de
repérer les interventions des architectes, et les parties
conservées du bâtiment original de Gill.*

Rafael Viñoly

Rafael Viñoly is an unusual figure in the world of contemporary architecture. Born in Montevideo, Uruguay in 1944, and having completed his studies in Buenos Aires in 1969, he formed the Estudio de Arquitectura with six associates, which ultimately became one of the largest architecture practices in South America. Invited to teach at Washington University in 1978, he changed countries, establishing Rafael Viñoly Architects in New York in 1983. Working for a decade on smaller projects, he won the competition for the Tokyo International Forum in 1989 and went on to become one of the first Western architects licensed to practice in Japan. Undoubtedly one of the most complex projects of the past decade anywhere in the world, because of its dimensions, and because of its decidedly cross-cultural origins, the Forum retains a geometric power that imposes its presence beyond the sheer physical volume of the structure. It was this that undoubtedly retained the attention of the prestigious jury. Rafael Viñoly's current projects include the Samsung World Pulse Headquarters, Seoul, Korea (1998) and the New Bronx Criminal Court Complex, Bronx, New York (2001).

Rafael Viñoly ist eine ungewöhnliche Persönlichkeit in der zeitgenössischen Architekturszene. Er wurde 1944 in Montevideo geboren und gründete nach Abschluß seines Studiums in Buenos Aires 1969 zusammen mit sechs Partnern das Estudio de Arquitectura, das sich zu einem der größten Architekturbüros Südamerikas entwickelte. Nach einem Lehrauftrag an der Washington University 1978 blieb er in den Vereinigten Staaten und gründete 1983 in New York Rafael Viñoly Architects. Nach einem Jahrzehnt der Arbeit an kleineren Projekten gewann Viñoly 1989 den Wettbewerb für das Tokyo International Forum und wurde einer der ersten westlichen Architekten, die eine Arbeitserlaubnis in Japan erhielten. Von Viñolys Forum, das aufgrund seiner Ausmaße und seiner bewußt multikulturellen Ursprünge zu den weltweit komplexesten Projekten der letzten zehn Jahre gehört, geht eine geometrische Kraft aus, die ihre Präsenz weit über den rein physikalischen Umfang des Gebäudes hinaus geltend macht und die zweifellos die Aufmerksamkeit der renommierten Jury auf sich gezogen haben dürfte. Zu Rafael Viñolys aktuellen Projekten zählen das Samsung World Pulse Headquarters, Seoul (1998) und der New Bronx Criminal Court Complex, Bronx, New York (2001).

Rafael Viñoly est une figure inhabituelle dans le monde de l'architecture contemporaine. Né à Montevideo, Uruguay, en 1944, il achève ses études à Buenos Aires en 1969, et crée avec six associés le Estudio de Arquitectura qui deviendra l'une des premières agences d'Amérique du Sud. Invité à enseigner à Washington University en 1978, il émigre et fonde Rafael Viñoly Architects à New York en 1983. Travaillant pendant dix ans sur de petits projets, il remporte le concours du Forum international de Tokyo en 1989, et sera l'un des premiers architectes occidentaux à pouvoir exercer au Japon. Certainement l'un des projets au monde les plus complexes de la décennie écoulée, et du fait de ses origines transculturelles, le Forum affiche la puissante présence d'une géométrie qui va bien au-delà du seul volume physique. C'est sans doute cet effet qui a retenu l'attention du prestigieux jury chargé de sélectionner un architecte. Les projets actuels de Rafael Viñoly concernent le Samsung World Pulse Headquarters, Séoul, Corée (1998), et le nouvel ensemble du tribunal correctionnel du Bronx, New York (2001).

Tokyo International Forum, Tokyo, Japan, 1989–96.
Tokyo International Forum, Tokio, Japan, 1989–96.
Forum international de Tokyo, Tokyo, Japon, 1989–96.

Tokyo International Forum
Tokyo, Japan, 1989–1996

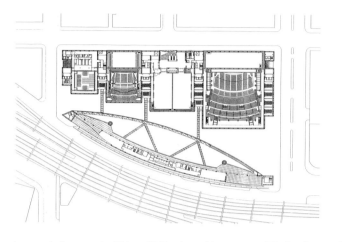

Located close to the Tokyo JR Station, this enormous 130,000 square meter complex will have cost more than $1.6 billion to build, making it one of the more visible and expensive monuments to the era of Japanese real estate optimism, a period referred to in Japan as the "Bubble years." Chosen from amongst 395 entries from fifty different countries, the project of Rafael Viñoly features the largest theater in Tokyo (5,000 seats) as well as a Glass Hall measuring 191 meters in length, 30 meters in width and no less than 57 meters in height. In a country where fears of seismic activity are well founded, such a 3,000 ton skylight is almost unheard of. Occupying the site of the former Tokyo City Hall built by Kenzo Tange in 1956, the International Forum benefits from a site of almost 3 hectares in a city renowned for its extremely restrictive real estate market. Although before the Forum even opened, it was charged that the complex is a "white elephant," the simple geometric vocabulary employed by the architect in a project that typically required as many as 3,000 construction workers at any one time is a testimony to the quality of the jury that chose Viñoly. It included such figures as Fumihiko Maki, I.M. Pei, Kenzo Tange, Vittorio Gregotti and Arthur Erickson.

Die Baukosten für den in unmittelbarer Nachbarschaft zur Tokyo JR Station gelegenen, 130 000 m² großen Komplex werden sich auf über 1,6 Milliarden Dollar belaufen, wodurch das Forum zu den besonders auffälligen und kostspieligen Monumenten einer Phase des Optimismus in der japanischen Immobilienwelt zählt, den sogenannten »Seifenblasen-Jahren«. Rafael Viñolys Projekt wurde aus insgesamt 395 Entwürfen aus 50 verschiedenen Ländern ausgewählt und umfaßt neben dem größten Theater Tokios (5 000 Plätze) auch eine »Glass Hall« von 191 m Länge, 30 m Breite und nicht weniger als 57 m Höhe. In einem Land mit beständiger Furcht vor Erdbeben stellt ein solches, 3 000 Tonnen schweres »Oberlicht« ein völliges Novum dar. Das auf dem ehemaligen Grundstück der von Kenzo Tange 1956 errichteten Tokyo City Hall gelegene International Forum profitiert von einem fast 3 ha großen Gelände in einer Stadt, die für ihren extrem restriktiven Immobilienmarkt bekannt ist. Obwohl das Forum noch kurz vor seiner Eröffnung als »teures, aber unerwünschtes und völlig nutzloses Bauwerk« eingestuft wurde, ist dieses Gebäude (an dessen Errichtung ständig 3 000 Bauarbeiter beteiligt waren) mit seiner schlichten geometrischen Formensprache ein Zeugnis für die Qualität der Jury – zu der u.a. Fumihiko Maki, I.M. Pei, Kenzo Tange, Vittorio Gregotti und Arthur Erickson gehörten.

Situé non loin de la gare JR de Tokyo, cet énorme complexe de 130 000 m² aura coûté plus de 1,6 milliard de $, ce qui en fait l'un des plus visibles et plus coûteux monuments de l'ère de l'optimisme immobilier japonais, période également appelée «bulle financière». Choisi au milieu de 395 participations issues de 50 pays, le projet de Rafael Viñoly comprend la plus grande salle de spectacle de Tokyo (5 000 places) et un Hall de verre de 191 m de long, 30 de large et 57 de haut. Dans un pays où la crainte des tremblements de terre est justifiée, une verrière de 3 000 tonnes était presque inimaginable. Occupant le site de l'ancien hôtel de ville de Tokyo construit par Kenzo Tange en 1956, ce Forum international bénéficie d'un terrain de près de 3 ha dans une ville renommée pour la rareté de l'espace. Bien que le Forum ait été qualifié «d'éléphant blanc», avant même qu'il ne soit inauguré, le langage géométrique simple utilisé par l'architecte pour un projet qui a vu plus de trois mille ouvriers travailler en même temps, témoigne de la perspicacité du jury qui a sélectionné Viñoly. Il comptait parmi ses membres des autorités comme Fumihiko Maki, I.M. Pei, Kenzo Tange, Vittorio Gregotti, et Arthur Erickson.

Page 152: *An image of the stairs and escalators leading into the space of the Glass Hall. The Hall is the oblong shape visible on the plan (top).*

Seite 152: *Ansicht der Treppen und Rolltreppen, die in den Bereich der Glass Hall führen. Die Glass Hall entspricht der langgestreckten Form auf dem oben abgebildeten Grundriß.*

Page 152: *Les escaliers et escaliers roulants menant au Hall de verre, évocateur d'un bateau ou d'un immense squelette de baleine. Le Hall est la forme oblongue figurant sur le plan (en haut).*

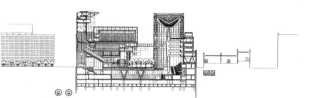

Below: Large trees have been planted in the open spaces between the buildings. The architect has created a contrast in both shape and materials between the curving Glass Hall and the more rigidly geometric boxes where the more functional spaces are concentrated.

Unten: Die offenen Bereiche zwischen den Gebäuden wurden mit großen Bäumen bepflanzt. Der Architekt schuf sowohl in Bezug auf die Form als auch bei der Materialverwendung einen Kontrast zwischen der gekrümmten Glass Hall und den geometrischen Kastenformen, die Funktionsräume beherbergen.

Ci-dessous: De grands arbres ont été plantés dans les espaces ouverts entre les bâtiments. L'architecte a créé un contraste à la fois de forme et de matériaux entre les courbes du Hall de verre et les «boîtes» plus géométriques qui contiennent les espaces fonctionnels.

Above: The space created between the curving shell of the Glass Hall and the more block-like forms of the convention spaces. The tracks leading to the Tokyo JR Station pass just behind the Forum.

Oben: Der Bereich zwischen der gekrümmten Schalenkonstruktion der Glass Hall und den Kongreßsälen. Die Gleise zur Tokyo JR Station verlaufen direkt hinter dem Forum.

Ci-dessus: L'espace créé entre la coquille du Hall de verre et les espaces plus rectilignes et en forme de bloc des espaces de congrès. Les voies d'accès à la gare JR de Tokyo passent juste derrière le Forum.

The Glass Hall, with its Piranesian bridges, is one of the more spectacular interior spaces to be created anywhere in the world in recent years. **Below:** The Forum's theaters and supporting structures.

Die Glass Hall mit ihren an Piranesi erinnernden Brückenkonstruktionen ist weltweit einer der aufsehenerregendsten Innenräume der letzten Jahre. **Unten:** Die Theatersäle und Stützpfeiler des Forums.

Le Hall de verre et ses passerelles piranésiennes est l'un des espaces intérieurs les plus spectaculaires créés dans le monde au cours de ces dernières années. **Ci-dessous:** Les salles du Forum, et les structures de soutènement.

Tod Williams,
Billie Tsien

Tod Williams was born in Detroit in 1943, and Billie Tsien in Ithaca, New York in 1949. After six years as an associate architect in the office of Richard Meier (1967–73), Williams founded his firm in New York in 1974., and created Tod Williams, Billie Tsien and Associates in 1986. Frequently linking the worlds of art and architecture, in 1989, Williams and Tsien organized a traveling exhibition in collaboration with the Walker Art Center on the theme "Domestic Arrangements: a La Report," about the relationship between the foundations of modernism and their reality in the contemporary environment. Their work includes Feinberg Hall (Princeton, New Jersey, 1986); New College, University of Virginia (Charlottesville, Virginia, 1992), with its strong, simple volumes in brick and glass; sets and costumes for "The World Upside Down," (Het Musiektheater, Amsterdam, The Netherlands, 1991) as well as the newly completed renovation and extension of the Museum of Fine Arts in Phoenix, Arizona. Williams has taught at Harvard, Yale, the University of Virginia, and the Southern California Institute of Architecture (SCI-Arc), while Billie Tsien has taught at Parsons School of Design, SCI-Arc, Harvard and Yale.

Tod Williams wurde 1943 in Detroit, Billie Tsien 1949 in Ithaca, New York geboren. Nach sechs Jahren als Mitarbeiter im Büro von Richard Meier (1967–73) gründete Williams 1974 in New York seine eigene Firma; 1986 entstand Tod Williams, Billie Tsien and Associates. 1989 organisierten Williams und Tsien – die häufig Kunst und Architektur miteinander verbinden – in Zusammenarbeit mit dem Walker Art Center eine Wanderausstellung unter dem Titel »Domestic Arrangements: a La Report«, die die Beziehungen zwischen den Grundlagen der Moderne und ihrer Wirklichkeit in der zeitgenössischen Umgebung zum Thema hatte. Zu Williams' und Tsiens Arbeiten gehören Feinberg Hall (Princeton, New Jersey, 1986); New College, University of Virginia (Charlottesville, Virginia, 1992), mit seinen kompakten, schlichten Baukörpern aus Ziegelstein und Glas; Bühnenausstattung und Kostüme für »The World Upside Down« (Het Muziektheater, Amsterdam, 1991) sowie die vor kurzem fertiggestellte Neugestaltung und Erweiterung des Museum of Fine Arts in Phoenix, Arizona. Williams unterrichtete in Harvard, Yale, an der University of Virginia sowie am Southern California Institute of Architecture (SCI-Arc), während Billie Tsien an der Parsons School of Design, am SCI-Arc, in Harvard und in Yale lehrte.

Ted Williams naît à Detroit en 1943, et Billie Tsien à Ithaca, New York, en 1949. Après six ans comme architecte associé dans l'agence de Richard Meier (1967–73), Williams crée son agence à New York en 1974, et Tod Williams, Billie Tsien and Associates en 1986. Reliant souvent les univers de l'art et de l'architecture, Williams et Tsien organisent une exposition itinérante en collaboration avec le Walker Art Center sur le thème: «Domestic Arrangements: a La Report», sur la relation entre les principes fondateurs du modernisme et leur réalité dans un environnement contemporain. Réalisations: Feinberg Hall (Princeton, New Jersey, 1986); New College, University of Virginia (Charlottesville, Virginie, 1992), aux solides et simples volumes de brique et de verre; décors et costumes pour «The World Upside Down», (Het Musiektheater, Amsterdam, Pays-Bas, 1991); restauration complète et extension du Museum of Fine Arts de Phoenix, Arizona. Williams a enseigné à Harvard, Yale, l'université de Virginie, et au Southern California Institute of Architecture (SCI-ARC), et Billie Tsien à la Parsons School of Design, SCI-ARC, Harvard et Yale.

Neurosciences Institute, San Diego, La Jolla, California, 1993–95.

Neurosciences Institute, San Diego, La Jolla, Kalifornien, 1993–95.

Neurosciences Institute, San Diego, La Jolla, Californie, 1993–95.

Neurosciences Institute

San Diego, La Jolla, California, 1993–1995

Intended by its founder, Nobel Prize winner Gerald Edelman, to be a "scientific monastery," the Neurosciences Institute is intentionally difficult to perceive in its totality. Unlike the Salk Institute (Louis Kahn, 1960), which is just up Torrey Pines Road, the NSI does not look to the kind of monumental simplicity for which the earlier building is justifiably famous. Rather, the 5,200 square meter, three-building complex offers a different aspect from any given point of view, although the composition does converge around a central court, intended as a place of meeting for the scientists working there. Edelman's theory of "Neural Darwinism," or the development of the capacity of the brain as a function of its individual circumstances, seems here to have found a natural counterpart in built form. The NSI includes a 1,675 square meter Theory Center, 2,340 square meters of laboratories, an auditorium and a utility building. Materials include Cordoba shell limestone, sandblasted concrete, natural split serpentine, honed serpentine, red wood veneers and solids, glass bead blasted stainless steel, and sandblasted and sealed laminated glass.

Das von seinem Gründer, dem Nobelpreisträger Gerald Edelman, als »Wissenschafts-Kloster« geplante Neurosciences Institute ist bewußt nur schwer als Ganzes zu erfassen. Im Gegensatz zum nahegelegenen Salk Institute (Louis Kahn, 1960) an der Torrey Pines Road strebt das NSI nicht die monumentale Schlichtheit an, für das das früher errichtete Bauwerk zurecht berühmt ist. Statt dessen bietet der 5200 m² große, aus drei Gebäuden bestehenden Komplex aus jedem Blickwinkel einen anderen Anblick – obwohl sich die Konstruktion um einen zentralen Innenhof gruppiert, der als Treffpunkt für die hier tätigen Wissenschaftler dienen soll. Edelmans Theorie des »Neuraldarwinismus« oder der Entwicklung des menschlichen Gehirns in Relation zu den individuellen Umständen scheint hier in der gebauten Form ein natürliches Pendant gefunden zu haben. Das NSI umfaßt ein 1 675 m² großes Theory Center, 2 340 m² Fläche für Laborräume sowie ein Auditorium und ein Versorgungsgebäude. Es wurde aus Cordoba-Muschelkalk, sandgestrahltem Beton, natürlich gespaltenem und glatt geschliffenem Serpentinmarmor, Furnieren und Massivholzbalken aus Rotholz, glasgestrahltem Edelstahl sowie sandgestrahltem Verbundglas errichtet.

Conçu par son fondateur, le Prix Nobel Gerald Edelman, comme un «monastère scientifique», c'est volontairement que le Neurosciences Institute est difficile à percevoir en totalité. À la différence du Salk Institute voisin (Louis Kahn, 1960), le NSI n'a pas recherché la simplicité monumentale qui a rendu à juste titre son voisin célèbre. Cet ensemble de trois bâtiments couvrant 5 200 m² offre au contraire des aspects très variés selon les points de vue, même si sa composition converge sur une cour centrale, lieu de réunion pour les chercheurs. La théorie d'Edelman du «darwinisme neuronal», ou du développement de la capacité du cerveau en fonction des circonstances individuelles, semble avoir trouvé là sa traduction architecturale. Le NSI comprend un Centre de théorie de 1 675 m², 2 340 m² de laboratoires, un auditorium, et un bâtiment pour les services. Les matériaux utilisés sont la pierre coquillière de Cordoba, le béton sablé, le marbre serpentin, le séquoia massif ou en placage, l'acier inoxydable traité aux billes de verre, le verre sablé et laminé.

The Neurosciences Institute was conceived as a "small campus organized around its own courtyard." According to the architects, "the primary feeling is one of active contemplation. The space is serene, but not static."

Das Neurosciences Institute wurde als »kleiner Campus rund um einen eigenen Innenhof« konzipiert. Laut Aussage der Architekten »verströmt es ein Gefühl der aktiven Kontemplation. Der Platz ist ruhig, aber nicht statisch.«

Le Neurosciences Institute a été conçu comme «un petit campus organisé autour de sa propre cour». Selon les architectes, «le sentiment premier est celui de contemplation active. L'espace est serein, mais non statique».

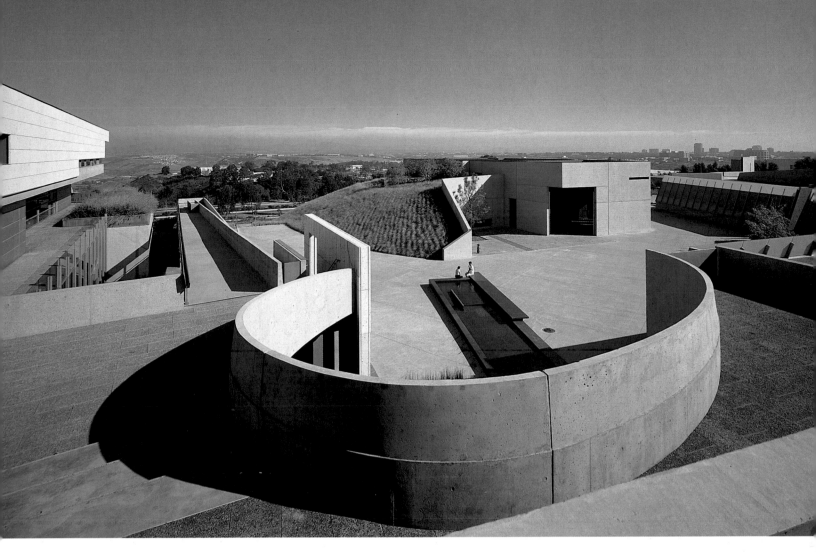

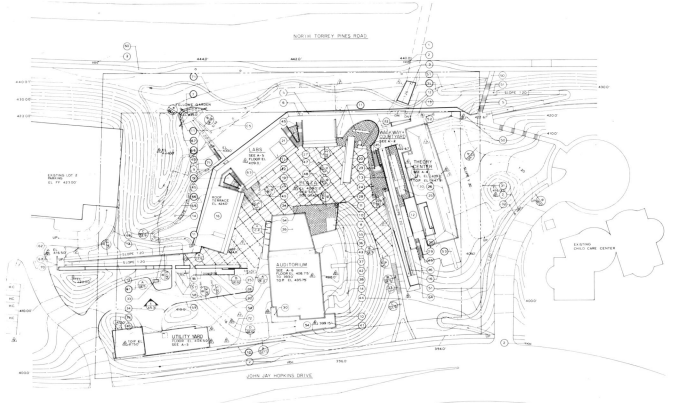

Extremely complex plans make clear the interaction of the various sections of the three-building complex which form a highly detailed and differentiated whole.

Komplexe Pläne veranschaulichen das Verhältnis der verschiedenen Bereiche des Drei-Gebäudekomplexes zueinander, die zusammen ein stark detailliertes und differenziertes Ganzes ergeben.

Les plans extrêmement complexes montrent clairement l'interaction des différentes sections de cet ensemble de trois bâtiments, qui forme un tout différencié et extrêmement détaillé.

Lebbeus Woods

Lebbeus Woods is by any measure of the term an unusual figure in the world of contemporary architecture. Born in 1940 in Lansing, Michigan, he was educated at Purdue University School of Engineering, and at the University of Illinois School of Architecture. After working with Eero Saarinen and Associates (later Roche Dinkeloo) on the John Deere and Ford Foundation Headquarters Building projects, he decided to become a theoretician after 1976, abandoning built works for progressively more and more remarkable drawings. Though some contemporary American architects like John Hejduk have exerted considerable influence while actually building very little, Woods is exceptional in that he puts his considerable talents as a draftsman trained in engineering and architecture to use creating imaginary environments that could, according to him, actually be built. He has done this in such projects as his Underground Berlin (1988), Zagreb Freespace Structure (1991), or more recent Apartment Blocks (1994) conceived for the reconstruction of war-damaged modernist apartment complexes in Sarajevo.

Lebbeus Woods kann mit Recht als ungewöhnliche Persönlichkeit in der zeitgenössischen Architekturszene bezeichnet werden. Der 1940 in Lansing, Michigan geborene Woods studierte an der School of Engineering der Purdue University und an der University of Illinois School of Architecture. Nachdem er im Büro von Eero Saarinen and Associates (später Roche Dinkeloo) an den Projekten für das John Deere and Ford Foundation Headquarters Building beteiligt war, entschloß er sich 1976, Theoretiker zu werden und das praktische Bauen zugunsten immer aufsehenerregender Entwürfe aufzugeben. Obwohl einige zeitgenössische amerikanische Architekten wie John Hejduk auch ohne nennenswerte eigene Bautätigkeit einen beträchtlichen Einfluß auf die Architektur ausübten, ist Woods insofern außergewöhnlich, als er seine erstaunlichen Fähigkeiten als bautechnischer Zeichner zur Gestaltung imaginärer bebauter Umgebungen nutzt, die seiner Ansicht nach auch tatsächlich realisiert werden könnten. So entstanden Projekte wie sein Underground Berlin (1988), Zagreb Freespace Structure (1991) oder, aus jüngster Zeit, Apartment Blocks (1994), das Woods für den Wiederaufbau der durch den Krieg beschädigten modernen Apartmentkomplexe in Sarajevo entwarf.

Lebbeus Woods est à tous égards un représentant inhabituel de l'univers de l'architecture contemporaine. Né en 1940 à Lansing, Michigan, il étudie à l'école d'ingénieurs de Purdue University et à l'école d'architecture de l'université de l'Illinois. Après avoir travaillé avec Eero Saarinen and Associates (devenu Roche Dinkeloo), sur les sièges sociaux de John Deere et de la Ford Foundation, il décide après 1976 de se consacrer à la théorie et à des dessins de plus en plus remarquables. Si d'autres architectes américains comme John Hejduk ont exercé une influence considérable sans réellement beaucoup construire, le cas de Woods est exceptionnel dans la mesure où il se sert de son considérable talent de dessinateur et de ses connaissances en architecture et en ingénierie pour créer des environnements imaginaires qui, selon lui, peuvent être construits. Il s'est ainsi exercé sur des projets comme Underground Berlin (1988), Zagreb Freespace Structure (1991), ou plus récemment ses Apartments Blocks (1994) pour la reconstruction d'immeubles modernistes ayant souffert de la guerre civile à Sarajevo.

Lebbeus Woods, Havana Project, Havana, Cuba, 1995.

Lebbeus Woods, Havana Project, Havanna, Kuba, 1995.

Lebbeus Woods, Havana Project, La Havane, Cuba, 1995.

Havana Project

Havana, Cuba, 1995

Lebbeus Woods has participated in several projects organized by Peter Noever, Director of the Österreichisches Museum für Angewandte Kunst in Vienna. The most recent of these, the International Conference on Contemporary Architecture, held in Havana, Cuba in January 1995, gave rise to his Havana Project, which is a proposal for a dynamic reassessment of the architectural needs of this city. The drawings of Woods, together with proposals on the same theme by Coop Himmelblau, Zaha Hadid, Steven Holl, Thom Mayne, Eric Owen Moss, and Carme Pinós, were conceived for a 1996 exhibition, held in the renovated Schindler House (1922) in Los Angeles, whose theme was the movement toward "architecture that comprises complexity, sensitivity, and dynamics; architecture that focuses on the human being and withstands commercial definitions; architecture that copes with new tasks as well as the old traditional ones – an everyday architecture that yet contains the claim of universality and topicality – architecture as a universal and unifying metaphor of space, time and body." Although they do bear some comparison to the work of cartoonists, the drawings of Lebbeus Woods are based on a solid knowledge of the technical aspects of architecture.

Lebbeus Woods nahm an mehreren von Peter Noever, dem Direktor des Österreichischen Museums für Angewandte Kunst in Wien organisierten Projekten teil. Die aktuellste dieser Veranstaltungen, die Internationale Konferenz für Zeitgenössische Architektur, fand im Januar 1995 in Havanna statt; dabei wurde das »Havana Project« ins Leben gerufen, das als Vorschlag für eine dynamische Neubeurteilung der architektonischen Bedürfnisse dieser Stadt konzipiert ist. Zusammen mit den Beiträgen von Coop Himmelblau, Zaha Hadid, Steven Holl, Thom Mayne, Eric Owen Moss und Carme Pinós wurden Lebbeus Woods Zeichnungen für eine Ausstellung entworfen, die 1996 im restaurierten Schindler House (1922) in Los Angeles stattfand und deren Thema die Entwicklung einer Architektur sein sollte, »die Komplexität, Sensibilität und Dynamik umfaßt; eine Architektur, die sich auf den Menschen konzentriert und kommerziellen Definitionen widersteht; eine Architektur, die die neuen Aufgaben ebenso meistert wie die alten, traditionellen – eine alltägliche Architektur, die dennoch den Anspruch der Universalität und Aktualität enthält – Architektur als universelle und vereinigende Metapher von Raum, Zeit und Gesellschaft.« Obwohl seine Zeichnungen eine gewisse Ähnlichkeit mit dem Werk eines Trickzeichners aufweisen, beruhen Lebbeus Woods Arbeiten auf einem fundierten Wissen der technischen Aspekte der Architektur.

Lebbeus Woods a participé à plusieurs projets organisés par Peter Noever, directeur de l'Österreichisches Museum für Angewandte Kunst de Vienne. Le plus récent d'entre eux, la conférence internationale d'architecture contemporaine, tenue à La Havane (Cuba) en janvier 1995, a permis à ce «Havana Project» de naître. Il s'agit d'une proposition de réévaluation dynamique des besoins architecturaux de cette ville. Les dessins de Woods, avec les propositions sur le même thème de Coop Himmelblau, Zaha Hadid, Steven Holl, Thom Mayne, Eric Owen Moss, et Carme Pinós, ont été conçus pour une exposition tenue en 1996 à Los Angeles dans la Schindler House rénovée, dont le thème était le mouvement vers «une architecture qui prenne en compte la complexité, la sensibilité et la dynamique; une architecture qui se concentre sur l'être humain, et résiste aux définitions commerciales; une architecture qui traite aussi bien des tâches nouvelles que des anciennes – une architecture de tous les jours qui maintienne néanmoins une prétention à l'universalité et à l'actualité – une architecture comme métaphore universelle et unificatrice de l'espace, du temps, et du corps». Bien qu'ils puissent être comparés à certaines bandes dessinées, les dessins de Lebbeus Woods reposent sur une solide connaissance des aspects techniques de l'architecture.

Although Lebbeus Woods does not go so far as to specifically choose construction materials for his imagined buildings, he does say that he would prefer metal or wood to brick, for example.

Obwohl Lebbeus Woods nicht so weit geht, spezielle Baumaterialien für seine erdachten Bauwerke vorzuschlagen, gibt er durchaus zu erkennen, daß er Metall oder Holz Ziegelstein vorziehen würde.

Si Lebbeus Woods ne va pas jusqu'à spécifiquement choisir les matériaux de construction des bâtiments qu'il imagine, il insiste sur le fait, qu'il préfère le métal où le bois à la brique.

Pages 168–169: *An overall view of the old part of Havana, with the wall-like structure imagined by Lebbeus Woods cutting past it, and marking its boundary from the newer areas of the city.*

Seite 168–169: *Gesamtansicht der Altstadt von Havanna, mit der von Lebbeus Woods erdachten, mauerartigen Konstruktion, die die Grenze zu neueren Stadtteilen markiert.*

Pages 168–169: *Vue générale des vieux quartiers de La Havane, avec la structure en forme de mur imaginée par Lebbeus Woods, qui marque une séparation avec les parties plus récentes de la ville.*

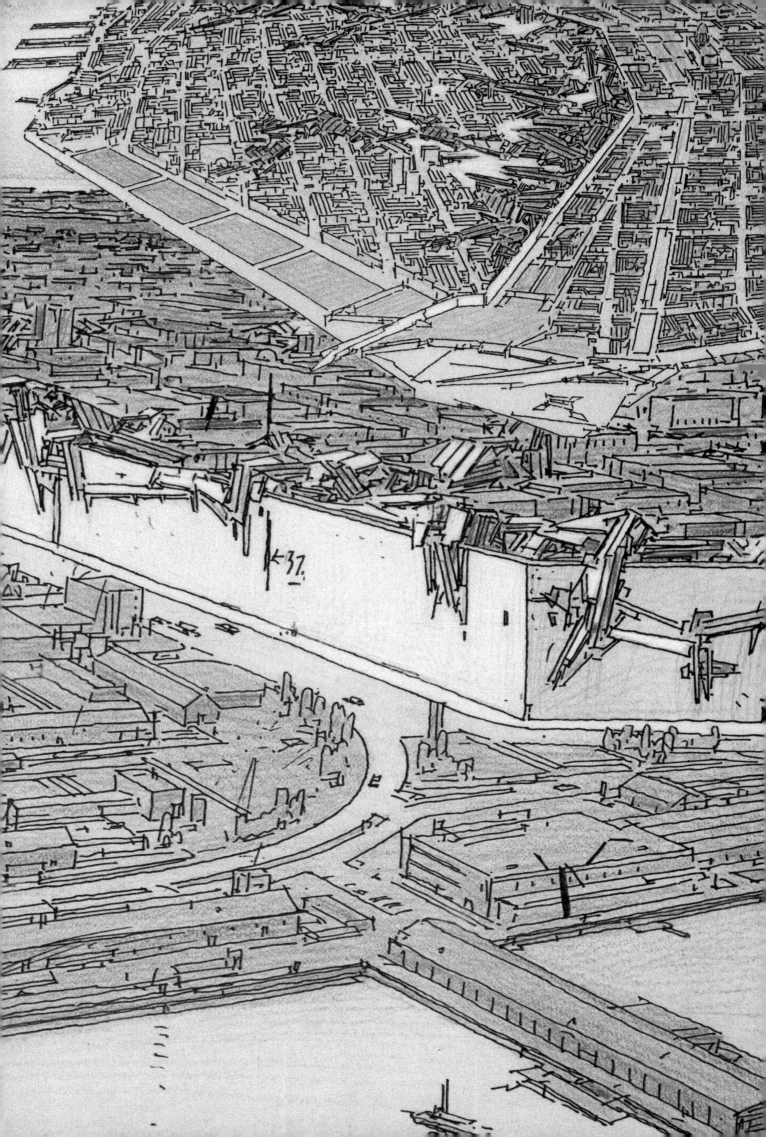

Arquitectonica
426 Jefferson Avenue
Miami Beach, Florida 33139
Tel: + 1 305 372 1812
Fax: + 1 305 372 1175

Centerbrook Architects
P.O. Box 955
Essex, Connecticut 06426
Tel: + 1 860 767 0175
Fax: + 1 860 767 8719

Steven Ehrlich Architects
2210 Colorado Avenue
Santa Monica, California 90404
Tel: + 1 310 828 6700
Fax: + 1 310 828 7710

Eisenman Architects
41 West 25th Street
New York, NY 10010
Tel: + 1 212 645 1400
Fax: + 1 212 645 0725

Frank O. Gehry & Associates
1520-B Cloverfield Boulevard
Santa Monica, California 90404
Tel: + 1 310 828 6088
Fax: + 1 310 828 2098

Arquitectonica

Bernardo Fort-Brescia was born in Lima, Peru in 1951. B. Arch., Princeton, 1973. M. Arch., Harvard, 1975. Principal of Arquitectonica since founding in 1977 in Miami. Laurinda Hope Spear was born in Rochester, Minnesota in 1950. M. Arch. Columbia, 1975. Master in City Planning, M.I.T. Principal of Arquitectonica with her husband since its founding. Major projects: Spear House, Miami (1976–78); The Atlantis, Miami (1980–82); Banco de Crédito, Lima, Peru (1983–88); North Dade Justice Center, Miami (1984–87); Banque de Luxembourg Headquarters, Luxembourg (1994). Current work includes a hotel tower in Times Square, New York, and Miami International Airport.

Bernardo Fort-Brescia wurde 1951 in Lima, Peru geboren. B. Arch. Princeton 1973; M. Arch., Harvard 1975. Er leitet Arquitectonica seit der Gründung 1977 in Miami. Laurinda Hope Spear wurde 1950 in Rochester, Minnesota geboren. Master of Architecture, Columbia University 1975, Master in City Planning am Massachusetts Institute of Technology. Leitet Arquitectonica seit der Gründung zusammen mit ihrem Mann. Projekte: Spear House, Miami (1976–78); The Atlantis, Miami (1980–82); Banco de Crédito, Lima, Peru (1983–88); North Dade Justice Center, Miami (1984–87); Zentrale der Banque de Luxembourg, Luxemburg (1994). Zu den aktuellen Projekten zählen ein Hotelturm am New Yorker Times Square und der Miami International Airport.

Bernardo Fort-Brescia naît à Lima, Pérou, en 1951. B. Arch. à Princeton en 1973, M. Arch. à Harvard, en 1975. Responsable d'Arquitectonica depuis sa fondation en 1977 à Miami. Laurinda Hope Spear naît à Rochester, Minnesota, en 1950. M. Arch. à Columbia, 1975. Master en urbanisme au M.I.T. Co-responsable d'Arquitectonica avec son mari, depuis sa fondation. Principales réalisations: Spear House, Miami (1976–78); The Atlantis, Miami (1980–82); Banco de Crédito, Lima, Pérou (1983–88); North Dade Justice Center, Miami (1984–87); siège de la Banque de Luxembourg, Luxembourg (1994). Ils travaillent actuellement sur une tour-hôtel à Times Square, New York, et l'aéroport international de Miami.

Centerbrook

Mark Simon received his B. A. in sculpture from Brandeis University (1968), and his M. Arch. from Yale (1972). He is one of five partners in Centerbrook Architects and Planners. Having initially worked as a cabinet maker, and later in the office of Warren Platner, Simon joined Charles Moore Associates (1974–75) and collaborated on a series of houses (1975–84). He became a partner in Moore Grover Harper (now Centerbrook) in 1978. The firm has built numerous private houses such as the Marsh Estate, East Coast (1991). They also built the Hood Museum of Art, Dartmouth College, Hanover, New Hampshire (1985). Current work includes a Chemistry Building at University of Connecticut (1997) and the University of Colorado Health Sciences Center and Campus Center, Denver, Colorado (2002).

Mark Simon studierte Bildhauerei an der Brandeis University (B. A. 1968) sowie Architektur in Yale (M. Arch. 1972) und ist heute einer der fünf Partner von Centerbrook Architects and Planners. Nachdem er zunächst als Möbeltischler und später im Büro von Warren Platner gearbeitet hatte, kam Simon zu Charles Moore Associates (1974–75), wo er an einer Reihe von Häusern mitarbeitete (1975–84). 1978 wurde Simon Partner bei Moore Grover Harper, dem heutigen Centerbrook. Diese Firma errichtete zahlreiche Privathäuser u.a. das Marsh Estate, Ostküste der USA (1991) sowie das Hood Museum of Art, Dartmouth College, Hanover, New Hampshire (1985). Aktuelle Projekte: Gebäude für die chemische Fakultät der University of Connecticut (1997) und University of Colorado Health Sciences Center and Campus Center, Denver, Colorado (2002).

Mark Simon reçoit son B. A. en sculpture de Brandeis University (1968), et son M. Arch. de Yale (1972). Il est l'un des cinq associés de Centerbrook Architects and Planners. Après avoir initialement travaillé comme ébéniste, puis dans l'agence de Warren Platner, il rejoint Charles Moore Associates (1974–75), et intervient sur une série de maisons (1975–84). Il devient associé de Moore Grover Harper (aujourd'hui Centerbrook) en 1978. L'agence a construit de nombreuses résidences privées comme le Marsh Estate (East Coast, 1991) et réalisé le Hood Museum of Art, Dartmouth College, Hanover, New Hampshire (1985). Elle travaille sur le bâtiment de la chimie à l'université du Connecticut (1997) et l'université du Colorado Health Sciences Center et le campus, Denver, Colorado (2002).

Steven Ehrlich

Born in Radburn, New Jersey in 1946, Steven Ehrlich received his B. Arch. degree from the Rensselaer Polytechnic Institute, Troy, New York (1969). He studied indigenous vernacular architecture in North and West Africa from 1969 to 1977, and taught for three years at Ahmadu Bello University in Zaria, Nigeria. He has completed numerous private residences, including the Friedman Residence (1986), the Ehrman-Coombs Residence, Santa Monica, California (1989–91) and the Schulman Residence, Brentwood (1989–92). Other built work includes the Shatto Recreation Center (1991) and Sony Music Entertainment Campus, Santa Monica, California (1993), and a Child Care Center, also for Sony, Culver City, California (1992–94).

Steven Ehrlich wurde 1946 in Radburn, New Jersey geboren und erhielt 1969 seinen B. Arch. am Rensselaer Polytechnic Institute, Troy, New York. Zwischen 1969 und 1977 beschäftigte er sich intensiv mit der Architektur Nord- und Westafrikas und lehrte drei Jahre an der Ahmadu Bello University in Zaria, Nigeria. Danach errichtete Ehrlich zahlreiche Privathäuser, einschließlich der Friedman Residence (1986), der Ehrman-Coombs Residence, Santa Monica (1989–91) und der Schulman Residence, Brentwood (1989–92). Zu seinen weiteren Werken zählen das Shatto Recreation Center (1991), der Sony Music Entertainment Campus, Santa Monica, Kalifornien (1993) und das Child Care Center, ebenfalls für Sony, Culver City, Kalifornien (1992–94).

Né à Radburn, New Jersey, en 1946, Steven Ehrlich est diplômé d'architecture du Rensselaer Polytechnic Institute, Troy, New York (1969). Il étudie l'architecture vernaculaire de l'Afrique du Nord et de l'Ouest de 1969 à 1977, et enseigne trois ans à l'Ahmadu Bello University de Zaria, Nigéria. Il a réalisé de nombreuses résidences privées, dont la Friedman Residence (1986), la Ehrman-Coombs Residence, Santa Monica, Californie (1989–91), et la Schulman Residence, Brentwood (1989–92). Il a également édifié le Shatto Recreation Center (1991), le Sony Music Entertainment Campus, Santa Monica, Californie (1993) et un Child Care Center, toujours pour Sony, Culver City, Californie (1992–94).

Peter Eisenman

Born in New York in 1932, B. Arch. Cornell, M. Arch. Columbia, Masters and Ph. D. degrees, University of Cambridge, England. Peter Eisenman has taught at Cambridge, Princeton, Yale and Harvard as well as the University of Illinois and Ohio State University. His major projects include the Wexner Center for the Visual Arts, Ohio State University, Columbus Ohio (1982–89); Greater Columbus Convention Center, Columbus, Ohio (1989– 93); Aronoff Center for Design and Art, University of Cincinnati, Cincinnati, Ohio (1988–96); and the unbuilt Max Reinhardt Haus, Berlin, Germany (1995). Current projects include the Center for the Arts, Emory University, Atlanta, Georgia.

Geboren 1932 in New York. B. Arch., Cornell University, M. Arch., Columbia University, Master und Promotion, University of Cambridge, England. Peter Eisenman lehrte in Cambridge, Princeton, Yale und Harvard, an der Universität von Illinois sowie an der Ohio State University. Zu seinen wichtigsten Projekten zählen: Wexner Center for the Visual Arts, Ohio State University, Columbus, Ohio (1982–89); Greater Columbus Convention Center, Columbus, Ohio (1989–93); Aronoff Center for Design and Art, University of Cincinnati, Cincinnati, Ohio (1988–96) sowie das nicht ausgeführte Max Reinhardt Haus in Berlin (1995). Gegenwärtig arbeitet Eisenman am Center for the Arts, Emory University, Atlanta, Georgia.

Né à New York en 1932, B. Arch. de Cornell, M. Arch. de Columbia, Masters et Ph. D. de l'université de Cambridge, Grande-Bretagne. Il enseigne à Cambridge, Princeton, Yale, Harvard, à l'université de l'Illinois et à l'Ohio State University. Principales réalisations: Wexner Center for the Visual Arts, Ohio State University, Columbus, Ohio (1982–89); Greater Columbus Convention Center, Columbus, Ohio (1989–93); Aronoff Center for Design and Art, University of Cincinnati, Cincinnati, Ohio (1988–96); Max Reinhardt Haus, Berlin, Allemagne (1995), non construit. Il travaille actuellement sur le projet du Center for the Arts de Emory University, Atlanta, Géorgie.

Frank O. Gehry

Born in Toronto, Canada in 1929, Frank O. Gehry studied at the University of Southern California, Los Angeles (1949–51), and at Harvard (1956–57). Principal of Frank O. Gehry and Associates, Inc., Los Angeles, since 1962, he received the 1989 Pritzker Prize. Some of his notable projects are: the Loyola Law School, Los Angeles (1981–84); the Norton Residence, Venice, California (1983); California Aerospace Museum, Los Angeles (1982–84); Schnabel Residence, Brentwood (1989); Festival Disney, Marne-la-Vallée, France (1989–92); American Center, Paris, France (1993); Nationale-Nederlanden Building, Prague, Czech Republic (1994–96); Disney Concert Hall, Los Angeles (construction temporarily halted); and the Guggenheim Museum, Bilbao, Spain (under construction).

Frank O. Gehry wurde 1929 in Toronto, Kanada geboren und studierte an der University of Southern California, Los Angeles (1949–51) sowie in Harvard (1956–57). Als Leiter von Frank O. Gehry and Associates, Inc., Los Angeles (seit 1962) erhielt er 1989 den Pritzker Preis. Wichtigste Projekte: Loyola Law School, Los Angeles (1981–84); Norton Residence, Venice, Kalifornien (1983); California Aerospace Museum, Los Angeles (1982–84); Schnabel Residence, Brentwood (1989); Festival Disney, Marne-la-Vallée, Frankreich (1989–92); American Center, Paris, Frankreich (1993); Gebäude der Nationale-Nederlanden, Prag, Tschechien (1994–96); Disney Concert Hall, Los Angeles (zeitweiliger Baustopp) sowie das Guggenheim Museum, Bilbao, Spanien (im Bau).

Né en 1929 à Toronto au Canada, Frank O. Gehry étudie l'architecture à l'University of Southern California, Los Angeles (1949–51) et Harvard (1956–57). Principal responsable de Frank O. Gehry and Associates, Inc., Los Angeles, depuis 1962, il reçoit le Prix Pritzker en 1989. Principales réalisations: Loyola Law School, Los Angeles (1981–84); Norton Residence, Venice, Californie (1983); le California Aerospace Museum, Los Angeles (1982–84); Schnabel Residence, Brentwood (1989); Festival Disney, Marne-la-Vallée, France (1989–92); l'American Center in Paris, France (1993); Nationale-Nederlanden Building, Prague, République Tchèque (1994–96); le Disney Concert Hall, Los Angeles (construction momentanément arrêtée), et le Guggenheim Museum, Bilbao, Espagne (en construction).

Philip Johnson, Ritchie & Fiore
885 Third Avenue
New York, NY 10022
Tel: +1 212 319 5880
Fax: +1 212 319 5881

Richard Meier & Partners
475 Tenth Avenue
New York, NY 10018
Tel: +1 212 967 6060
Fax: +1 212 967 3207

Eric Owen Moss Architects
8557 Higuera Street
Culver City, California 90232
Tel: +1 310 839 1199
Fax: +1 310 839 7922

Pei Cobb Freed & Partners
600 Madison Avenue
New York, NY 10022
Tel: +1 212 751-3122
Fax: +1 212 872 5443

Cesar Pelli & Associates Inc
1056 Chapel Street
New Haven, Connecticut 06510
Tel: +1 203 777 2515
Fax: +1 203 787 2856

Philip Johnson

Born in Cleveland, Ohio (1906). Harvard, B. A. (1930), Harvard, B. Arch. (1943). Founder and Director, Department of Architecture, Museum of Modern Art, New York (1932–34 and 1945–54). Wrote *The International Style* with Henry-Russell Hitchcock (1932) 1979 Pritzker Prize. Organized 1988 exhibition *Deconstructivist Architecture* at MoMA with Mark Wigley. Works: Philip Johnson House, New Canaan, Connecticut (1949); Seagram Building, New York (with Ludwig Mies van der Rohe, 1958); Boston Public Library, addition (with Architects Design Group, 1973); Pennzoil Place, Houston (1976); AT&T Headquarters Building, New York (1979); IBM Tower, Atlanta, Georgia (1987); Cathedral of Hope, Dallas, Texas (1996–2000).

Philip Johnson wurde 1906 in Cleveland, Ohio geboren; B. A., Harvard 1930, B. Arch., Harvard, 1943. Gründer und Direktor des Department of Architecture am New Yorker Museum of Modern Art (1932–34 und 1945–54). 1932 schrieb er zusammen mit Henry-Russell Hitchcock das Buch »The International Style«. Pritzker Preis 1979. 1988 organisierte Johnson am MoMA, zusammen mit Mark Wigley, die Ausstellung »Deconstructivist Architecture«. Werke: Philip Johnson House, New Canaan, Connecticut (1949); Seagram Building, New York (mit Ludwig Mies van der Rohe, 1958); Anbau zur Boston Public Library (mit Architects Design Group, 1973); Pennzoil Place, Houston (1976); AT&T Headquarters Building, New York (1979); IBM Tower, Atlanta, Georgia (1987), Cathedral of Hope, Dallas, Texas (1996–2000).

Né à Cleveland, Ohio, en 1906. B. A., Harvard (1930), B.Arch., Harvard (1943). Fondateur et directeur du département d'architecture du Museum of Modern Art de New York (1932–34 et 1945–54). Écrit «The International Style» avec Henry-Russell Hitchcock (1932). Prix Pritzker 1979. Organise en 1988 l'exposition «Deconstructivist Architecture», au MoMA, avec Mark Wigley. Réalisations: Philip Johnson House, New Canaan, Connecticut (1949); Seagram Building, New York (avec Ludwig Mies van der Rohe, 1958); extension de la Boston Public Library (avec Architects Design Group, 1973); Pennzoil Place, Houston (1976); siège d'AT&T, New York (1979); IBM Tower, Atlanta, Géorgie (1987); Cathedral of Hope, Dallas, Texas (1996–2000).

Richard Meier

Born in Newark, New Jersey in 1934. Richard Meier received his architectural training at Cornell University, and worked in the office of Marcel Breuer (1960–63) before establishing his own practice in 1963. Pritzker Prize, 1984; Royal Gold Medal, 1988. Major buildings: The Atheneum, New Harmony, Indiana (1975–79); Museum for the Decorative Arts, Frankfurt, Germany (1979–85); High Museum of Art, Atlanta, Georgia (1980–83); Getty Center, Los Angeles, California (1985–97); City Hall and Library, The Hague, Netherlands (1986–95); Barcelona Museum of Contemporary Art, Barcelona, Spain (1987–95); U.S. Federal Courthouse, Phoenix, Arizona (1995–2000); Church of the Year 2000, Rome, Italy (1996–2000).

Richard Meier wurde 1934 in Newark, New Jersey geboren. Nach seiner Ausbildung an der Cornell University arbeitete er im Büro von Marcel Breuer (1960–63), bevor er 1963 sein eigenes Büro eröffnete. 1984 gewann er den Pritzker Preis, 1988 die Royal Gold Medal. Wichtige Bauten: The Atheneum, New Harmony, Indiana (1975–79); Museum für Kunsthandwerk, Frankfurt a.M. (1979–85); High Museum of Art, Atlanta, Georgia (1980–83); Getty Center, Los Angeles, Kalifornien (1985–97); Rathaus und Zentralbibliothek, Den Haag, Niederlande (1986–95); Museum für zeitgenössische Kunst, Barcelona, Spanien (1987–95); U.S. Federal Courthouse, Phoenix, Arizona (1995–2000); Church of the Year 2000, Rom, Italia (1996–2000).

Né à Newark, New Jersey, en 1934, Richard Meier étudie à Cornell University, et travaille dans l'agence de Marcel Breuer (1960–63), avant de se mettre à son compte en 1963. Prix Pritzker 1984; Royal Gold Medal, 1988. Principales réalisations: The Atheneum, New Harmony, Indiana, (1975–79); Musée des arts décoratifs de Francfort-sur-le-Main (1979–85); High Museum of Art, Atlanta, Géorgie (1980–83); Getty Center, Los Angeles, Californie (1985–97); Musée d'art contemporain de Barcelone, Espagne (1987–95); hôtel de ville et bibliothèque, La Haye, Pays-Bas (1986–95); U.S. Federal Courthouse, Phoenix, Arizona (1995–2000); église de l'an 2000, Rome, Italie (1996–2000).

Eric Owen Moss

Born in Los Angeles, California in 1943, Eric Owen Moss received his B. A. degree from UCLA in 1965, and his M. Arch. in 1968. He also received a M. Arch. degree at Harvard in 1972. He has been a Professor of Design at the Southern California Institute of Architecture since 1974. He opened his own firm in Culver City in 1976. His built work includes the Central Housing Office, University of California at Irvine, Irvine (1986–89); Lindblade Tower, Culver City (1987–89); Paramount Laundry, Culver City (1987–89); Gary Group, Culver City (1988–90), The Box, Culver City (1990–94) and the IRS Building, also in Culver City (1993–94). Current projects include the Ince Theater (Culver City); Stealth (Culver City); Pittard, Sullivan (Culver City).

Eric Owen Moss wurde 1943 in Los Angeles, Kalifornien geboren und erhielt 1965 seinen B. A. an der UCLA, 1968 seinen M. Arch. sowie 1972 seinen M. Arch. in Harvard. Seit 1974 ist Moss als Professor of Design am Southern California Institute of Architecture tätig. 1976 gründete er in Culver City seine eigene Firma. Wichtige Bauten: Central Housing Office, University of California at Irvine, Irvine (1986–89); Lindblade Tower, Culver City (1987–89); Paramount Laundry, Culver City (1987–89); Gary Group, Culver City (1988–90); The Box, Culver City (1990–94) und das IRS Building, ebenfalls Culver City (1993–94). Zu Moss' aktuellen Projekten zählen das Ince Theater, Culver City; Stealth, Culver City; Pittard, Sullivan, Culver City.

Né en 1943 à Los Angeles, Eric Owen Moss est diplômé en architecture de l'UCLA (B. A., 1965) et reçoit deux masters en architecture en 1968, et en 1972 à Harvard. Il enseigne le dessin d'architecture au SCI-Arc depuis 1974, et crée sa propre agence à Culver City en 1976. Parmi ses réalisations: Central Housing Office, University of California at Irvine, Irvine (1986–89); Lindblade Tower, Culver City (1987–89); Paramount Laundry, Culver City (1987–89); Gary Group, Culver City (1988–90); The Box, Culver City (1990–94) et l'IRS Building, toujours à Culver City (1993–94). Ses projets actuels comprennent l'Ince Theater (Culver City); Stealth (Culver City); Pittard Sullivan (Culver City).

James Ingo Freed

One of three design principals at Pei Cobb Freed & Partners, James Ingo Freed joined the office in 1956. Born in Germany, he received his architectural degree from Illinois Institute of Technology in 1953 and two decades later (1975–78) returned as Dean of the School of Architecture. Before joining I.M. Pei, he worked in Chicago and New York, notably in the office of Ludwig Mies van der Rohe. In addition to the San Francisco Public Library, Freed's recently completed projects include the United States Holocaust Memorial Museum (1993); the expansion and modernization of the Los Angeles Convention Center; and First Bank Place, a fifty-five-story tower in Minneapolis. Works in progress include the United States Air Force Memorial Museum in Arlington Cemetery; the Science and Engineering Quad at Stanford University; the United States Courthouse in Omaha, Nebraska.

James Ingo Freed, heute einer der drei für das Design verantwortlichen Partner bei Pei Cobb Freed & Partners, trat der Firma 1956 bei. Der in Deutschland geborene Freed machte 1953 seinen Abschluß in Architektur am Illinois Institute of Technology, an das er zwei Jahrzehnte später als Dekan der Architekturfakultät zurückkehrte (1975–78). Vor seiner Zusammenarbeit mit I.M. Pei arbeitete er in Chicago und New York, vor allem im Büro von Ludwig Mies van der Rohe. Wichtige Bauten: San Francisco Public Library, United States Holocaust Memorial Museum (1993), die Erweiterung und Modernisierung des Los Angeles Convention Center sowie First Bank Place in Minneapolis. Aktuelle Projekte: United States Air Force Memorial Museum, Arlington Cemetery; Science and Engineering Quad, Stanford University; United States Courthouse, Omaha, Nebraska.

L'un des trois associés de Pei Cobb Freed & Partners, James Ingo Freed a rejoint l'agence en 1956. Né en Allemagne, il est architecte diplômé de l'Illinois Institute of Technology en 1953, et deux décennies plus tard (1975–78) retourne à son université comme doyen de l'école d'architecture. Avant de s'associer à I.M. Pei, il travaille à Chicago et New York, en particulier avec Mies van der Rohe. En dehors de la San Francisco Public Library, Freed a récemment achevé l'United States Holocaust Memorial Museum (1993), l'extension et la modernisation du Centre de congrès de Los Angeles et First Bank Place à Minneapolis. Parmi ses travaux en cours: l'United States Air Force Memorial Museum au cimetière d'Arlington, le Science and Engineering Quad à Stanford University, la cour fédérale de justice d'Omaha, Nebraska.

Cesar Pelli

Born in 1926 in Tucuman, Argentina, studied at Tucuman University, Dip. Arch. (1949). Emigrated to the U.S. (1952) and attended University of Illinois, M.S. Arch. (1954). Worked in office of Eero Saarinen and Associates, (1954–64), project designer for the TWA Terminal, Kennedy Airport, New York, and Vivian Beaumont Theater, New York. From 1968 to 1977, Pelli was partner in charge of design at Gruen Associates, Los Angeles, where he completed the Pacific Design Center, Los Angeles (1975). After becoming Dean of the School of Architecture at Yale in 1977, he opened Cesar Pelli and Associates, in New Haven. Notable buildings include: residential tower and gallery expansion, Museum of Modern Art, New York (1977); World Financial Center, New York (1980–88); Canary Wharf Tower, London (1987–91); NTT Shinjuku Headquarters Building, Tokyo, Japan (1990–95); Kuala Lumpur City Center Phase 1, Malaysia (1992–96).

Geboren 1926 in Tucuman, Argentinien. Studierte an der Universität Tucuman; Diplomarchitekt 1949. Nach Einwanderung in die USA (1952) Besuch der University of Illinois; M. S. Arch. 1954. Arbeitete für das Büro von Eero Saarinen and Associates (1954–64); Projektdesigner für das TWA Terminal, Kennedy Airport, New York sowie für das Vivian Beaumont Theater, New York; von 1968 bis 1977 für das Design veranwortlicher Partner bei Gruen Associates, Los Angeles, in deren Auftrag er das Pacific Design Center in Los Angeles (1975) fertigstellte. Nachdem er 1977 zum Dekan der School of Architecture in Yale ernannt worden war, gründete Pelli in New Haven, Connecticut Cesar Pelli and Associates. Wichtigste Bauten: Wohnturm und Erweiterung des Museum of Modern Art, New York (1977); World Financial Center, New York (1980–88); Canary Wharf Tower, London (1987–91); NTT Shinjuku Headquarters Building, Tokio (1990–95); Kuala Lumpur City Centre Phase 1, Malaysia (1992–96).

Né en 1926 à Tucuman, Argentine. Diplôme d'architecture de l'université de Tucuman (1949). Émigre aux États-Unis (1952), et passe son Master en architecture en 1954 (University of Illinois). Travaille pour Eero Saarinen & Associates (1954–64), dessinateur de projet pour le terminal TWA de l'aéroport Kennedy, New York, et le Vivian Beaumont Theater, New York. De 1968 à 1977, Pelli est associé chargé de la conception chez Gruen Associates, Los Angeles, pour qui il réalise le Pacific Design Center à Los Angeles (1975). Devenu doyen de l'école d'architecture de Yale en 1977, il ouvre Cesar Pelli & Associates, à New Haven, Connecticut. Réalisations importantes: tour d'appartements et extension du Museum of Modern Art, New York (1977); World Financial Center, New York (1980–88); Canary Wharf Tower, Londres (1987–91); siège de NTT Shinjuku, Tokyo, Japon (1990–95); Kuala Lumpur City Centre Phase 1, Malaisie (1992–96).

Polshek and Partners
320 West 13th Street
New York, NY 10014-1278
Tel: + 1 212 807 7171
Fax: + 1 212 807 5917

James Stewart Polshek

James Stewart Polshek was born in Akron, Ohio in 1930. Case Western Reserve University, Cleveland, Ohio (1951); M. Arch. Yale (1955); established his own practice in New York in 1963. Dean of Graduate School of Architecture, Columbia University, New York (1972–87). Recent projects include: Seamen's Church Institute in the South Street Seaport Historic District, New York (1991); renovation of Carnegie Hall, Center for the Arts Theater at Yerba Buena Gardens, San Francisco (1993); Government Office Building, Chambery-le Haut, France (1994); renovation and expansion of Brooklyn Museum. Current projects include: American Museum of Natural History, New York; Cooper Hewitt National Design Museum renovation, New York; National Museum of the American Indian, Cultural Resources Center, Suitland, Maryland.

James Stewart Polshek wurde 1930 in Akron, Ohio geboren. Case Western Reserve University, Cleveland, Ohio (1951); M. Arch., Yale (1955); Gründung seiner eigenen Firma in New York 1963. Von 1972–87 war Polshek Dekan der Graduate School of Architecture an der New Yorker Columbia University. Wichtigste Bauten: Seamen's Church Institute im South Street Seaport Historic District, New York (1991); Neugestaltung der Carnegie Hall, Center for the Arts Theater in Yerba Buena Gardens, San Francisco (1993); Bürogebäude der französischen Regierung, Chambery-le-Haut (1994); Neugestaltung und Erweiterung des Brooklyn Museum. Aktuelle Projekte: American Museum of Natural History, New York; Neugestaltung des Cooper Hewitt National Design Museum, New York; National Museum of the American Indian, Cultural Resources Center, Suitland, Maryland.

James Stewart Polshek est né à Akron, Ohio, en 1930. Après des études à Case Western Reserve University, Cleveland, Ohio (1951) et un M. Arch. à Yale (1955), il ouvre son agence à New York en 1963. Il a été doyen de la Graduate School of Architecture, Columbia University, New York, de 1972 à 1987. Récents projets: le Seamen's Church Institute du South Street Seaport Historic District, New York (1991); la rénovation de Carnegie Hall, le Center for the Arts à Yerba Buena Gardens, San Francisco (1993); immeuble administratif à Chambéry-le-Haut, France (1994); la rénovation et l'extension du Brooklyn Museum. Projets actuels: l'American Museum of National History, New York; rénovation du Cooper Hewitt National Design Museum, New York; le National Museum of the American Indian, Cultural Ressources Center, Suitland, Maryland.

Bart Prince Architect
3501 Monte Vista NE
Albuquerque, New Mexico 87106
Tel: + 1 505 256 1961
Fax: + 1 505 268 9045

Bart Prince

Born in Albuquerque, New Mexico in 1947. B. Arch., Arizona State University (1970). Worked with Bruce Goff from 1968 to 1973; assisted him in the design of the Pavilion for Japanese Art, Los Angeles County Museum of Art, Los Angeles, CA (1978–89), and completed the building after Goff's death in 1982. Opened his own architectural practice in 1973. Main buildings: Bart Prince Residence and studio, Albuquerque, New Mexico (1983); Brad and June Prince House, Albuquerque (1988); Mead/Penhall Residence, Albuquerque (1994); Hight Residence, Mendocino County, California (1995); Sziklai Residence, Carefree, Arizona (1997); Skilken Residence, Columbus, Ohio (1997).

Geboren 1947 in Albuquerque, New Mexico. 1970 B. Arch. an der Arizona State University. Von 1968 bis 1973 arbeitete Prince mit Bruce Goff zusammen, assistierte ihm beim Entwurf des Pavillons für japanische Kunst des Los Angeles County Museum of Art, Los Angeles, Kalifornien (1978–89) und stellte das Gebäude nach Goffs Tod 1982 fertig. Eröffnete 1973 ein eigenes Büro. Wichtige Bauten: Bart Prince Residence and Studio, Albuquerque, New Mexico (1983); Brad and June Prince House, Albuquerque, New Mexico (1988); Mead/Penhall Residence, Albuquerque, New Mexico (1994); Hight Residence, Mendocino County, Kalifornien (1995); Sziklai Residence, Carefree, Arizona (1997); Skilken Residence, Columbus, Ohio (1997).

Né à Albuquerque, Nouveau-Mexique, en 1947. B. Arch., Arizona State University (1970). Travaille avec Bruce Goff de 1968 à 1973, et l'assiste dans la conception du pavillon de l'art japonais du Los Angeles County Museum of Art, Los Angeles (1978–89), qu'il achève après la mort de Goff en 1982. Principales réalisations: Bart Prince Residence and Studio, Albuquerque, Nouveau-Mexique (1983); Brad and June Prince House, Albuquerque, Nouveau-Mexique (1988); Mead/Penhall Residence, Albuquerque, Nouveau-Mexique (1994); Hight Residence, Mendocino County, Californie (1995); Sziklai Residence, Carefree, Arizona (1997); Skilken Residence, Columbus, Ohio (1997).

Richard Rauh & Associates
3400 Peachtree Road, NE, Suite 817
Atlanta, Georgia 30326-1107
Tel: + 1 404 233 9447
Fax: + 1 404 233 1833

Richard Rauh

Born in Kentucky, Richard Rauh studied art history at Columbia (B. A., 1970); B. Arch., M. Arch., Harvard University GSD, 1970–74. A teaching fellow at Harvard (1971–74) and later a research associate (1976), before becoming an assistant professor of architecture at the University of Kentucky (1976–80), he was principal of Carpenter/Rauh Architects in Lexington, Kentucky (1978–81) before moving to Atlanta (RHPMHR) and finally creating Richard Rauh & Associates in 1984. Projects include: Carew Tower Office Building adaptive reuse, Cincinnati, Ohio; restoration of Omni Netherlands Plaza Hotel, Cincinnati, Ohio; and the Caribbean Gardens Center, Naples, Florida. Current work includes Preston Road Cineplex, Louisville, Kentucky (1997); Military Circle Cineplex, Norfolk, Virginia (1997).

Richard Rauh wurde in Kentucky geboren und studierte Kunstgeschichte an der New Yorker Columbia University (B. A. 1970), gefolgt von einem Studium in Harvard (1970–74 B. Arch., M. Arch., Harvard University GSD), Assistenzprofessor für Architektur an der University of Kentucky (1976–80). Von 1978 bis 1981 leitete Rauh Carpenter/Rauh Architects in Lexington, Kentucky, bevor er nach Atlanta zog (RHPMHR) und schließlich 1984 Richard Rauh & Associates gründete. Projekte: Umbau und Neugestaltung des Carew Tower Office Building, Cincinnati, Ohio; Restaurierung des Omni Netherlands Plaza Hotel, Cincinnati, Ohio; sowie des Caribbean Gardens Center, Naples, Florida. Aktuelle Projekte: Preston Road Cineplex, Louisville, Kentucky (1997); Military Circle Cineplex, Norfolk, Virginia (1997).

Né dans le Kentucky, Richard Rauh étudie l'histoire de l'art à Columbia University (B. A., 1970); B. Arch., M. Arch., Harvard University Graduate School of Design, 1970–74. Assistant à Harvard puis chercheur, avant de devenir professeur assistant en architecture à l'université du Kentucky (1976– 80), il dirige l'agence Carpenter/ Rauh Architects à Lexington, Kentucky (1978–81), puis s'installe à Atlanta (RHPMHR) et fonde Richard Rauh & Associates en 1984. Projets: la Carew Tower Office Building, une rénovation, Cincinnati, Ohio; la restauration de l'Omni Netherlands Plaza Hotel, Cincinnati, Ohio; et le Caribbean Gardens Center, Naples, Floride. Projets actuels: Preston Road Cineplex, Louisville, Kentucky (1997); Military Circle Cineplex, Norfolk, Virginie (1997).

Siegel Diamond Architects
605 W. Olympic Boulevard #820
Los Angeles, California 90015
Tel: + 1 213 627 7170
Fax: + 1 213 627 7069

Katherine Diamond

Born in 1954, in Chicago, Illinois, Katherine Diamond has dual citizenship (USA, Israel), and was a 1st Lieutenant Israeli Air Force Engineering Corps. She received her B. Arch. from The Technion, Israel Institute of Technology (1978); worked on a Masters in Psychology, UCLA (1981–83). First woman president of Los Angeles Chapter of American Institute of Architects (1993–94). Design Studio Instructor at the University of Southern California School of Architecture since 1995. Projects since 1985: Universal City Metro Red Line Subway Station; Baldwin Park Commuter Rail Station, also in Los Angeles; four elevated light rail stations for Los Angeles/ Long Beach Metro Blue Line (1989); University of California Davis Medical Center Plant with Cogeneration. LAX Control Tower, Los Angeles (Design Architect).

Die 1954 in Chicago, Illinois geborene Katherine Diamond besitzt zwei Staatsbürgerschaften (Vereinigte Staaten, Israel) und diente als Oberleutnant bei der israelischen Luftwaffe. Sie machte ihren B. Arch. am Technion, dem Israel Institute of Technology (1978), und studierte von 1981–83 Psychologie an der UCLA in Los Angeles. Erste Präsidentin des Los Angeles Chapter des American Institute of Architects (1993–94). Seit 1995 als Design Studio Instructor an der School of Architecture der University of Southern California tätig. Projekte seit 1985: Untergrundbahnhof für die Universal City Metro Red Line, Baldwin Park Commuter Rail Station in Los Angeles; vier Hochbahnstationen der Los Angeles/Long Beach Metro Blue Line (1989); University of California Davis Medical Center Plant, zusammen mit Cogeneration. LAX Control Tower, Los Angeles (Designarchitekt).

Née en 1954 à Chicago, Illinois, Katherine Diamond possède la double nationalité américaine et israélienne, et a même été lieutenant de l'armée d'Israël. Elle est diplômée en architecture de l'Institut israélien de technologie (1978), et a préparé une maîtrise en psychologie à UCLA (1981–83). Elle est la première femme a avoir présidé le chapitre de Los Angeles de l'American Institute of Architects (1993–94). Depuis 1985, elle a travaillé sur la station de métro d'Universal City, la Baldwin Park Commuter Rail Station également à Los Angeles, quatre stations légères sur la ligne bleue du métro Los Angeles/Long Beach (1989), et le Davis Medical Center Plant de l'université de Californie avec Cogeneration. LAX Control Tower, Los Angeles (architecte-concepteur).

Venturi, Scott Brown and Associates
4236 Main Street, Philadelphia,
Pennsylvania 19127–1696
Tel: + 1 215 487 0400
Fax: + 1 215 487 2520

Venturi, Scott Brown

Robert Venturi, born in 1925 in Philadelphia; B. A. (1947) and M. F. A. (1950), Princeton. Spent two years at American Academy in Rome (1954–56). Worked for Louis Kahn and Eliel Saarinen. Venturi Rauch (1964–67), Venturi Rauch Scott Brown (1967–92), since 1992 Venturi, Scott Brown and Associates. *Complexity and Contradiction in Architecture* (1966) translated into sixteen languages. 1991 Pritzker Prize. Denise Scott Brown born in 1931 in Nkana, Zambia. Graduated from Architectural Association, London (1955), M.C.P. University of Pennsylvania (1960); M. Arch. University of Pennsylvania (1965). Fellow at Princeton, Butler College since 1983. Participated in *Learning from Las Vegas* (1972). Projects: Molecular Biology Building, Princeton (1985); Clinical Research Building, University of Pennsylvania, Philadelphia (1990); National Gallery Sainsbury Wing, London (1991); Seattle Art Museum, Seattle (1991). Current projects include: student centers at Harvard and the University of Delaware; lab buildings at Princeton, Yale, and UCLA; and an office building for Disney in Orlando, Florida.

Robert Venturi wurde 1925 in Philadelphia geboren; B. A. 1947, Master of Fine Arts 1950, Princeton University. Er studierte zwei Jahre an der American Academy in Rom (1954–56) und arbeitete für Louis Kahn und Eliel Saarinen. Venturi Rauch (1964– 67), Venturi Rauch Scott Brown (1967–92), seit 1992 Venturi, Scott Brown and Associates. »Complexity and Contradiction in Architecture« (1966) wurde in 16 Sprachen übersetzt. Pritzker Preis 1991. Denise Scott Brown wurde 1931 in Nkana, Zambia geboren; Abschluß an der Architectural Association, London (1955). M.C.P. University of Pennsylvania (1960); M. Arch., University of Pennsylvania (1965). Seit 1983 Mitglied des Butler College, Princeton University. Mitautorin von »Learning from Las Vegas« (1972). Wichtige Bauten: Molecular Biology Building, Princeton (1985); Clinical Research Building, University of Pennsylvania, Philadelphia (1990); National Gallery Sainsbury Wing, London (1991); Seattle Art Museum, Seattle (1991). Gegenwärtige Projekte: Studentenzentren in Harvard und an der University of Delaware, Laborgebäude in Princeton, Yale, an der UCLA und der University of Pennsylvania sowie ein Bürogebäude für Disney in Orlando, Florida.

Rafael Viñoly Architects
50 Vandam Street
New York, NY 10013
Tel: + 1 212 924 5060
Fax: + 1 212 924 5858

Tod Williams, Billie Tsien and
Associates, 222 Central Park South
New York, NY 10019
Tel: + 1 212 582 2385
Fax: + 1 212 245 1984

Lebbeus Woods
7 Bond Street, 6B
New York, NY 10012
Tel: + 1 212 677 6974
Fax: + 1 212 674 2238

Rafael Viñoly

Tod Williams, Billie Tsien

Lebbeus Woods

Robert Venturi, né à Philadelphie en 1925, B. A. (1947) et M. F. A. (1950), à Princeton. Il passe deux années à l'American Academy de Rome (1954–56) puis travaille pour Louis Kahn et Eliel Saarinen avant de créer l'agence Venturi Rauch (1964–67), puis Venturi Rauch Scott Brown (1967–92), devenue Venturi, Scott Brown and Associates. Son ouvrage «Complexité et contradiction en architecture» (1966) est traduit en 16 langues. Lauréat du Prix Pritzker en 1991. Denise Scott Brown est née en 1931 à Nkana, Zambie. Diplômée de l'Architectural Association, Londres (1955), M.C.P., University of Pennsylvania (1960); M. Arch. University of Pennsylvania (1965). Assistante au Butler College, Princeton, depuis 1983. Participe à l'ouvrage «L'Enseignement de Las Vegas» (1972). Réalisations: Molecular Biology Building, Princeton (1985); Clinical Research Building, University of Pennsylvania, Philadelphie (1990); National Gallery Sainsbury Wing, Londres (1991); Seattle Art Museum, Seattle (1991). Ils travaillent actuellement sur des centres pour étudiants à Harvard et à l'université du Delaware, des laboratoires à Princeton, Yale, et l'UCLA, et un immeuble de bureaux pour Disney à Orlando, Floride.

Born in 1944 in Montevideo, Uruguay. Son of the artistic director of the Sodre Opera Theater, spent early years in Uruguay and Argentina. Considered career as concert pianist before architecture. M. Arch. University of Buenos Aires (1969). Formed the Estudio de Arquitectura which became one of the largest practices in South America. 1978, invited to teach at Washington University and then at Harvard GSD. Established Rafael Viñoly Architects in 1983 in New York. Notable buildings include: Bank of the City of Buenos Aires, Buenos Aires, Argentina (1968); Mendoza Sports Complex, Buenos Aires, Argentina (1978); NYNEX, New York (1989); Queens Museum Reconstruction, Flushing Meadow Park, Flushing, Queens (1994); Samsung World Pulse Headquarters, Seoul, Korea (1998); New Bronx Criminal Court Complex, Bronx, New York (2001).

Rafael Viñoly wurde 1944 in Montevideo geboren, als Sohn des künstlerischen Leiters des Sodre Opera Theater verbrachte er seine Kindheit in Uruguay und Argentinien. Strebte vor dem Architekturstudium eine Karriere als Konzertpianist an. M. Arch., Universität Buenos Aires (1969). Gründete das Estudio de Arquitectura, das sich zu einem der größten Architekturbüros Südamerikas entwickelte. 1978 Lehrauftrag an der Washington University und am Harvard GSD. Gründete 1983 in New York Rafael Viñoly Architects. Bekannteste Bauten: Bank der Stadt Buenos Aires, Buenos Aires (1968); Mendoza Sportkomplex, Buenos Aires (1978); NYNEX, New York (1989); Umbau des Queens Museum, Flushing Meadow Park, Flushing, Queens (1994); Samsung World Pulse Headquarters, Seoul (1998); New Bronx Criminal Court Complex, Bronx, New York (2001).

Né à Montevideo, Uruguay, en 1944. Fils du directeur artistique de l'opéra Sodre, il passe la première partie de sa vie en Uruguay et en Argentine, et pense entreprendre une carrière de pianiste de concert. M. Arch. de l'université de Buenos Aires (1969). Crée le Estudio de Arquitectura qui devient l'une des plus importantes agences d'Amérique du Sud. En 1978, il est invité à enseigner à Washington University puis à Harvard. Il fonde Rafael Viñoly Architects à New York en 1983. Principales réalisations: Banque de la ville de Buenos Aires, Buenos Aires, Argentine (1968); complexe sportif de Mendoza, Buenos Aires, Argentine (1978); NYNEX, New York (1989); reconstruction du Queens Museum, Flushing Meadow Park, Flushing, Queens (1994); siège de Samsung World Pulse, Séoul, Corée du Sud (1998); nouvel ensemble du tribunal correctionnel du Bronx, New York (2001).

Tod Williams, born in Detroit in 1943, B. A. 1965, M. F. A., 1967 Princeton University. After six years as associate architect in the office of Richard Meier in New York, he began his own practice in New York in 1974. Taught at Cooper Union for more than fifteen years and has also taught at Harvard, Yale, the University of Virginia, and Southern California Institute of Architecture. Mid-career Prix de Rome in 1983. Billie Tsien, born in Ithaca, New York in 1949, B. A., Yale, M. Arch., UCLA, 1977. She has been a painter, and graphic designer (1971–75). Taught at Parsons School of Design, (SCI-Arc), Harvard and Yale. Work includes: Feinberg Hall, Princeton, New Jersey (1986); New College, University of Virginia, Charlottesville, Virginia (1992); as well as the newly completed renovation and extension of the Museum of Fine Arts in Phoenix, Arizona.

Tod Williams wurde 1943 in Detroit geboren. B. A. 1965, M. F. A. 1967, Princeton University. Nach sechs Jahren Mitarbeit im Büro von Richard Meier gründete Williams 1974 in New York seine eigene Firma. Williams unterrichtete an der Cooper Union sowie in Harvard, Yale, an der University of Virginia sowie am SCI-Arc. Prix de Rome 1983. Billie Tsien wurde 1949 in Ithaca, New York geboren. B. A. in Yale, M. Arch., UCLA, 1977. Sie arbeitete als Malerin und Graphikdesignerin (1971–75) und unterrichtete an der Parsons School of Design, am SCI-Arc, in Harvard und in Yale. Bauten: Feinberg Hall, Princeton, New Jersey (1986); New College, University of Virginia, Charlottesville, Virginia (1992) sowie die kürzlich fertiggestellte Neugestaltung und Erweiterung des Museum of Fine Arts in Phoenix, Arizona.

Tod Williams, né à Detroit en 1943, B. A. en 1965, M. F. A., 1967, Princeton University. Après six ans comme architecte associé dans l'agence de Richard Meier il crée son cabinet à New York en 1974, enseigne à Harvard, Yale, l'université de Virginie, et au SCI-Arc. Prix de Rome (mid-career) en 1983. Billie Tsien, née à Ithaca, New York, en 1949, B. A., Yale, M. Arch., UCLA, 1977. Elle a été peintre et graphiste de 1971 à 1975. Enseigne à la Parsons School of Design, SCI-Arc, Harvard et Yale. Ils ont réalisé: Feinberg Hall, Princeton, New Jersey (1986); New College, University of Virginia, Charlottesville, Virginia (1992); restauration complète et extension du Museum of Fine Arts de Phoenix, Arizona.

Born in 1940 in Lansing, Michigan. Educated at Purdue University School of Engineering and the University of Illinois School of Architecture. After working with Eero Saarinen and Associates (later Roche Dinkeloo) on the John Deere and Ford Foundation Headquarters Building in the 1960s, he has been a visiting professor of architecture at Cooper Union, SCI-Arc, and Columbia University. Major solo exhibitions: "Origins," Architectural Associaton, London 1985; "Berlin: Denkmal oder Denkmodell," Paris 1989, Berlin 1989, Krakow 1990 and Moscow 1991. Major projects: Underground Berlin (1988), Zagreb Freespace Structure (1991), and the recent Sarajevo Apartment Blocks (1994).

1940 in Lansing, Michigan geboren. Studium an der School of Engineering der Purdue University und an der University of Illinois School of Architecture. Nachdem er in den 60er Jahren mit Eero Saarinen and Associates (später Roche Dinkeloo) am John Deere and Ford Foundation Headquarters Building gearbeitet hatte, unterrichtete Woods als Gastprofessor für Architektur an der Cooper Union, am SCI-Arc sowie an der Columbia University. Bedeutende Einzelausstellungen: »Origins«, Architectural Association, London 1985; »Berlin: Denkmal oder Denkmodell«, Paris 1989, Berlin 1989, Krakau 1990 und Moskau 1991. Bedeutende Projekte: Underground Berlin (1988), Zagreb Freespace Structure (1991) und das kürzlich entstandene Sarajevo Apartment Blocks (1994).

Né en 1940 à Lansing, Michigan. Études à l'école d'ingénieurs de Purdue University et à l'école d'architecture de l'université de l'Illinois. Après avoir travaillé avec Eero Saarinen and Associates (devenu Roche Dinkeloo), sur les sièges sociaux de John Deere et de la Ford Foundation, il est professeur invité d'architecture à Cooper Union à SCI-Arc, et à Columbia University. Principales expositions personnelles: «Origins», Architectural Association, Londres 1985; «Berlin: Denkmal oder Denkmodell», Paris 1989, Berlin 1989, Cracovie 1990, et Moscou 1991. Principaux projets: Underground Berlin (1988), Zagreb Freespace Structure (1991) et, plus récemment, les Apartments Blocks de Sarajevo (1994).

Bibliography | Bibliographie

Bédard, Jean-François (editor): *Cities of Artificial Excavation, The Work of Peter Eisenman, 1978–1988.* Rizzoli International, Singapore, 1994.

Buchanan, Peter: "Aloof Abstraction," *Architecture,* February 1996.

Collins, Brad (compiled by): *Eric Owen Moss, Buildings and Projects 2.* Rizzoli, New York, 1996.

Crosbie, Michael: *Centerbrook, Reinventing American Architecture.* AIA Press, New York, 1993.

Dietsch, Deborah: "Philip's Folly," *Architecture,* November 1995.

Dietsch, Deborah: "Monastery of the Mind," *Architecture,* March 1996.

Dixon, John Morris: "The Santa Monica School. What's Its Lasting Contribution?" *Progressive Architecture,* May 1995.

Dixon, John Morris: "Urban Showplace," *Progressive Architecture,* September 1995.

Edelman, Gerald: "The Wordless Metaphor: Visual Art and the Brain," in: *1995 Biennal Exhibition.* Whitney Museum of American Art. New York, 1995.

Filler, Martin: "Husbands and Wives," *Architecture,* June 1996.

Frampton, Kenneth, Charles Jencks and Richard Meier: *Richard Meier, Buildings and Projects, 1979–1989.* St. Martin's Press, New York, 1990.

Frampton, Kenneth and Joseph Rykwert: *Richard Meier Architect, 1985/1991.* Rizzoli, New York, 1991.

Freiman, Ziva: "The Brain Exchange," *Progressive Architecture,* April 1995.

Futagawa, Yukio (editor): "Frank O. Gehry," *GA Architect 10.* A.D.A. Edita, Tokyo, 1993.

Gebhard, David and Robert Winter: *Los Angeles, An Architectural Guide.* Gibbs-Smith, Salt Lake City, 1994.

Giovannini, Joseph: "Is Richard Meier Really Modern?," *Architecture,* February 1996.

Goldberger, Paul: "Refashioning the Old With All Due Respect," *The New York Times,* May 5, 1996.

Jerde, Jon, (preface): *Steven Ehrlich, Contemporary World Architects.* Rockport Publishers, Rockport, Massachusetts, 1995.

Johnson, Philip and Mark Wigley: *Deconstructivist Architecture.* Museum of Modern Art, New York, 1988.

Kipnis, Jeffrey: *Philip Johnson, Recent Work,* Architectural Monographs n° 44. Academy Editions, London, 1996.

Kroloff, Reed: "Reinventing Akron," *Architecture,* December 1995.

Kwinter, Sanford (introduction): *Eisenman Architects.* Images Publishing, Mulgrave, Australia, 1995.

Muschamp, Herbert: "Viñoly's Vision for Tokyo and for the Identity of Japan," *The New York Times,* July 16, 1993.

Muschamp, Herbert: "A Man Who Lives in Glass Houses," *The New York Times,* October 17, 1993.

Muschamp, Herbert: "To a Neuroscientist's Liking: Calm, yet Complex," *The New York Times,* October 22, 1995.

Muschamp, Herbert: "Room for Imagination in a Temple of Reason," *The New York Times,* May 12, 1996.

Polledri, Paolo (editor): *Visionary San Francisco.* Prestel-Verlag, Munich, 1990.

Ryan, Raymund: "Brainwatch," *Blueprint,* February 1996.

Schulze, Franz: *Philip Johnson, Life and Work.* Knopf, New York, 1994.

Steele, James: *Eric Owen Moss,* Architectural Monographs, n° 29. Academy Editions, Ernst & Sohn, London, 1993.

Steele, James: *Salk Institute.* Phaidon, London, 1993.

Venturi, Robert: *Complexity and Contradiction in Architecture.* The Museum of Modern Art, New York, 1966.

Whitney, David (editor): *Philip Johnson, The Glass House.* Pantheon Books, New York, 1993.

Woods, Lebbeus: *The New City.* Simon & Schuster, New York, 1992.

Woods, Lebbeus: *War and Architecture.* Pamphlet Architecture 15, Princeton Architectural Press, New York, 1993.

Zaera, Alejandro: "*Frank O. Gehry,*" *El Croquis,* 74/75, Madrid, 1995.

Index

Credits | Fotonachweis | Crédits photographiques

l. = left | links | à gauche
r. = right | rechts | à droite
t. = top | oben | ci-dessus
c. = center | Mitte | centre
b. = bottom | unten | ci-dessous

2	© Photo: Peter Mauss/Esto
7	© Photo: 1995 Norman McGrath
9	© Photo: Christian Richters
10, 13	© Photo: Jeff Goldberg/Esto
14	© Polshek and Partners
17	© Photo: Peter Mauss/Esto
18	© Eric Owen Moss Architects
21	© Photo: Tom Bonner
22	© Photo: Michael Moran
25	© Rendering by Peter Dozal
26	© Photo: Timothy Hursley
28	© Venturi, Scott Brown and Associates
31	© Courtesy of KLCC
32, 35	© Photo: Masashi Kudo
37–41	© Photo: Jeff Goldberg/Esto
42	© Frank O. Gehry & Associates
45	© Photo: 1995 Norman McGrath
46	© Photo: Peter Aaron/Esto
49 t.	© Photo: Scott Frances/Esto
49 b.	© Richard Meier & Partners
51	© Photo: Timothy Hursley
52	© Photo: Alan Weintraub
55	© Photo: Timothy Hursley
56–61	© Lebbeus Woods
62	© Photo: Peter Aaron/Esto
63	© Arquitectonica
64/65	© Photo: Peter Aaron/Esto
66	© Photo: Jeff Goldberg/Esto
67	© Photo: Jeannette Montgomery Barron
68–71	© Photo: Jeff Goldberg/Esto
72–73	© Photo: Jeff Goldberg/Esto
73 c.	© Photo: Jeff Goldberg/Esto
73 b.	© Centerbrook
74	© Photo: Tom Bonner
75	© Photo: Douglas Slone
77–79	© Photo: Tom Bonner
80	© Photo: Jeff Goldberg/Esto
81	© Photo: Jason Schmidt
82	© Photo: Jeff Goldberg/Esto
84 t.	© Photo: Jeff Goldberg/Esto
84 b.	© Peter Eisenman
85	© Photo: Jeff Goldberg/Esto
86	© Photo: Christian Richters
87	© Courtesy of Frank O. Gehry & Associates
88	© Frank O. Gehry & Associates
89–92	© Photo: Christian Richters
93 t.	© Photo: Christian Richters
93 b.	© Frank O. Gehry & Associates
94	© Photo: 1995 Norman McGrath
95	© Photo: Greg Gorman
96	© Photo: 1995 Norman McGrath
97 t.	© Photo: 1995 Norman McGrath

97 b.	© Philip Johnson
98	© Photo: Scott Frances/Esto
99	© Photo: Luca Vignelli
101	© Photo: Scott Frances/Esto
102 t.	© Photo: Scott Frances/Esto
102 b.	© Richard Meier & Partners
103	© Photo: Scott Frances/Esto
104	© Photo: Tom Bonner
105	© Photo: Cervin Robinson 1991
106	© Eric Owen Moss Architects
107–109	© Photo: Tom Bonner
109 b.	© Eric Owen Moss Architects
110–111	© Photo: Tom Bonner
112	© Photo: Timothy Hursley
113	© Photo: Serge Hambourg
115	© Photo: Timothy Hursley
116 t.	© Pei Cobb Freed & Partners
116–117	© Photo: Timothy Hursley
118/119	© Cesar Pelli & Associates
120 t.	© Courtesy of KLCC
120 b.	© Cesar Pelli & Associates
121	© Cesar Pelli & Associates
122	© Photo: Jeff Goldberg/Esto
123	© Photo: Isaiah Wyner
125 t.	© Polshek and Partners
125 b.	© Photo: Jeff Goldberg/Esto
126/127	© Photo: Alan Weintraub
128	© Bart Prince
129–131	© Photo: Alan Weintraub
131 b.	© Bart Prince
132	© Photo: Peter Mauss/Esto
133	© Richard Rauh & Associates/Photo: Studio One
134	© Photo: Peter Mauss/Esto
135	© Richard Rauh & Associates
136 t.	© Photo: Peter Mauss/Esto
136–137	© Richard Rauh & Associates/Photo: Double Vision
137 t.	© Photo: Peter Mauss/Esto
137 b.	© Richard Rauh & Associates
138 t.	© Richard Rauh & Associates/Photo: Double Vision
138 b.	© Richard Rauh & Associates
139	© Richard Rauh & Associates/Photo: Double Vision
140	© Photo: Timothy Hursley
141	© Siegel Diamond Architects
142	© Siegel Diamond Architects/ Holmes & Narver Inc
143–144	© Photo: Timothy Hursley
145	© Photo: John T. Miller
146	© Venturi, Scott Brown and Associates

147–150	© Photo: Timothy Hursley
151	© Photo: Lucas Michael
152	© Photo: Pauline Jalil
153	© Rafael Viñoly Architects
154–155	© Photo: Timothy Hursley
156–157	© Photo: Pauline Jalil
158	© Photo: Timothy Hursley
159	© Photo: Michael O'Brien
160	© Photo: Michael Moran
161	© Photo: Timothy Hursley
162 t.	© Photo: Timothy Hursley
162 b.	© Tod Williams, Billie Tsien and Associates
163	© Photo: Michael Moran
164	© Lebbeus Woods
165	© Photo: Tom Wool
167–169	© Photo: Lebbeus Woods

The publisher and author wish to thank each of the architects and photographers for their kind assistance.